COOPERATIVE LEARNING IN PHYSICAL EDUCATION AND PHYSICAL ACTIVITY

This book introduces Cooperative Learning as a research-informed, practical way of engaging children and young people in lifelong physical activity. Written by authors with over 40 years' experience as teachers and researchers, it addresses the practicalities of using Cooperative Learning in the teaching of physical education and physical activity at any age range.

Cooperative Learning in Physical Education and Physical Activity will help teachers and students of physical education to master research-informed strategies for teaching. By using school-based and real-world examples, it allows teachers to quickly understand the educational benefits of Cooperative Learning. Divided into four parts, this book provides insight into:

- key aspects of Cooperative Learning as a pedagogical practice in physical education and physical activity
- strategies for implementing Cooperative Learning at elementary school level
- approaches to using Cooperative Learning at middle and high school level
- the challenges and advantages of practising Cooperative Learning.

Including lesson plans, activities, and tasks, this is the first comprehensive guide to Cooperative Learning as a pedagogical practice for physical educators. It is essential reading for all students, teachers, and trainee teachers of physical education and will also benefit coaches, outdoor educators, and people who work with youth in the community.

Ben Dyson is an Associate Professor in Health and Physical Education at the University of Auckland, New Zealand. He has carried out research and taught for over twenty years in Canada, the USA and New Zealand. Ben has taught at McGill University, Montreal, Canada; the University of New Hampshire, NH;

the University of Memphis, TN; and the University of Auckland, New Zealand. His research interests include research on innovative curriculum and pedagogy, and Cooperative Learning as a pedagogical practice. Ben is the current senior co-editor of the Journal of Teaching in Physical Education.

Ashley Casey is a Senior Lecturer in Pedagogy at Loughborough University, UK. His research explores pedagogical models, teacher development through social media and pedagogies of technology. He can be found on Twitter as @DrAshCasey, where he writes about teaching and research in physical education.

COOPERATIVE LEARNING IN PHYSICAL EDUCATION AND PHYSICAL ACTIVITY

A practical introduction

Ben Dyson
and
Ashley Casey

Routledge
Taylor & Francis Group

LONDON AND NEW YORK

First published 2016
by Routledge
2 Park Square, Milton Park, Abingdon, Oxon OX14 4RN

and by Routledge
711 Third Avenue, New York, NY 10017

Routledge is an imprint of the Taylor & Francis Group, an informa business

British Library Cataloguing-in-Publication Data
A catalogue record for this book is available from the British Library

Library of Congress Cataloging in Publication Data
A catalog record for this book has been requested

ISBN: 978-1-138-82618-2 (hbk)
ISBN: 978-1-138-82619-9 (pbk)
ISBN: 978-1-315-73949-6 (ebk)

Typeset in Bembo
by Fakenham Prepress Solutions, Fakenham, Norfolk NR21 8NN
Printed and bound in Great Britain by
Ashford Colour Press Ltd, Gosport, Hampshire

Dedication

Ben – To Lisa, Brennan, and Lily – my supportive and patient family.

Ash – To Sarah, Thomas and Maddie, and to Mum – those who've supported me unfailingly and unselfishly while I've pursued my dreams.

CONTENTS

ILLUSTRATIONS

Figures

Tables

Boxes

Worksheets

Diagrams

FOREWORD

In this immensely useful and practical book, authors Ben Dyson and Ash Casey, who are both experts in the field, describe Cooperative Learning as a pedagogical model rather than a teaching model by focusing on the junction of teaching, learning and curriculum and five critical elements including: (a) Positive Interdependence, (b) Individual Accountability, (c) Promotive Face-to-Face Interaction, (d) Interpersonal and Small Group Skills, and (e) Group Processing (Dyson & Casey, 2012). Metzler (2011) in his popular textbook on teaching models for Physical Education called Cooperative Learning one of the models for the future of Physical Education. Others have called it the fastest growing teaching model for Physical Education. Notable critical student outcomes for our Physical Education programs from this pedagogical model include improved self-efficacy and motivation or psychological health, better participation or engagement with tasks, development of communication skills, and increased skill levels and academic achievement through understanding and applying content (Casey & Goodyear, 2015, p. 57).

Although Cooperative Learning has been used for about 50 years, primarily in Science, Math and Literacy programs (e.g. Cohen, 1994), it is a model for the future in Physical Education. Activities such as 'Jigsaw Perform' may not be new; however, they are new in their use in Physical Education and physical activity settings. The authors show us how this pedagogical model can be used in active settings to enhance students' experiences and learning outcomes.

The authors published a companion book to this text in 2012 that focused on Cooperative Learning as a research-based approach. This current book is one of the first (along with an out-of-print guide, Grineski, 1996) to inform teachers and teacher educators about how to teach Physical Education and physical activity using the Cooperative Learning model from a practitioner's perspective. This book will be immensely useful for teachers and teacher educators alike.

The authors bring expertise in both research and practice, thus enabling them to bridge the theory–practice gap. Thus, the authors present research-grounded information and sample activities in practical ways that are easy for teachers and teacher educators to immediately use in their teaching settings (e.g. gymnasium, playing fields, community space, or university). Many of the chapters have useful teacher friendly sections, such as, 'we believe that', 'thinking outside the box', 'give it a go', 'imagine the scene', 'self-processing / a time to reflect', and 'our reflections'. In 'our reflections', for example, the authors share their own perspectives and experiences in very personal ways that immediately connect the reader to the authors' stories.

Similarly, in the sections of 'imagine the scene', actual Cooperative Learning teaching experiences are shared. Reading about these scenes made me feel like Larry Locke (1989) describing beginning studies in qualitative research in the 1980s. 'I [too] can almost smell the sneakers' – such are the examples that allow the reader to imagine what this teaching–learning experience was like and how they can immediately use this pedagogical practice in her/his classes. There are numerous examples under 'imagine the scene' that present real student and teacher experiences, such as the following excerpt from Chapter 3:

> The students' eyes light up when they realize they are in charge of the equipment and that they can let their imagination run wild with what types of jumping obstacles they can build. Cathy walks around the gym watching the students working together to form the obstacles. She notices the group with the jump ropes is playing limbo and not practicing jumping skills. She poses a question to the group, 'What skill are we working on today?' The students reply 'Jumping!' and then quickly realize that the obstacle they are building is not accomplishing the task. One student suggests that they talk about how they can use the jump ropes in different ways.

These types of authentic classroom examples make the book come alive and will encourage and enable teachers to adopt this pedagogical model. The textbook is also written in accessible language for teachers and teacher educators, while challenging teachers to reflect on their current teaching practices.

All teaching levels are addressed in this text from elementary/primary levels through university levels and it is also written from an international perspective. The authors' experiences working with teachers and researchers on Cooperative Learning across levels and many cultural settings (e.g. Asia, Europe, North America, the Pacific and the Middle East) adds to the applicability of these materials for teachers and teacher educators around the world.

All Physical Education and physical activity teachers should have this ready-to-use tool on their bookshelf. This text will lead to developing the teaching skills to make Cooperative Learning part of their Physical Education and physical activity teaching repertoire.

References

Casey, A. & Goodyear, V. (2015). Can Cooperative Learning Achieve the Four Learning Outcomes of Physical Education? A Review of Literature, *Quest, 67*(1), 56-72, DOI:1 0.1080/00336297.2014.984733.

Cohen, E. G. (1994). Restructuring the classroom: Conditions for productive small groups. *Review of Educational Research, 64*(1), 1-35.

Dyson, B. & Casey, A. (2012). *Cooperative learning in physical education: A research-based approach.* London: Routledge.

Grineski, S. (1996). *Cooperative learning in physical education.* Champaign, IL: Human Kinetics 1996.

Locke, L. F. (1989). Qualitative research as a form of scientific inquiry in sport and physical education. *Research Quarterly for Exercise and Sport, 60*, 1-20.

Metzler, M. W. (2011). *Instructional models for physical education* (3rd ed.). Scottsdale, AZ: Holcomb Hathaway.

Professor Pamela Hodges-Kulinna,
Arizona State University, USA.
September 2015

ACKNOWLEDGEMENTS

To all the teachers, student teachers, and students we have worked with over the years in many different countries and many different contexts: you have interacted with us and challenged us to rethink our pedagogies and dared us to think and do in different, more learner-centered ways. Our heartfelt thanks to you all.

To our colleagues and friends who have supported us in this and other endeavors: most noticeably (but not exclusively) – Vicky Goodyear, Pamela Hodges-Kulinna, Pat Yeaton, Michelle Grenier, all those authors who worked with us on the companion book, Simon Whitmore, and William Bailey.

1

COOPERATIVE LEARNING AS A PEDAGOGICAL MODEL IN PHYSICAL EDUCATION

Chapter overview

This chapter provides an introduction to Cooperative Learning as a pedagogical practice. It explores the five key elements and characteristics of Cooperative Learning and positions them within Physical Education. Drawing on our substantial experience of Cooperative Learning, the chapter presents the research in layman's terms and offers the reader a chance to engage with the ideas behind the model. This chapter also examines and describes different approaches to teaching and makes clear and understandable links between these approaches and practice.

Key aspects of Cooperative Learning as a pedagogical practice

In our experiences of teaching through, and researching about, Cooperative Learning in Physical Education over the years we have come to value and believe a few things. At the beginning of each chapter we present things that we believe about Cooperative Learning.

We believe that

1. Physical Education needs to be raised to a higher status in the education system. As educators we are tasked to facilitate student learning and student success.
2. Being a teacher, an outdoor educator, and/or a community worker is important and makes a vital contribution to society.
3. Physical Education and Outdoor Education are important subject areas that can make a valuable contribution to the education of all students.

4. Teachers can improve students' physical, cognitive, affective, and social skills through the creation of a positive learning environment.
5. All students deserve high-quality Physical Education and physical activity programs. That is, we believe in truly inclusive Physical Education programs.
6. Teaching through Cooperative Learning in Physical Education is *not* 'business as usual'.
7. Cooperative Learning generates interest for young people in Physical Education and physical activity settings.

Imagine the scene

The gym is alive with activity and students are divided into their Cooperative Learning Teams, with four students in each group. Students in this class of 14-year-olds are working on their training programs both in the gym and outside. Each group has a coach, a manager, an equipment organizer, and an encourager. As you watch the teacher, Jackson, asks his class 'What's your Learning Team's training goal for today? Are you going to meet your team target today?' The students reply loudly 'Yes we are!!!' Each group has a clipboard with their tasks hand-written by the group on it. It is to these tasks that they now turn.

Some groups start by running shuttles, some by lifting weights, while others are doing plyometrics (box jumping in this instance). The groups stop their activity at a time of their choosing, sit in a small huddle, and engage in an inclusive interchange of ideas. After observing these individual group discussions for a while you can see that all students in these mixed groups (mixed by ability, gender, and race, etc.) are contributing to the discussion. They are intensely engaged in talking about what they need to do today to reach the targets they have set for each other. One group asks Jackson, 'Can we combine different training programs?' Jackson smiles and replies, 'That's your choice, but think about the best way to ensure you get the full benefit from what you have planned.' Jackson, a former college rower, has taught the students about periodization for different training programs for different activities like triathlon, dance, kayaking, and martial arts – among others – and they have the knowledge to perform different activities safely.

As you continue to watch you see that Jackson is very active as a teacher, moving quickly to each group to monitor and interact with each of his students, while resisting the urge to tell them exactly what to learn. Stopping briefly to scan the whole class, Jackson sees something he thinks is important and quickly moves closer to one of the teams, the 'Wanderers'. He is watching all groups, but standing closer to the Wanderers, listening to their discussion. He is ready to provide different ideas to help them fine-tune their target for their Cooperative Learning Structure Learning Teams. You sense that Jackson wants to make a comment based on what he sees but he tries to stand back and listen. Eventually, sensing an impasse in their discussion, he makes a suggestion, 'Why don't you try it and see what happens and then change it if you need to?' Jackson sees them safely back into action and then moves to the other end of the gym and to another team, the 'Vibes'.

Before he steps in with a prompt, one of the group members makes the suggestion that they should vote on how hard they should push themselves and what training targets they should set for themselves in their practice time today. Jackson steps back and looks around at his class, who he finds working hard, problem-solving, and working together at their own pace on the activities. Some teams are still discussing their workout, while the Wanderers have started a 10m shuttle run on the gym court. Jackson's intended learning outcome for this lesson was for students to apply the knowledge they had learned to create a training program for their choice of activity (triathlon, dance, kayaking, or martial arts, etc.), and set an appropriate training goal for today for their Learning Team. Looking around the gym one last time you would agree that everyone appears to work together in their group with the unifying aim of the group to contribute to achievement of their mutually agreed group goal.

Introduction

If it works here (and we have multiple examples of it working to share with you in this book), maybe it could work in your gymnasium, on your playing fields, or in your community setting. But before we share these examples we need to explore what Cooperative Learning is and examine the overarching idea that operates at the junction between teaching, learning, and curriculum – what we define as pedagogy for the purposes of this book. By the end of this chapter you will have a better understanding of Cooperative Learning, be able to describe different elements and approaches to using Cooperative Learning, and begin to understand its possible contributions to enhancing learning in Physical Education and physical activity. You will be able to explain the educative goals of Cooperative Learning and, using the resources for teaching that will be provided, you will be able to try it yourself. The Organisation for Economic Co-operation and Development's (OECD) (2013) Futures Report suggested that Cooperative Learning is one of the six innovative pedagogical approaches that should be used to create effective student-centered learning environments in the twenty-first century.

In the rest of the chapter we will begin by briefly defining Cooperative Learning and then discuss more thoroughly, through our experiences and reflection, the notion that it is a pedagogical model that deliberately considers the divergent needs of teaching, learning, and curriculum. We will show how it can be applied to different content areas, and with different age groups, and in different schools and educational settings. We will use examples throughout and provide resources to help you get started. We hope you enjoy using Cooperative Learning and get as much out of using it as we have in our teaching, in our collective work with teachers across three continents, and in many diverse settings.

What is Cooperative Learning? The five elements

For us Cooperative Learning is a dynamic pedagogical model that allows the teacher to be flexible in their choice of which of the three aspects of pedagogy to favor. Consequently Cooperative Learning can teach diverse content to students at different grade levels. Students work together in small, structured, heterogeneous (in other words mixed by ability, race, gender, socio-economic background, and so on) groups to master subject matter content (Dyson, Linehan, & Hastie, 2010). The students are not only responsible for learning the material, but also for helping their group-mates learn (Cohen, 1994; Dyson & Casey, 2012). In the act of taking on the role of teacher, the students are better positioned to understand what is being learned.

Just putting students in groups, however, is not Cooperative Learning. We would like to emphasize, as Velazquez–Callado (2012) has argued, that Cooperative Learning is not just students working in groups, playing cooperative games, or being involved in team building activities. Johnson and Johnson (1999, p. 68) presented concerns about students working in groups:

> Seating people together and calling them a cooperative group does not make them one. Study groups, project groups, lab groups, home-rooms, and reading groups are groups, but they are not necessarily cooperative. Even with the best of intentions, teachers may be using traditional classroom learning groups rather than cooperative learning groups. To ensure that a group is cooperative, educators must understand the different ways cooperative learning may be used and the basic elements that need to be used and the basic elements that need to be carefully structured within every cooperative activity.

Practitioners often state that they are doing Cooperative Learning but this is based on the fact that students are grouped together or are working together. Yet this doesn't mean they are doing Cooperative Learning. In order to actually be using Cooperative Learning as a pedagogical model, and not just collaborative learning, cooperative games, or team games, there are five critical elements of the model (Dyson & Casey, 2012; Johnson & Johnson, 2009) that we believe act as explicit guidelines in the successful implementation of Cooperative Learning in Physical Education, as seen in Figure 1.1.

These elements will be introduced here and will appear throughout this book, as they are critical in the successful implementation of Cooperative Learning in your lessons. They form the backbone of the pedagogical aspects of this model and will serve as indicators that you are 'doing it right', so to speak. That is not to say that these are inflexible markers against which your work will be judged. Instead they should be considered as guidelines against which you can start to examine your practice.

1. Clearly perceived Positive Interdependence.
2. Considerable Promotive (Face-to-Face) Interaction.
3. Clearly perceived Individual Accountability and personal responsibility to achieve the group's goals.
4. Frequent use of the relevant Interpersonal and Small Group Skills.
5. Frequent and regular Group Processing of current functioning to improve the group's future effectiveness.

FIGURE 1.1 Cooperative Learning elements

In many ways as educators we are already experts when it comes to the first element of Cooperative Learning – *Positive Interdependence.* Success is only achieved when students work together in teams and rely on each other to complete the task. Only in this way are students or players positively interdependent on each other. That is to say that students rely on each other to complete the pre-designed task, i.e. 'we sink or swim together' (Johnson & Johnson, 1999). In Physical Education and Outdoor Education and community sport we are familiar with many examples of Positive Interdependence. In fact, every team sport requires it to be successful. For example, whether it is working in a volleyball team to develop three hits, or performing part of a dance, or holding up the rugby scrum, students or players are positively interdependent on each other.

In your Physical Education program, whenever students rely on each other to complete the task, they are being positively interdependent. Positive Interdependence exists when students perceive that they are linked to group members in such a way that they cannot succeed unless all the other group members do. That is, students rely on each other to complete the pre-designed task or class goal. As social interdependence guru Deutsch (1949) has suggested, Positive Interdependence is a sense of being 'on the same side'.

Yet this is not something that just happens when you play as part of a team. Learning to cooperate is not an explicit outcome of asking kids to work together. In fact, Hellison and Wright (2003) suggest that no one has actually ever demonstrated the commonly held belief that team games teach cooperation and teamwork. In contrast, these 'working together' skills are meaningfully developed in a Cooperative Learning classroom and not simply left to chance. For example, ask a class of students to score five points in a basketball task and the most able player will complete the objective in as few as two shots while the least able might not achieve the task in the whole lesson. Ask a group of players to score twenty points together with no one player scoring more than their share of the points and suddenly students are positively interdependent on each other to complete the task. The focus of this text is based on 'how to teach' the elements, Cooperative Learning Structures, and characteristics of Cooperative Learning.

In Cooperative Learning in Physical Education and physical activity settings we present Cooperative Learning Structures to move students towards *Individual Accountability.* In these settings we hope that students are individually accountable or answerable to some improvement (Lund & Tannehil, 2015) but in reality, if we are honest with ourselves and our students (in schools or universities), we are often making educated guesses and don't require appropriate evidence to determine assessments. That is, we are not quite sure or we don't really have the evidence to demonstrate that our students have developed in any of the domains of learning, have better social skills, or have improved on their defense or learned a motor skill. Individual Accountability refers to students taking responsibility for completing their part of the task for their group and learning something in the process. For example, we recommend accountability strategies like 'student task sheets' that can hold students individually accountable and create a situation where assigned tasks are more explicit for students. In a well-designed Cooperative Learning class, accountability strategies try to minimize what Tousignant and Siedentop (1984) called 'competent bystanders' (see Chapter 12) in Physical Education and what Slavin (1996) referred to as 'free riders' in Math and Reading.

The next Cooperative Learning element, *Promotive Face-to-Face Interaction*, is often undervalued and misunderstood. In the Cooperative Learning classroom (and our definition of classroom is broad: it could be a gymnasium, a community swimming pool, a playing field or court, or an Adventure Education camp) we want students to feel physically and emotionally safe (Dyson & Sutherland, 2015). That is, small groups or teams are nurtured and created to have an explicit role to encourage one another. Often this occurs generally in the group and everyone is asked (and expected to encourage) but equally individuals might have a specific role in their group. This role, the encourager, would be someone in close proximity who gives promotive or positive comments to other members of the group. Students in their groups or teams should be literally head-to-head, toe-to-toe, knee-to-knee, that is, in close proximity to each other. Students should be providing positive comments and engaging in a positive and supportive dialogue with other members of their group. Using the role of encourager with your students can support Promotive Face-to-Face Interaction, but it's not the only way of doing it.

The next element, *Interpersonal and Small Group Skills*, is especially related to the development of social skills and is listed as a goal of curricula and national standards across the globe. Look at Strand 5 and 6 from the US National Standards or the curricula from New Zealand, the UK, Australia, Korea, France, Germany, Spain, China and Israel, to name a few countries that we have worked in, and you will see the need for these skills. Interpersonal and Small Group Skills are student behaviors that allow comfortable and relaxed communication between group mates. We would argue that in our modern, electronically enhanced world, students and teachers (of elementary, middle school, high school, or university age) do not have strong interpersonal and social skills. These skills are developed through the tasks in which students participate and may include listening, shared decision making, taking responsibility, giving and receiving feedback, leading, following, and encouraging each other. Research suggests that positive interaction and the development of social skills greatly influences successful school participation and achievement (Cornelius–White, 2007; Wang, Haertel, & Walberg, 1993).

The most unique and perhaps the most important element for Cooperative Learning is *Group Processing*. Our definition of Group Processing is borrowed from Outdoor Education and Project Adventure (Dyson, 1995; Sutherland, 2012). Group Processing is best understood as a reflective, guided discussion that is student-centered, that is, guided by the students rather than driven by the teacher. Group Processing is a social and cognitive task and often is represented during the Physical Education lesson as 'strategizing', that is, the students in their team talk about and create an offensive or defensive strategy (Dyson et al., 2010). In Group Processing, team members work towards constructing meaning from the task, activity, or game they have just participated in. Sutherland (2012) suggests that this Group Processing differs from the notion of Group Processing in general education (Johnson & Johnson, 1989), which has more of an emphasis on student evaluation. Through the experience of Group Processing students learn to apply this meaning to other situations in their lives. This transfer of learning to another setting could be in another class, outside in the playground, or at home with their family. When a teacher or coach is highly skilled at Group Processing they can use this teaching strategy throughout their lesson, not just as a debrief or closure portion of a lesson.

In summary, the five main elements of Cooperative Learning are: Positive Interdependence (working well together); Individual Accountability (taking responsibility for your own contribution and effort); Promotive Face-to-Face Interaction (helping each other to learn); interpersonal and small-group skills (being able to work together, negotiate, and compromise for the greater good of the group); and Group Processing (being able to critically reflect on the development of the group and move ideas forward). The next step is to apply these five main elements of Cooperative Learning in your Physical Education, Outdoor Education, or community sports program. Ultimately, and drawing on the work of Johnson and Johnson (1994, p. 5):

> Cooperative efforts result in participants' recognizing that all group members share a common fate (We all sink or swim together), striving for mutual benefit so that all group members benefit from each other's efforts (Your efforts benefit me and my efforts benefit you), recognizing that one's performance is mutually caused by oneself and one's colleagues (United we stand, divided we fall), empowering each other (Together we can achieve anything), and feeling proud and jointly celebrating when a group member is recognized for achievement (You got an A! That's terrific!).

Pedagogy, Cooperative Learning, and removing the 'me' from 'team'

We believe that for learning to occur in a classroom it has to involve each and every student. An obvious statement perhaps, but we believe that for many students learning in education is not always positive. Unfortunately, this belief is supported by a multitude of studies in our field (see for example the work of Ennis, 2014). Indeed, under a traditional approach to teaching Physical Education many students learn that they are not capable, that even their best efforts are not enough to beat even the most half-hearted of efforts from some of their more able peers, and that teachers often use increased amounts of praise to encourage the least able students. Therefore, while students quickly learn that performance and ability are the measures of worth in Physical Education (see Chapter 7 and Chapter 11 for a fuller discussion), they also learn that ability is defined in narrow terms around performance in traditional team sports such as basketball, soccer, cricket, and American football.

In contrast, Cooperative Learning, when it's done well and when it uses all of its attributes, goes a long way to ensure that success is about more than just performance. Success is defined in terms of team or group achievement and not individual prowess, and it (i.e. success) can only be achieved when everyone works together for a shared purpose. To put it more simply, it encompasses everything that is good about team sports while deliberately removing the 'me' from 'team'. Yes, individuals can still shine, but only when they work as part of the team. Just like the star quarterback is made ineffectual without the wide receiver to catch the pass, the offensive line to hold back the blitz, and the linebacker to sack the other quarterback, so the most able student in Cooperative Learning is dependent on his or her teammates to succeed.

We want to emphasize from the beginning that we are both very passionate about high-quality Physical Education, Outdoor Education, and community sport. Unfortunately, many programs around the world (at elementary, middle, and high school age settings) are characterized by traditional practices. These practices are representative of a 'multi-activity' approach (Metzler, 2011) that lacks in-depth learning and focuses on large-group competitive activities that offer minimal opportunities for individual students to grow and develop. We believe that *all students* should be valued in, and have the opportunity to learn in, Physical Education and other settings. To be more inclusive Physical Education, Outdoor Education, sports, and community professionals need to acknowledge the inter-connectivity between teaching, learning, and curriculum. In other words, we need to focus on pedagogy.

In this book we purposely use the term 'pedagogical model' rather than 'instructional model' or 'curriculum model' to describe Cooperative Learning. The terms 'instructional model' and 'curriculum model' are too narrow a definition for our understanding of Cooperative Learning (Haerens et al., 2011). When we teach through Cooperative Learning we are not just referring to the teacher's instruction but also to the students' response to that instruction and the context where something is taught. We believe Cooperative Learning to be an 'equity pedagogy', i.e. more inclusive for the teacher and more inclusive for *all* students as equal participants in the learning. Cooperative Learning works as an 'inclusive' practice that encourages and supports student learning thorough the process of all students working together in their group to complete the task or to achieve the group's goals (Alton-Lee, 2011). With this equity pedagogy we hope to develop a 'positive learning environment' (which will be discussed in Chapter 4).

Pedagogy is a term that is becoming increasingly popular in education and yet it is seldom accompanied by a definition (Tinning, 2008). For our purposes, we present pedagogy as a three-way relationship connecting teacher, students, and the knowledge to be taught and learned (Amade-Escot, 2006). In Figure 1.2 the notion of pedagogy that we are using is best defined by its three components: teaching, learning, and curriculum.

In reconsidering the traditional approach – indeed the original notion of pedagogy – we would suggest that teaching has held the topmost hierarchical

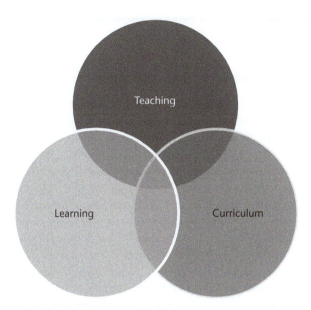

FIGURE 1.2   The three components of pedagogy

position in this relationship, followed by curriculum and finally by learning. Put another way, teachers have been shown to have a preferred teaching style that is normally commanding in nature, and they take this into every classroom. With the style of teaching chosen, next comes the curriculum choice. Evidence suggests that this is predominantly focused on team games and sports techniques, which are well suited to a command style approach to teaching. The learning – more specifically the learner – comes last in this relationship and they are expected to adapt to the teaching style and curricula choice.

When considering the wider notion of pedagogy, and applying it to the education of our young people, we believe that learning ceases to be subordinate to teaching and curriculum. Consequently teachers are able to make informed decisions about a number of issues. For example, the teacher wants to teach the fundamental skill of the overhead throw. This decision is made because it is felt that mastery of this skill will transfer to many other situations, such as serving in tennis, throwing the javelin, and/or the quarterback pass. The throw becomes the learning outcome for the session and is then placed within an appropriate curriculum setting that could be games or could be track and field. Finally, the teacher decides that the prior learning of these students in throwing is adequate so decides to use a peer-teaching approach. In this way the learning choice is made first, the curriculum second, and the teaching third. However, for this to happen there needs to be thoughtful planning, teaching, assessing, and critical ongoing reflection of what Physical Education is and does, so that it makes a valuable contribution to the lives of students. We think Cooperative Learning has the potential to support and encourage teachers in this process and in the next section we will explore how Cooperative Learning achieves this by exploring the model and its five elements.

Apply this understanding to your classrooms and gymnasia

As a pedagogical model, Cooperative Learning is a relatively new area of research in Physical Education, Outdoor Education, and community sport (Casey & Goodyear, 2015). However, we are encouraged to see that there is a growing amount of research in Physical Education, which we will present in the next chapter. The intention of presenting the findings from evidenced-based research is to expand your understanding and support your use of Cooperative Learning. However, we know that change in your context is very difficult. We agree with Hargreaves and Fullan (2009) that change in schools is never *simplistic* or *linear* but is always *chaotic* and *messy*. In our research over the last 20 years in schools we have come to realize that the change that we present in this book is complex and will be a conceptual shift for you and your students (Casey, 2013; Dyson et al., 2004). In what remains of this book we hope to make that process easier by scaffolding your efforts with examples, research-informed ideas and common sense approaches. One way in which we will do this is by asking you to take some time to reflect. We use the term 'self-processing' to represent a time when you take the time to reflect on your reading. We hope that some of the ideas in this book will spur your interest. We hope that you can allocate some time to reflect on one or two of the questions posed at the end of each chapter or on an issue, concern, and/or question that you have during your reading.

Many folks have only a superficial understanding of the knowledge and the practice of Cooperative Learning in general education (Antil et al., 1998) and particularly in Physical Education. In terms of general education, Cooperative Learning has been around for over 50 years (Casey & Dyson, 2012; Cohen, 1994; Johnson & Johnson, 2009; Kagan & Kagan, 2009; Slavin, 1996) and it is likely that you might have seen teachers using it in core subjects such as Math, Literacy, and Science. In 1996 Steve Grineski brought Cooperative Learning to Physical Education in a book of the same name. More recently, there has been a revitalization of Cooperative Learning in Physical Education, and we have published our own book *Cooperative learning in physical education: A research based approach* (2012). That text defines the model, examines the implementation of Cooperative Learning in a variety of educational settings, and presents research from eight different countries. We believe that the previous book demonstrates that Cooperative Learning is 'alive and well' in several different countries and has achieved success in multiple contexts with thousands of students. The research on Cooperative Learning has found many benefits to teachers' instruction and to students' learning in all the domains of learning (Casey & Goodyear, 2015). More details about the research are provided in Chapter 2. If you are not interested in the evidence found to support Cooperative Learning through research we suggest that you skip the next chapter.

If you do choose to skip to the next chapter then please bear the following in mind. There are a number of benefits of Cooperative Learning and the research or evidence to support these are provided in Chapter 2. However, a brief summary of some of the educational benefits of Cooperative Learning: There is improvement in the physical, social, and cognitive skills of learners (Casey & Goodyear, 2015). Teachers notice an increase in positive instructions that encourage students to give more effort, and this facilitates an increase in interpersonal skills and purposeful discussion. Research also suggests that Cooperative Learning can decrease negative teacher or coach behaviors, such as overcorrecting students, disciplining students, interrupting students, and hurrying students in their activities too much.

Self-processing / A time to reflect

Self-processing questions

1. What motivated you to become a physical educator or teacher, outdoor educator or coach, or community worker?
2. Google 'Positive Interdependence'. What are some of the examples you have found? How might they be applied in your classes and with your students?
3. What is your prior experience with Cooperative Learning?
4. Do you think Cooperative Learning can work in your program?

Our reflections

Ben

When observing Cooperative Learning in Physical Education I have seen students: helping each other, patting each other on the back, listening to each other, cheering for each other, giving specific skills feedback to each other, and laughing loudly with each other. This highlights to me the value of an inclusive and 'student-centered' pedagogy.

Ash

I wonder when I moved from learning about Cooperative Learning myself in my gymnasium to helping other teachers to learn how to use it. It seems like such a big step and yet such an obvious one. When I learned how to use Cooperative Learning – before I learned about pedagogy and research – I had to rely on a few books from general education and the papers that Ben had written. The rest I had to make up as I went along. This book, to me, represents the evolution of the model in our subject and allows me to do what I'm best at – teach. It allows me to use my decade or more of using Cooperative Learning to help others to 'get to grips' with it and develop their own pedagogies.

References

Alton-Lee, A. (2011). (Using) evidence for educational improvement. *Cambridge Journal of Education*, *41*(3), 303–329. http://doi.org/10.1080/0305764X.2011.607150

Amade-Escot, C. (2006). Student Learning within the Didactique Tradition. In D. Kirk, D. MacDonald, M. O'Sullivan (Eds.), *The handbook of physical education* (pp. 347–366). London: Sage. http://doi.org/http://dx.doi.org.ezproxy.auckland.ac.nz/10.4135/9781848608009.n20

Antil, L. R., Jenkins, J. R., Wayne, S. K., & Vadasy, P. F. (1998). Cooperative learning: prevalence, conceptualizations, and the relation between research and practice. *American Educational Research Journal*, *35*(3), 419–454. http://doi.org/10.3102/00028312035003419

Casey, A. (2013). 'Seeing the trees not just the wood': Steps and not just journeys in teacher action research. *Educational Action Research*, *21*(2), 147–163. http://doi.org/10.1080/09650792.2013.789704

Casey, A. & Dyson, B. (2012). Putting Cooperative Learning and physical activity into practice with primary students. In B. Dyson & A. Casey (Eds.), *Cooperative learning in physical education: A research-based approach* (pp. 59–74). London: Routledge.

Casey, A. & Goodyear, V. A. (2015). Can Cooperative Learning achieve the four learning outcomes of physical education? A review of literature. *Quest*, *67*(1), 56–72. http://doi.org/10.1080/00336297.2014.984733

Cohen, E. G. (1994). Restructuring the classroom: Conditions for productive small groups. *Review of Educational Research*, *64*(1), 1–35. http://doi.org/10.3102/00346543064001001

Cornelius-White, J. (2007). Learner-centered teacher-student relationships are effective: A meta-analysis. *Review of Educational Research*, *77*(1), 113–143. http://doi.org/10.3102/003465430298563

Deutsch, M. (1949). A theory of co-operation and competition. *Human Relations*, *2*(2), 129–152. http://doi.org/10.1177/001872674900200204

Dyson, B. (1995). Students' voices in two alternative elementary physical education programs. *Journal of Teaching in Physical Education*, *14*(4), 394–407. Retrieved from http://ezproxy.auckland.ac.nz/login?url=http://search.ebscohost.com/login.aspx?direct=true&db=sph&AN=20752003&site=ehost-live&scope=site

Dyson, B. & Casey, A. (2012). *Cooperative learning in physical education: A research-based approach*. London: Routledge.

Dyson, B. & Sutherland, S. (2015). Adventure based learning. In J. Lund & D. Tannehill (Eds.), *Standards-based curriculum development* ((3rd ed.), pp. 56–68). Boston, MA: Jones Bartlett.

Dyson, B., Griffin, L. L., & Hastie, P. (2004). Sport education, tactical games, and cooperative learning: Theoretical and pedagogical considerations. *Quest*, *56*(2), 226–240.

Dyson, B., Linehan, N. R., & Hastie, P. A. (2010). The ecology of Cooperative Learning in elementary physical education classes. *Journal of Teaching in Physical Education*, *29*, 113–130.

Ennis, C. D. (2014). The role of students and content in teacher effectiveness. *Research Quarterly for Exercise and Sport*, *85*(1), 6–13. http://doi.org/10.1080/02701367.2014.872979

Haerens, L., Kirk, D., Cardon, G., & De Bourdeaudhuij, I. (2011). Toward the development of a pedagogical model for health-based physical education. *Quest*, *63*(3), 321–338. http://doi.org/10.1080/00336297.2011.10483684

Hargreaves, A. & Fullan, M. (Eds.). (2009). *Change wars*. Bloomington, IN: Solution Tree.

Hellison, D. & Wright, P. (2003). Retention in an urban extended day program: A process-based assessment. *Journal of Teaching in Physical Education*, *22*(4), 369–381.

Johnson, D. W. & Johnson, R. T. (1989). *Cooperation and competition: Theory and research.* Edina, MN: Interaction Book.

Johnson, D. W. & Johnson, R.T. (1994). *Learning together and alone: cooperative, competitive, and individualistic learning.* London: Allyn and Bacon.

Johnson, D. W. & Johnson, R. T. (1999). Making cooperative learning work. *Theory Into Practice, 38*(2), 67–73. http://doi.org/10.1080/00405849909543834

Johnson, D. W. & Johnson, R. T. (2009). An educational psychology success story: Social interdependence theory and cooperative learning. *Educational Researcher, 38*(5), 365–379. http://doi.org/10.3102/0013189X09339057

Kagan, S. & Kagan, M. (2009). *Kagan cooperative learning.* San Clemente, CA: Kagan.

Lund, J. & Tannehil, D. (2015). *Standards-based physical education curriulum development* (3rd ed.). Barlett and Jones.

Metzler, M. W. (2011). *Instructional models for physical education* (3rd ed.). Scottsdale, AZ: Holcomb Hathaway.

OECD. (2013). *Innovative learning environments.* Paris: OECD. Retrieved from http://dx.doi.org/10.1787/9789264203488-2-en

Slavin, R. E. (1996). Research for the future on on Cooperative Learning and achievement: What we know, what we need to know. *Contemporary Educational Psychology, 69*(1), 43–69. http://doi.org/http://dx.doi.org/10.1006/ceps.1996.0004

Sutherland, S. (2012). Borrowing strategies from adventure-based learning to enhance group processing in cooperative learning. In B. Dyson & A. Casey (Eds.), *Cooperative learning in physical education: A research-based approach* (pp. 103–118). London: Routledge.

Tinning, R. (2008). Pedagogy, sport pedagogy, and the field of kinesiology. *Quest, 60*(3), 405–424. http://doi.org/10.1080/00336297.2008.10483589

Tousignant, M. & Siedentop, D. (1984). A qualitative analysis of task structures in required secondary physical education classes. *Journal of Teaching in Physical Education, 3*(1), 47–57.

Velazquez-Callado, C. (2012). Cooperative learning and physical activity into practice with primary students. In B. Dyson & A. Casey (Eds.), *Cooperative learning in physical education: A research-based approach* (pp. 59–74). London: Routledge.

Wang, M. C., Haertel, G. D., & Walberg, H. J. (1993). Toward a knowledge base for school learning. *Review of Educational Research, 63*(3), 249–294. http://doi.org/10.3102/00346543063003249

2

RESEARCHED BENEFITS OF COOPERATIVE LEARNING AS A PEDAGOGICAL PRACTICE

Chapter overview

Drawing on the work of authors across multiple settings and countries, this chapter explores the research findings associated with using Cooperative Learning in Physical Education and physical activity settings. Using examples from classrooms and the community, the chapter explores key findings around the benefits of using the approach and uses the voices of teachers and students to show its effectiveness (Dyson & Casey, 2012). Cooperative Learning is a pedagogical model suitable for generating change in schools because of its focus on cognitive and social goals (Alton-Lee, 2011; Johnson & Johnson, 2009; Slavin, 2010). In addition to this dual focus, when Cooperative Learning is used in Physical Education, the psycho-motor domain of learning, that is, motor and tactical goals, are added as learning intentions (Dyson, Linehan, & Hastie, 2010). Recently, Casey and Goodyear (2015) extended this notion to include learning in the physical, cognitive, social, and affective domains. The amalgamation of these goals means that Cooperative Learning is capable of helping students to develop physically and cognitively, while also enhancing the quality of their social interactions and their group work.

Why research informed pedagogy?

In writing about and advocating for research-informed choices in the form of pedagogy we understand the need to make our choices from a position of understanding. While research has been seen as something that teachers don't read (Hargreaves & Fullan, 2009) it might be more accurate to suggest that it is something they cannot access. However, working from a research-informed position and experience allows us to state our beliefs.

We believe that

1. Educators benefit from a knowledge and understanding of research.
2. Research can provide knowledge to educators to guide them to make a greater contribution to the education of our children.
3. With support and guidance teachers can carry out worthwhile and meaningful research in their teaching setting.
4. Cooperative Learning used as a pedagogical practice can enhance students' physical, cognitive, and social skills, and their affective development.
5. Cooperative Learning has much potential in Physical Education, Outdoor Education, and community programs. We also believe that you can be part of the team to further develop Cooperative Learning as a pedagogical practice.

Research on Cooperative Learning

What can we learn from the general Cooperative Learning research?

In the last 40 years much of the research in Physical Education has developed from research in other subject areas in education. Our definitions and initial formats or instructional guidelines for our research come from general education. For example, in the 1970s Academic Learning Time in PE (ALT-PE) research emerged from Academic Learning Time (ALT) research (Fisher, 1981) and the ecology of the gymnasium research on Cooperative Learning originated in work in Dyson, Linehan, and Hastie (2010). Similarly, the huge body of literature from general education on Cooperative Learning (see for example Cohen, 1994; Gillies & Haynes, 2011; Johnson & Johnson, 1989, 2009; Slavin, 1996, 2010) has informed the work in Physical Education (Casey & Goodyear, 2015).

Research in general education (from areas such as Literacy, Social Studies, Art, Technology, Math, and Science) has reported that using Cooperative Learning has improved the classroom environment, academic achievement, active learning, social–skill development, and classroom equity (Cohen, 1994; Cohen & Lotan, 2004; Gillies & Haynes, 2011; Johnson & Johnson, 1989, 2009; Slavin, 1996, 2010). Gillies and Haynes (2011) suggested that Cooperative Learning can provide instruction that leads students to more authentic learning experiences, allows for more active participation, is more meaningful, and empowers students to learn complex content. In general education Cooperative Learning has a dual learning emphasis on social and academic goals (Antil, Jenkins, Wayne, & Vadasy, 1998; Cohen, 1994; Sharan, 2010). However, when Cooperative Learning is taught in Physical Education, the psychomotor domain of learning is added as a learning priority (Casey & Goodyear, 2015; Dyson et al., 2010; Metzler, 2011).

In our book *Cooperative Learning in physical education: A research-based approach* (Dyson & Casey, 2012), we extend the knowledge and understanding of Cooperative Learning as a research base and practical pedagogical model in Physical Education. In that book we explore elementary, middle, and high school settings and university classrooms with research from Australia, France, Germany, Israel, New Zealand, Spain, the UK, and the USA. That text provides a rich variety of global theory and practice contexts from the leading educators and authors working with Cooperative Learning in Physical Education. We are excited and encouraged by this research base but more impressed with the practical work that is going on around the world. Slavin (2010), a leading expert on Cooperative Learning, recently commented about global school reform, stating that he still believes that Cooperative Learning 'is relatively inexpensive and easily adopted'. Unfortunately he also suggests that 'thirty years after much of the foundational research was completed, it remains at the edge of school policy' (p. 174).

The general education research has supported the concept that social skills need to be taught explicitly (Sapon-Shevin, 1994; Sharan, 2010). Teachers must plan specifically to develop social skills, i.e. listening to others, resolving conflict, supporting and encouraging, working together, taking turns, expressing enjoyment in the success of others, and demonstrating the ability to criticize ideas, not individuals (Johnson et al., 1984). Cooperative Learning teams are especially beneficial in developing 'harmonious interracial relations' (Cohen, 1994, p. 17). Students make the greatest gains in learning when teachers delegate responsibility so that more students can talk and work together at multiple learning centers (Cohen, 1994).

Recently, Gillies, Nichols and Asaduzzaman (2015) studied the impact of cooperative contemporary inquiry-science on primary students' education. This research stated that students had more time to engage in the tasks, be a part of cooperative peer discussions, and receive encouragement and guidance from their teachers. The students' individual understanding of earthquakes was improved based on the comprehensive feedback they received from each other within their groups.

What can we learn from the Cooperative Learning research in Physical Education?

Casey and Goodyear (2015), in a recent review of the Cooperative Learning literature on Physical Education, summarized the learning outcomes of Physical Education:

> as academic achievement (an ability to apply and understand content), inter-personal skill development and relations (communication skills and/or peer relations), enhanced participation (engagement with learning tasks), and an improvement in young people's psychological health (self-esteem and/or motivation).
>
> *(p. 57)*

The research on Cooperative Learning in Physical Education has reported the improvement of interpersonal and social skills within a positive and supportive learning environment (Barrett, 2005; Bayraktar, 2011; Darnis & Lafont, 2013; Casey et al., 2009; Dyson, 2001, 2002; Dyson et al., 2010; Goudas & Magotsiou, 2009; Casey & Goodyear, 2015). For example, in his work Barrett (2005) found that Cooperative Learning increased students' correct trials during practice with task cards, compared to traditional whole-group instruction, and motivated students to increase their appropriate motor practice. Similarly, Goudas and Magotsiou (2009) reported that Cooperative Learning helped to develop students' social skills and attitudes toward group work in Physical Education. Furthermore they found that the Cooperative Learning groups not only developed motor skills but also empathy with and to other students, which in turn decreased their disruptive behaviors. In other words, Cooperative Learning enhanced their social skills and attitudes toward group work compared to a control group and increased their preference for working in groups.

In the US, Dyson et al. (2010) studied the ecological environment of Cooperative Learning in Physical Education classes. More specifically, they studied instruction time, management time, and social tasks in Physical Education lessons. Group Processing, which can be a form of cognitive and social tasks, was observed in every lesson and appeared to contribute to student learning. Organization and management of students, student roles, student physical skill development, and students developing strategies, or 'strategizing', were reported as promoting student learning. To highlight the Cooperative Learning element of *Individual Accountability* (see Chapter 1), the study discussed the teacher using task sheets, assigning Cooperative Learning roles, keeping group sizes small, randomly choosing students to demonstrate their skills, and frequently asking students to teach their teammates strategies and motor skills.

Casey, Goodyear, and Dyson (2015) extended this work by studying model fidelity and students' responses to Cooperative Learning lessons. The Cooperative Learning Validation Tool was used to confirm model fidelity (i.e. how closely the teacher – Ash in this case – adhered to the model and its elements). Useful teaching themes were drawn from the evidence collected: *scaffolding student learning*, *working together*, and *deeper learning*. These teaching strategies were closely connected to the use of Cooperative Learning in a school setting. Casey et al. (2015) suggest that in model-based research we should use more rigor and quality in the research to create more authentic representations of models in different contexts. That said, this book is about helping you to use Cooperative Learning rather than ensuring you do it exactly right. To teach Cooperative Learning 'by the book' might be an aspiration in the longer term but in the first instance we are hopeful that you want to give it a chance.

Ovens, Dyson, and Smith (2012) presented the co-construction of Cooperative Learning classrooms in two primary and three secondary schools in New Zealand. They argued that teachers needed to be able to utilize innovative pedagogical practices that are in line with current research findings in order to support student success. Ovens et al. (2012) attempted to develop a professional learning community based on Cooperative Learning as a pedagogical practice in Physical

Education programs. They found that Cooperative Learning was a feasible pedagogical model to meet the social-critical curriculum of the New Zealand Curriculum (Ministry of Education (MOE), 2007).

Bähr and Wibowo (2012) reported two driving forces for Cooperative Learning in Physical Education in Germany. Firstly, there is an explanation of how Cooperative Learning is translated in the German context. This representation positioned sport pedagogy as a student-centered instructional focus where the teacher is the 'guide' on the side, not the leader of instruction. In other words, the student is the leader in his or her own learning. In addition to current sport and movement culture that focuses on motor achievement ('Education *to* Sport') in German sport pedagogy, the Cooperative Learning Model allows for personality development to move into an equal focus ('Education *by* Sport'). Secondly, Bähr and Wibowo (2012) present instructional practices that include learning 'in' and 'through' the physical. In their empirical study regarding the learning effects in Cooperative Learning during Physical Education classes, they propose that using Cooperative Learning structures can provide a strategy for learning when teaching.

Velazquez-Callado (2012) described the practical application of Cooperative Learning in an elementary school in Spain. He used several Cooperative Learning structures and teaching strategies – such as working in groups, cooperative games, or team building activities – to underpin his work as a teacher. His research presented strategies and techniques to help students learn to analyze skills and correct errors in a supportive, encouraging environment. His teaching tasks encouraged students to problem solve within their Cooperative Learning lessons. He suggests that when we highlight social and emotional learning there is a clear focus for Cooperative Learning in Physical Education. Velazquez–Callado (2012) also stresses the need for teachers to invest time to learn Cooperative Learning as a pedagogical practice in order to create a positive and inclusive learning environment for students.

In their research in France, Darnis and Lafont (2013) reported that motor and tactical skills could be developed through discussions among peers regarding the goals and strategies in basketball units. Similarly, Lafont (2012) presented examples of tasks that meet the recommendations of the French National Curriculum. Her research is a microanalysis of the pedagogical processes of French Physical Education classes. Lafont's research on *verbal interactions* and *debate of ideas* using small Cooperative Learning groups and partners provides examples of how Cooperative Learning can improve students' social interaction. Her research from physical exercises, basketball, handball, acrobatics, and table tennis provide multiple examples of social-skill development. Lafont (2012) argues that by analyzing student interactions, taking turns speaking, and students participating in verbal discourse we gain an understanding of how Cooperative Learning can contribute to the development of Interpersonal and Small Group Skills.

From an Adventure-Based Learning perspective, Sutherland (2012) has examined the benefits and value of the Cooperative Learning element *Group Processing* at Ohio State University. She discusses the inherent value of Group Processing, which we draw from the extensive work in the Adventure Education field (Brown, 2006). Sutherland, Stuhr, and Ressler (2014) illustrate the challenging time constraints that teachers face on a daily basis when developing Group Processing as a part of the regular Physical Education practice. She illuminates Group Processing with the idea of the Sunday drive, a vivid metaphor to represent the benefits of this salient Cooperative Learning element. The goal is to create an open reflective dialogue that benefits both student and teacher but which, like a Sunday afternoon drive, has no purpose beyond the enjoyment of the drive itself. Sutherland, Stuhr, and Ressler (2014) contest that to develop Cooperative Learning to its fullest potential, the use of quality Group Processing experience is required.

An area of immense importance to education and to our field is working with persons with disabilities. Grenier and Yeaton (2012) from New Hampshire have worked together as a research team for 20 years to better understand how best to create a positive and inclusive learning environment for students. Their research supports the use of Cooperative Learning as a powerful pedagogical practice when working with persons with disabilities. Cooperative Learning structures provide learning intentions that promote student learning and this is most apparent in the development of Interpersonal and Small Group Skills. For students with disabilities they foreground the teaching strategy of differentiated learning. Differentiated learning is defined as a teaching process that requires the educator to teach to the individual needs of the student (Hattie, 2012). This differentiated learning is often designed to begin with partner work and then progress to small group tasks. Grenier and Yeaton (2012) argue that within Cooperative Learning structures, students can work together towards group goals through what they call the 'natural supports' of peers and a shared understanding of learning intentions. Cooperative Learning fosters sensitivity to student disabilities and cultural awareness is facilitated by the many interactions with the students' group mates. Grenier and Yeaton (2015) create a positive learning environment of tolerance and respect for students with disabilities. The Cooperative Learning tasks are designed so that all students have meaningful roles to promote student learning in partner work or in small groups of four students.

Dowler's (2012, 2014) research foregrounds differentiated Cooperative Learning tasks to develop the social skills and Small Group Skills of students with mild intellectual disability and the students they practice with who do not have a documented disability. She highlights work from Australia that shows the challenges of implementing Cooperative Learning in secondary school inclusive Physical Education classes. Her research supports the use of Cooperative Learning to develop interpersonal skills and small group skills between students, whether they have a documented disability or not. Her research shows that equal status interactions are promoted when students contribute equally, and share roles and resources as they pursue common goals in a Cooperative Learning task. Dowler's (2014) work details an inclusive program in which students use shared roles, and have a shared contribution and shared equipment and resources in an equity pedagogy. She illustrates tasks that promote and tasks that discourage social skill development. In a similar vein, André, Louvet, and Deneuve (2013) have found that *Cooperative Groups* facilitate the inclusion of students with learning disabilities in risk-taking activities.

Working at the university level in Israel, Zach and Cohen (2012) argue that social interaction and social activities should be structured into the Physical Education Teacher Education (PETE) processes. They highlight that many PETE programs globally teach and promote Models-Based Practice in Physical Education: Sport Education, Teaching Games of Understanding, Teaching Personal and Social Responsibility and/or Cooperative Learning. There is a growing amount of research but still a paucity of evidence from research on teaching in PETE programs. Zach and Cohen (2012) point to a common dilemma in PETE programs, that is, inadequate amounts of content knowledge and pedagogical knowledge being taught to pre-service teachers. The Israeli government, similarly to many other countries, expects children to learn Interpersonal and Small Group Skills in the school setting. We agree that Cooperative Learning can enhance the attainment of national standards and curriculum (Goodyear, 2013; Retter, Goodyear, & Casey, 2014). Zach and Cohen (2012) provide learning intentions in Gymnastics, Orienteering, and Basketball lessons. In addition, Zach and Cohen (2012) highlight the theory–practice gap in their discussion on content knowledge and pedagogical knowledge in PETE programs. Developing this argument, Retter, Goodyear, and Casey (2014) present a strong expectation when they state that 'with the apparent synergy between the model's outcomes and governmental expectations for teaching and learning, Cooperative Learning presents itself as an important and meaningful inclusion into Physical Education programs' (p. 33).

In recent research Ash (Casey, 2012, 2013, 2014) illuminated his journey as a teacher and how Cooperative Learning has facilitated a conceptual shift in the way he teaches in the UK. Ash's major contribution is an ability to connect his pedagogy with his students as they co-construct their own Physical Education tasks. He has explored the pedagogical changes that occur when using Cooperative Learning and the impact Cooperative Learning has on student learning. Ash (2013) demonstrated how continued commitment to using the model was key for him as teacher and for his students when learning how to teach and learn through the model.

Goodyear and Casey (2015) conclude that more research is required in Cooperative Learning 'on students' learning, teachers' use of the model, Cooperative Learning structures, and how a school's contextual factors constrain or facilitate teachers' use of a model' (p. 68). They endorse the notion that teachers and researchers need to move 'beyond the honeymoon' (Goodyear & Casey, 2015, p. 186) period of implementation of this innovative model, i.e. the time when the initial euphoria and excitement has passed and when the realities of life are reasserting themselves.

Apply this understanding to your classrooms and gymnasia

Throughout this text we have argued (and will continue to argue) that there is a growing amount of school-based research in Physical Education that endorses the use of Cooperative Learning. Recently, many futurists in Physical Education pedagogy or sport pedagogy have argued for the increased use of instructional models or pedagogical models in Physical Education (Metzler et al., 2008; Metzler, 2011; Kirk 2010, 2013). While we strongly support the argument that teachers should be equipped to use a number of pedagogical models in Physical Education (for example, Direct Instruction, Sport Education, Teaching Games for Understanding, Adventure-Based Learning, Personal and Social Responsibility, and so on) we are concerned that in practice, many researchers and teachers have a superficial understanding of these pedagogical models or instructional approaches. This limited understanding limits their research, their teacher preparation, and their continuing professional development as educators.

In the Physical Education setting students need to learn skills progressively. Research and practice suggests that teachers need to learn to scaffold their learning experiences to allow children to gain a progressive and deeper understanding of Cooperative Learning as a pedagogical practice in their classroom or gymnasium (Casey et al., 2015; Dyson & Casey, 2012). We will argue that the teacher has to learn Cooperative Learning progressively and also learn to scaffold their learning experiences to gain a progressive and deeper understanding of Cooperative Learning as a pedagogical practice in their classroom, gymnasium, or in the community. Throughout this book we will present a number of practical student and teacher experiences to articulate the ideas that form the background to the Cooperative Learning model. Hopefully the students' or players' enjoyment and success will serve as impetus for using this approach in your gymnasium and physical activity setting.

In Physical Education, teachers often state that they are doing Cooperative Learning, but this is based on the fact that students are grouped together or are working together. Yet this does not mean they are doing Cooperative Learning. We have found through our observations that typically activities are not explicitly structured to be Cooperative Learning groups (Dyson & Grineski, 2001). If the reader tries to use the Cooperative Learning activities without a thorough understanding of the five elements of Cooperative Learning, Cooperative Learning Structures, and three additional procedures[1] (Goodyear, 2015) and does not teach using a Cooperative Learning Structure; then the teacher will probably not be able to facilitate the activity successfully and the goal of implementing Cooperative Learning will remain tenuous at best. In other words, while the students might work collaboratively they are not learning cooperatively in the ways suggested by the research.

Self-processing / A time to reflect

We know that research is often out there and not connected to the everyday world of the teacher, the coach, the outdoor educator, and the community worker. That said, over the years we (Ben and Ash) have done a great deal of Group Processing with others and 'self-processing' to come to a better user-friendly application of research for teachers. We hope we challenged you a *wee bit* as you read through the research but also hope that you gained some understanding of the strong support for Cooperative Learning in educational research.

Self-processing questions

1. What research or evidence do you use as a physical educator, teacher, coach, or community worker to support your practice?
2. What are some of the examples you have found from research that apply to your teaching and learning?
3. With your busy schedule, have you carried out research on your own teaching or pedagogy?
4. What kinds of research could you carry out on your future pedagogy? Or what kinds of evidence could you collect about your own teaching or coaching?
5. If you could collect some information or evidence about your pedagogy, what would be most useful for you and what evidence would be most useful for your students?

Our reflections

Ben

I have always been a bit of a research geek. My first research project was for a final project as an undergraduate. I and another student, Werner van Hassalaar, went out to a primary school twice a week for a semester, and I taught the kids Physical Education and he videotaped every lesson. My goal was to teach well. We coded every lesson using ALT-PE (Metzler, 1983). What I learned from that experience was that I had to reduce my management time as a teacher if I was going to provide the students with more practice time. I also learned that if I had concise learning intentions as instructions the students engaged in the tasks. So that was my modest beginning. But if you learn one thing from every little investigation, or piece of information, or inquiry on your teaching and put that knowledge into practice, then you will continue to be a better teacher. I look forward to learning more from your research experiences.

Ash

What I found most appealing, in my early days of using Cooperative Learning, was my ability to read something at lunchtime and apply it in my next lesson. I used research evidence from other schools – often Ben's work – and then observed how my students reacted to this new pedagogy. It was the applicability of what I was reading to my teaching and, more importantly, my students' learning, that I found most interesting. It wasn't straightforward. I had to adapt and modify what I was reading and learning so that it worked in my school and with my students. That was my job and what I was good at. Having the ideas and applying them was where I struggled and it was one of the reasons I said, even then, more than a decade ago, that we needed a book on how to use Cooperative Learning in Physical Education.

Notes

1 Goodyear (2015) recently suggested that three additional procedures could be used to help guide teachers in their use of Cooperative Learning. These were deduced from the literature in general education and in Physical Education and included small (4 to 5 members) heterogeneous teams, group goals, and teacher-as-facilitator. These procedures are additional elements that help to develop a Cooperative Learning classroom.

References

Alton-Lee, A. (2011). (Using) evidence for educational improvement. *Cambridge Journal of Education, 41*(3), 303–329. http://doi.org/10.1080/0305764X.2011.607150

André, A., Louvet, B., & Deneuve, P. (2013). Cooperative group, risk-taking and inclusion of pupils with learning disabilities in physical education. *British Educational Research Journal, 39*(4), 677–693.

Antil, L. R., Jenkins, J. R., Wayne, S. K., & Vadasy, P. F. (1998). Cooperative learning: prevalence, conceptualizations, and the relation between research and practice. *American Educational Research Journal, 35*(3), 419–163. http://doi.org/10.32102/00028312035003419

Bähr, I. & Wibowo, J. (2012). Teacher action in the cooperative learning model in the physical education classroom. In B. Dyson & A. Casey (Eds.) *Cooperative learning in physical education: A research-based approach* (pp. 27–41). London, England: Routledge.

Barrett, T. (2005). Effects of cooperative learning on the performance of sixth-grade physicaleducation students. Journal of Teaching in Physical Education, 24(1), 88–102.

Bayraktar, G. (2011). The effect of cooperative learning on students' approach to general gymnastics course and academic achievements. *Educational Research and Reviews, 6*(1), 62–71.

Brown, M. (2006). Adventure education in physical education. In D. Kirk, D. MacDonald, & M. Sullivan (Eds.), *Handbook of physical education* (pp. 685–702). London: Sage.

Casey, A. (2012). A self-study using action research: changing site expectations and practice stereotypes. *Educational Action Research, 20*(2), 219–232.

Casey, A. (2013). 'Seeing the trees not just the wood': Steps and not just journeys in teacher action research. *Educational Action Research.* 21 (2), 146-162.

Casey, A. (2014). Through the looking glass: distortions of self and context in teacher education. In A. Ovens & T. Fletcher (Eds.), *Self-study in physical education: Exploring the interplay of practice and scholarship.* London: Springer.

Casey, A. & Goodyear, V. (2015). Can Cooperative Learning Achieve the Four Learning Outcomes of Physical Education? A Review of Literature, *Quest, 67*(1), 56-72, DOI:1 0.1080/00336297.2014.984733.

Casey, A., Dyson, B., & Campbell, A. (2009). Action research in physical education: Focusing beyond myself through cooperative learning. *Educational Action Research, 17*(3), 407-423.

Casey, A., Goodyear, V. A., & Dyson, B. (2015). Model fidelity and students' responses to an authenticated unit of cooperative learning. *Journal of Teaching in Physical Education, 34,* 642–660.

Cohen, E. G. (1994). Restructuring the classroom: Conditions for productive small groups. *Review of Educational Research, 64*(1), 1-35.

Cohen, E. G., & Lotan, R. A. (2004). Equity in heterogeneous classrooms. In J. Banks &

C. McGee Banks (Eds.), *Handbook of Research on Multicultural Education* (2nd ed., pp. 736–749). San Francisco, CA: Jossey-Bass.

Darnis, F., & Lafont, L. (2013). Cooperative learning and dyadic interactions: Two modes of knowledge construction in socio-constructivist settings for team-sport teaching. *Physical Education & Sport Pedagogy*, 20(5), 459–473.

Dowler, W. (2012). Cooperative learning and interactions in inclusive secondary school physical education classes in Australia. In B. Dyson & A. Casey (Eds.), *Cooperative learning in physical education: A research-based approach.* (pp. 159–165). London: Routledge.

Dowler, W. (2014). Cooperative learning as a promising approach for the inclusion of students with disabilities. *ACHPER Active and Healthy Magazine, 21*(2), 19–24.

Dyson, B. (2001). Cooperative Learning in an elementary physical education program. *Journal of Teaching in Physical Education, 20*, 264–281.

Dyson, B. (2002). The implementation of cooperative learning in an elementary physical education program. *Journal of Teaching in Physical Education, 22*(1), 69–85.

Dyson, B. & Grineski, S. (2001). Using cooperative learning structures in physical education. *The Journal of Physical Education, Recreation & Dance, 72*(2), 28-31.

Dyson, B. & Casey, A. (2012). *Cooperative learning in physical education: A research-based approach.* London: Routledge.

Dyson, B., Linehan, N., & Hastie, P. (2010). The ecology of cooperative learning in elementary physical education classes. *Journal of Teaching in Physical Education, 29*(2), 113-130.

Fisher, C. W. (1981). Teaching behaviors, academic learning time, and student achievement: An overview. *Journal of Classroom Interaction, 17*(1), 2-15.

Gillies, R. M. & Haynes, M. (2011). Increasing explanatory behavior, problem-solving, and reasoning within classes using cooperative group work. *Instr Sci, 39*, 349-366.

Gillies, R. M., Nichols, K. & Asaduzzaman, K. (2015). The effects of scientific representations on primary students' development of scientific discourse and conceptual understandings during cooperative contemporary inquiry-science. Cambridge Journal of Education, DOI: 10.1080/0305764X.2014.988681.

Goodyear, V. A. (2013) Participatory action research: challenging the dominant practice architectures of physical education. Unpublished doctoral thesis, University of Bedfordshire.

Goodyear, V. (2015). Developing students' promotive interactions over time: Teachers' adaptions to and interactions within the cooperative learning model. AIESEP International Conference. July 2015, Madrid, Spain.

Goodyear, V. A. & Casey, A. (2015). Innovation with change: Developing a community of practice to help teachers move beyond the 'honeymoon' of pedagogical renovation. Physical Education and Sport Pedagogy, 20(2), 186–203. doi:10.1080/17408989.2013 .817012.

Goudas, M. & Magotsiou, E. (2009). The effects of a cooperative physical education program on students' social skills. *Journal of Applied Sport Psychology, 21*(3), 356–364. http://doi.org/10.1080/10413200903026058

Grenier, M. & Yeaton, P. (2012). Cooperative learning as an inclusive pedagogical practice in physical education. In B. Dyson & A. Casey (Eds.), *Cooperative learning in physical education: A research-based approach* (pp. 119–135). London: Routledge.

Hargreaves, A. & Fullan, M. (Eds.). (2009). *Change wars.* Bloomington, IN: Solution Tree.

Hattie, J. (2012). *Visible learning for teachers: Maximizing impact on learning.* New York: Routledge.

Johnson, D. W. & Johnson, R. T. (1989). *Cooperation and competition: Theory and research.* Edina, MN: Interaction Book.

Johnson, D. W. & Johnson, R. T. (2009). An educational psychology success story: Social interdependence theory and cooperative learning. *Educational Researcher, 38*(5), 365–379.

Johnson, D. W., Johnson, R. T., Johnson-Holubec, E., and Roy, P. (1984). *Circles of learning: Cooperation in the classroom.* Alexandria, VA: Association for Supervision and Curriculum Development.

Kirk, D. (2010). *Physical education futures.* London: Routledge.

Kirk, D. (2013). Educational value and models-based practice in physical education. *Educational Philosophy and Theory, 45,* 973–986. doi:10.1080/00131857.2013.785352

Lafont, L. (2012). Cooperative learning and tutoring in sports and physical activities. In B. Dyson & A. Casey (Eds.). *Cooperative learning in physical education: A research-based approach* (pp. 136–149). London: Routledge.

Metzler, M. (1983). ALT-PE for inservice teachers: Questions and insights. *Journal of Teaching in Physical Education, Summer Monograph, 1,* 17–21.

Metzler, M. (2011). *Instructional models for physical education* (3rd ed.). Scottsdale, AZ: Halcomb Hathaway.

Metzler, M. W., Lund, J. L., & Gurvitch, R. (2008). Adoption of instructional innovation across teachers' career stages. *Journal of Teaching in Physical Education, 27,* 457–465.

Ministry of Education (MOE) (2007). *The New Zealand Curriculum.* Wellington: New Zealand: Learning Media.

Ovens, A., Dyson, B., & Smith, W. (2012). Cooperative learning in physical education in New Zealand schools. In B. Dyson & A. Casey (Eds.). *Cooperative learning in physical education: A research-based approach.* London: Routledge.

Retter, V., Goodyear, V. & Casey, A. (2014). 'It's just an OfSTED Lesson': A pre-preservice teacher's experience of using cooperative learning to teach physical education. *ACHPER Active and Healthy Magazine, 21*(2), 33-38.

Sapon-Shevin, M. K. (1994). Cooperative learning and middle schools: What would it take to really do it right? *Theory into Practice, 33,* 183–190.

Sharan, Y. (2010). Cooperative learning for academic and social gains: Valued pedagogy, problematic practice. *European Journal of Education, 45*(2), 300–313.

Slavin, R. E. (1996). Research on cooperative learning and achievement: What we know, what we need to know. *Contemporary educational psychology, 21*(1), 43–69.

Slavin, R. E. (2010). Co-operative learning: what makes group-work work?. In H. Dumont, D. Instance & F. Benavides (Eds.), *The nature of learning: Using research to inspire practice.* Paris: OECD.

Sutherland, S. (2012). Borrowing strategies from adventure-based learning to enhance group processing in cooperative learning. In B. Dyson & A. Casey (Eds.). *Cooperative learning in physical education: A research-based approach* (pp. 103–118). London: Routledge.

Sutherland, S., Stuhr, P., & Ressler, J. (2014). Group processing in cooperative learning: Using the Sunday afternoon drive debrief model. *Australian Council for Health Physical Education and Recreation, 21,* 12–15.

Velazquez-Callado, C. (2012). Putting cooperative learning and physical activity into practice with primary students. In B. Dyson & A. Casey (Eds.). *Cooperative learning in physical education: A research-based approach* (pp. 59–74). London: Routledge.

Yeaton, P. (2015). Essential inclusive practices. The SHAPE National US Conference, April, Seattle.

Zach, S. & Cohen, R. (2012). Using the cooperative learning in physical education teacher education: From theory into practice. In B. Dyson & A. Casey (Eds.), *Cooperative learning in physical education: A research-based approach* (pp. 88-100). London: Routledge.

3

COOPERATIVE LEARNING STRUCTURES IN PHYSICAL EDUCATION AND PHYSICAL ACTIVITY SETTINGS

Chapter overview

This chapter examines Cooperative Learning Structures in classroom practice and in Physical Education and physical activity. Traditionally in Physical Education, cooperation has been focused around, for example, the Reciprocal Teaching Style (Mosston & Ashworth, 2008). This chapter seeks to offer a much broader perspective on how students can work together for mutual benefit. Physical Education teachers, outdoor educators, community workers, or coaches might pose questions such as: What is a Cooperative Learning Structure to improve students' social skills? This chapter contains detailed explanations of different structures and how students can come together to answer such questions. It provides examples of how Cooperative Learning Structures have been used in context to illustrate the learning that occurs as a consequence of using these approaches in Physical Education and physical activity settings. Several Cooperative Learning Structures are presented in this chapter, such as: Round Robin; Tip Tip, Coach; Numbered Heads Together; Think, Pair, Share; Jigsaw Perform; and Learning Teams.

We believe

1. Cooperative Learning Structures can be used effectively in Physical Education, Outdoor Education, coaching, and/or the community.
2. Most teachers are not aware of Cooperative Learning Structures.
3. Teachers and students can learn a number of Cooperative Learning Structures.
4. Teachers and students can learn how Cooperative Learning Structures can make an important contribution to their teaching and learning.
5. Learning Cooperative Learning Structures takes time and involves *ongoing practice* in your gymnasium or educational setting.
6. It is difficult to learn Cooperative Learning without guidance and support, and this is a process full of challenges.

Imagine the scene

Emma and her classmates burst into the gym and immediately get into their Cooperative Learning groups of four. The students are in a class of very excited 7-year-olds. They are anticipating what types of jumping challenges they will be working on today. The teacher, Cathy, is very impressed with how the students have taken ownership in their groups to develop skills. She comments that the students take a sense of pride in being the 'expert' for a certain type of jump. Today is the culminating activity of the unit: a jumping obstacle course. The students break off into their assigned number groups (1, 2, 3, or 4) for a Jigsaw Cooperative Learning Structure (see Chapter 7). Each group is given a different piece of equipment – hula hoop, jump rope, poly spot, or cones – to build their part of the obstacle course. The students' eyes light up when they realize they are in charge of the equipment and that they can let their imagination run wild with what types of jumping obstacles they can build. Cathy walks around the gym watching the students working together to form the obstacles. She notices the group with the jump ropes is playing limbo and not practicing jumping skills. She poses a question to the group, 'What skill are we working on today?' The students reply 'Jumping!' and then quickly realize that the obstacle they are building is not accomplishing the task. One student suggests that they talk about how they can use the jump ropes in different ways.

Cathy moves onto a different group that is engaged in making a pattern with the poly spots. She is happy to hear one student say 'Let's move them farther apart so we can jump for distance', as that is one of the major skills the students had been working on in that unit. The students then go back into their original Cooperative Learning groups from their expert groups to connect the parts together to form the entire obstacle course. Students are observed adapting the obstacles to meet the needs of their group members. At the end of the lesson Cathy and the students sit down in a circle for a class chat (Group Processing). During Group Processing one student says, 'I felt great doing the obstacle course because my friends helped me through and moved the hula hoops lower so I could jump over them.'

Cathy is a classroom teacher who is not a Physical Education specialist and is very happy with the class. She comments: 'It went excellent, I couldn't believe how engaged they were. It was really good because I can see how they can start creating their ideas, generating more ideas, and generating more discussion.'

Introduction

Cooperation has always been integral to a quality Physical Education, Outdoor Education, coaching, and community programs. Partner or pair work has been examined for over 40 years in Physical Education (Mosston, 1981). Mosston's commonly known 'teaching styles in Physical Education' have been researched and practiced for years (Mosston & Ashworth, 2008). In fact, Muska Mosston, with his publication of *Teaching Styles* in 1966, was a physical educator way ahead of his time and yet is not fully recognized by mainstream education. We have used this approach in Physical Education and coaching for years, way before Palinscar and Brown (1984) in general education were credited for developing Reciprocal

Teaching. One of the frequently used student-centered teaching styles is the Reciprocal Teaching Style of teaching (Mosston, 1981). Reciprocal Teaching is a collaborative teaching strategy that allows students to work together in pairs. Partners take turns with the pre-assigned task, ask questions of each other, and receive feedback from each other. Reciprocal Teaching embraces the idea that students can effectively learn from each other. Reciprocal Teaching was also highlighted as one of the most effective teaching strategies in a recent meta-analysis of education research (Hattie, 2012). Many of you will be familiar with Reciprocal Teaching and you will have used it in your teaching and coaching. Reciprocal Teaching can be described as a Cooperative Learning Structure, and one example in the Cooperative Learning literature is the 'Pair-Check-Perform' Cooperative Learning Structure (described in Box 3.1).

In this chapter we focus on Cooperative Learning Structures such as this. Cooperative Learning Structures can be defined as methods of teaching that utilize strategies for the organization of content and social interaction of students in a classroom or educational setting (Kagan, 1989). The specific step-by-step procedures of Cooperative Learning Structures are used to present, practice,

---

BOX 3.1: PAIR-CHECK-PERFORM

In the *Pair-Check-Perform* Cooperative Learning Structure, students are required to work with each other to perform and check information. Pair Check is a great strategy for assessment of students (= Individual Accountability).

1. The instructor explains, demonstrates, and checks for understanding of a selected sports skill or teaching skill.
2. The instructor describes student performance outcomes and social, cognitive, and/or physical skills necessary to achieve the goal.
3. The instructor places students in groups of four, divided into two pairs.
4. In each pair one student practices the skill while the other student provides encouragement and helps the performer correctly perform the skill.
5. When one student has performed the skill correctly, roles are reversed.
6. When students in each pair have performed correctly, they join together with the other pair, in their group of four, and each student from each pair performs. If all students agree that the performance was correct, the pairs can move onto the next skill. If there is disagreement, the students must continue working on the performance until they all agree.

For example, the *Pair-Check-Perform* Cooperative Learning Structure is useful when assessing the learning cues for the forearm pass in volleyball: Bend knees, flat platform, move to the ball, and square to target.

and assess content. Some enhance interactions between pairs, whereas others are designed for small group work, and others for a larger group (Kagan & Kagan, 2009). Our research (Dyson & Casey, 2012) and the research of others (Cohen, 1994; Gillies & Boyle, 2011; Johnson & Johnson, 2009; Sharan, 2010; Slavin, 1996) suggests that small groups of three to five students produce the most reliable results when using Cooperative Learning Structures. Therefore, in this text when we discuss Cooperative Learning Structures we are referring to students working in small groups of three to five students, unless otherwise stated. Johnson and Johnson (1999) talked about the base or home Cooperative Group. By this they mean the basic Cooperative Learning group that students return to every day. In this chapter the Base/Home Cooperative Group is described as the small group, basic unit group, of students who work together to achieve the task or the group goal.

Kagan's Structures

We feel that it's important to credit Spencer Kagan for his work in naming and developing and refining many Cooperative Learning Structures. Kagan (1989) first highlighted and defined the structural approach that was 'based on the creation, analysis, and systematic application of *structures*, or content-free ways of organizing social interaction in the classroom. Structures usually involve a series of steps, with prescribed behavior at each step' (p. 12). Teachers and coaches can use structures as a content-free way to organize their learning environments. Structures can be employed with many different classroom subjects, physical activities, or Outdoor Education tasks. Teachers, coaches, and outdoor educators can develop learning intentions in all domains of learning and different Cooperative Learning Structures can correspond with different focuses of learning intentions.

In 1996 Steve Grineski published a text on Cooperative Learning in Physical Education that presented several Cooperative Learning Structures and provided a useful resource for teachers. Later in a journal article Dyson and Grineski (2001) presented several Cooperative Learning Structures for Physical Education: *Think-Share-Perform*, *Pair-Check-Perform*, *Jigsaw Perform*, *Co-op Play*, and *Learning Teams*. In our research and work with teachers we have found that some of the Cooperative Learning Structures have not changed much (*Think-Share-Perform* and *Co-op Play*), while others have been modified and adapted a great deal (*Pair-Check-Perform*, *Jigsaw Perform*, *Learning Teams*, and *Collective Group Score*). This chapter introduces and describes several Cooperative Learning Structures.

Think-Pair-Perform

Think-Pair-Perform is modified from Think-Share-Perform (Dyson & Grineski, 2001). Over the years we have adapted and modified these Cooperative Learning Structures and we encourage you to do the same. When you practice a Cooperative Learning Structure we suggest that you should make it your own, with specific variations for your students and your context. So start small with one or two of the five critical elements of Cooperative Learning (see Chapter 6). We have observed that often teachers follow a prescriptive Kagan method of structures that only requires short and simplistic Cooperative Learning Structures (Kagan & Kagan, 2009). An example of a simple Cooperative Learning Structure would be *Think-Pair-Perform*. In this structure, students might be asked to *Think* of the learning cues for kicking a soccer ball, then join up with a partner (*Pair*) and discuss the learning cues, then *Perform*, or practice, kicking the soccer ball to each other. This may act as a warm-up and not take a great deal of lesson time. This is, however, a good way to start using Cooperative Learning Structures. Later in this chapter we describe more complex Cooperative Learning Structures, such as *Learning Teams* and *Jigsaw*. In the next section we present structures that educators can use as an introduction, warm-up, or in a short amount of time during a lesson. The next sections describe a number of less complicated Cooperative Learning Structures such as: *Tip, Tip, Coach*; *Rally Robin*; *Rally Coach*; *Round Robin*; *Timed Round Robin*; and *Numbered Heads Together Perform*. Teachers or coaches can start using these simple structures before moving on to complicated Cooperative Learning Structures.

Tip, Tip, Coach

Tip, Tip, Coach can be used in multiple settings. In *Tip, Tip, Coach*, partners alternate between two roles (coach and player) to be successful with the task or activity.

Partner A (in the player role) has a first attempt at an activity while partner B (in the coach role) is watching. If partner A is unsure or partner B notices they need help, partner A can get help. That is, partner B can give partner A one (coaching) tip (but can't give them the answer or do it for them). Partner A tries again, and can ask for another tip. On the third attempt, partner B can now start coaching partner A to refine their task towards success. After success with the task, students swap roles. Partner A and partner B will need some guidance, and we have found that task sheets or task cards provide a useful visual representation of the task. This is common in Physical Education, coaching, and community settings where adults are giving specific feedback to the learner. We have found *Tip, Tip, Coach* to be really useful in Physical Education (PE) and coaching when we give our partner specific feedback.

For example, in the soccer skill of passing, the learning cues are written on a task card: use your instep/inside of foot, plant the non-kicking foot beside the ball, strike the middle of the ball, and follow through. Partner A (in the player role) has a first attempt at passing while partner B (in the coach role) is observing. If partner A is unsure or partner B notices they need help, partner A can ask for help. That is, partner B can give partner A one tip (use your in step/inside of foot). Partner A tries again, and can ask for another tip (plant non-kicking foot beside the ball). On the third attempt, partner B can now start coaching partner A to refine their passing. After partner A passes using at least three of the four cues, students swap roles.

Rally Robin Perform

Rally Robin has been used in general education for a number of years (Kagan, 1994). Students work in pairs and take turns to provide a verbal response to each other's questions. This is a similar strategy to Reciprocal Teaching. In Physical Education we have been doing this for a number of years but in this chapter we call it *Rally Robin Perform*. That is, students work in pairs to take turns to provide a physical response to a challenge or a question. For example, we are learning a dance move and the task is to create your best dance moves, such as 'move like a giraffe'. Student A shows student B his giraffe moves and then student B shows student A her giraffe moves and the students can ask questions or set challenges, e.g. how does that represent a giraffe, or can you think about the way a giraffe moves? This is a form of Reciprocal Teaching. At the end of the task the teacher can ask the students to provide a physical response, that is, 'Show me your giraffe moves.' This could lead into a Group Processing session with students after the activity about how our movement can mimic that of a giraffe.

Rally Coach

Partners take turns, with one student solving a problem while the other coaches. Again this is a form of Reciprocal Teaching but could be seen as a progression from *Tip, Tip, Coach* since this uses more of an 'open ended' feedback structure. Students bat ideas back and forth and then practice a task, for example, forearm passing a volleyball to each other and reminding each other to start the hit square to the target. This is practice that is common in Physical Education and coaching settings, we are just providing a term to describe this type of teaching strategy which perhaps many of you already use. The difference between Rally Robin and Round Robin, the next structure, is that in Rally Robin students work in pairs like a singles rally in tennis but in Round Robin they work in their Cooperative Base Group of three to five students.

Round Robin

Physical educators and coaches have used the term 'Round Robin' for years to mean that students will participate in an everyone-plays-everyone-else tournament. When we use Round Robin as a Cooperative Learning Structure it has a different meaning. In the Cooperative Learning Structure *Round Robin*, students practice a task 'around' their small Cooperative Base Group. In Round Robin students take turns responding orally and/or physically. That is, each student takes turns in his or her Cooperative Base Group, for example, students or players brainstorming the learning cues for passing a ball with a floor hockey stick: stick on the ground, swing stick back, push through the ball, keep blade facing target, and follow through target.

Each student in the group is required to make at least one suggestion of a specific cue. Another example can be that everyone in the group is passed to as a requirement of the task. Again this is a strategy frequently used by effective teachers and coaches. For example, trying to keep a balloon in the air in your group of four. Every time a person volleys the ball one point is scored.

Timed Round Robin

Students take turns for specific time, much like a political debate. Each teammate is allocated a specific amount of time to contribute to the group discussion. This could be used as a strategy to ensure everyone contributes in a Group Processing session, for example, quick questions for each student to answer: What did you do well? What do you need to work on?

Numbered Heads Together Perform

This is a modification of Kagan's (1994) Numbered Heads Together. The teacher poses a problem, e.g. 'What are the best learning cues to bump a volleyball?' Each student thinks of the correct response. Then the teammates literally and physically put their heads together to reach consensus to answer the question. The teacher varies the time allocated for this task depending on the needs of the students and the complexity of the task. To think about and answer the question, students stand up and put their heads together in their group, sharing answers and discussing. Students sit down when everyone knows the answers. The teacher calls a number, and the student who has that number assigned to them in the group answers the question. There are several ways students might respond: a physical demonstration, thumbs up, thumbs down, response cards, whiteboard/chalkboard responses, or an individual explanation. If the student is struggling to answer they could 'phone a friend' in their group to come to their aid. This is one of the supportive elements inherent in Cooperative Learning. Yes, we want to hold students individually accountable for their contribution, but this is 'sink or swim together' and therefore the group is always there to offer help and support to a group mate.

Alternative format for *Numbered Heads Together Perform*: for example, in a practical example where the students are practicing the forearm passes in volleyball there are some basic mistakes being made. During the practice task the ball may be not going towards the target. That is, the teacher notices a common error related to the learning cues or success criteria of volleyball: the students are not square to the target. The teacher might pose a question, for example: 'How do we solve this problem?' The answer generated by the student team should help the students to perform better and might be as simple as students saying they need to stay 'square to the target'. The final act is that all students should be able to perform their suggested answer to the teacher's question.

There are many variations of *Numbered Heads Together Perform*. The general concept is that the teacher poses a problem. The students independently and quietly think about a solution, join their teammates in a group, and communicate or discuss their answer together. Then the whole group must reach a consensus about the answer (which creates opportunities to develop small group and inter-personal skills and engage in Promotive Face-to-Face Interactions). At that time the students indicate that they are ready to answer the question. This strategy is similar to the Cooperative Learning Strategy *Think-Share-Perform* but in *Numbered Heads Together Perform* students are numbered off in order to hold each student accountable. The teacher calls a random number and every member of the group must be ready to answer the question. In Outdoor Education, coaching, or Physical Education, examples could include: creating your own game/s, creating your own dance/s, and creating your own obstacle courses. This structure encourages problem solving for practical games and sport tactics or strategies.

The following Cooperative Learning Structures (*Pair-Check-Perform*, *Jigsaw Perform*, *Learning Teams*, and *Collective Group Score*) are more complicated and should be taught in small progressions. That is, the teacher or coach should scaffold the ideas in and build them progressively into the task. We suggest that you use Reciprocal Teaching or one of the previously mentioned Cooperative Learning Structures to begin your experience with Cooperative Learning.

Pair-Check-Perform

There have been several modifications to *Pair-Check-Perform* over the last 15 years. One version below emphasizes or focuses on Individual Accountability. We have observed that *Pair-Check-Perform* has also been used by several teachers as a peer assessment strategy. Below is an example used by Rachel Colby at Conner's Emerson School in Maine, USA. Assessment will be discussed in more detail in Chapter 12, on Cooperative Learning and Assessment.

In the Cooperative Learning Structure *Pair-Check-Perform*, students are required to work with each other to perform the task but also check on their teammate's response to the task. Students work in their Base/Home Cooperative Group of four students. *Pair-Check-Perform* is a great strategy for assessment of students and a way to hold students individually accountable.

Rachel uses *Pair-Check-Perform* to focus on her psychomotor learning objectives for guiding students to learn the forearm pass in volleyball (Box 3.2). The task is to use *Pair-Check-Perform* as an assessment of learning cues for the forearm pass in volleyball: bend knees, flat platform, move to the ball, and body angled towards target.

In using this approach Rachel felt that she was able to do a better job of teaching students the forearm pass for volleyball. Rachel has noticed that students at the upper elementary level have a huge range in ability for volleyball skills. She uses *Pair-Check-Perform* to check that her students have learned this skill well enough to play in a modified game with their peers.

BOX 3.2: PAIR-CHECK-PERFORM: FOREARM PASS IN VOLLEYBALL

1. The instructor explains, demonstrates, and checks for the understanding of the forearm pass.
2. The instructor describes student performance outcomes and social, cognitive, and/or physical skills necessary to achieve the goal.
3. The instructor places students in groups of four, divided into two pairs.
4. In each group one student practices the skill while the other student provides encouragement and helps the other student correctly perform the skill. You might use *Tip, Tip, Coach* here as well.
5. When one student has performed the pass correctly, roles are reversed.
6. When students in each pair have performed correctly, they join together with the other pair, in their group of four, and each student from each pair performs. If all students agree that the forearm pass was correct, the pairs can move onto the next skill. If there is disagreement, the students must continue working on the pass until they all agree on the form.

Jigsaw Perform

There are many different variations and adaptions to the Jigsaw Cooperative Learning Structure (Aronson, 1978; Kagan & Kagan, 2009) that will be discussed in Chapter 9. If you are thinking of using Jigsaw it might be worth heading over to Chapter 9 and familiarizing yourself with the structure.

There are many ways to modify the Jigsaw Perform. In a basic *Jigsaw Perform Structure* each student is responsible for learning a portion of content and then teaching that content to other members of their group. Students work in their Base Cooperative Group. The teacher assigns a task to groups; this task is divided into four separate parts and numbers the students: 1, 2, 3, and 4. All students assigned to be 1s work together, all 2s work together, all 3s work together, and all 4s work together. These expert groups are different from the base group. Each member of the four groups learns a skill, learning cue, or part of the movement. Then students go back to their original base group, and each student takes it in turn to teach their part of the skill or movement to rest of the group.

For example, when teaching the task of creating a dance routine at the elementary level: the 1s work on arms together in one large group, 2s work on legs, 3s work on body and hip movements, and 4s work on head movements. Students work in their expert groups to practice the different movements. Once all students have practiced their body part and feel confident to teach their group mates, students move back to their original base groups and teach their body part movement to their group mates. When the 1, 2, 3, and 4s get back together in their Base Cooperative Group they can now combine all the movements into one coherent dance.

In another example below, Jacquie Greenslade at Papatoetoe South School in New Zealand used Jigsaw to encourage her students to practice and learn four different jumps. The learning intention for this task was to practice four different jumps: one foot to two feet, two feet to one foot, jump for distance, jump for height. Jacquie wanted her students to practice different kinds of jumping by drawing on their creativity. She wanted her Year 4 (aged 9 to 11 years) students to present and practice different kinds of jumping with each other without getting off task (Box 3.3).

By using *Jigsaw Perform* to teach four different jumps Jacquie was able to more easily manage the students. She could walk around the gymnasium observing students performing their jumps in their groups. If there were student groups who were not talking about jumping or practicing jumping she was able to redirect them. When she found students off task she would ask student groups questions like: 'Are you working on jumping?' or 'Can you tell me what you are working on?' or 'Can you show me how to jump in different ways?' Jacquie wanted to challenge the students to practice at their level. She was excited when students adapted and modified the activities to suit the needs of all group members. Near the end of most lessons Jacquie tried to remember to ask group members a couple of questions like: 'What went well today?' and 'What do you need to work on?' Then after a short while she asks the entire class to sit in a

---

BOX 3.3: JIGSAW PERFORM: PRACTICING FOUR DIFFERENT JUMPS

1. The students start out in their Learning Teams and number themselves 1–4.

2. The teacher assigns a portion of the content to each number. For example in a Jumping and Landing Lesson: The Number 1s learn how to do a two-foot take-off, one-foot landing jump. Number 2s learn how to do a one-foot take-off, two-foot landing jump. Number 3s learn how to jump for height. Number 4s learn how to jump for distance.

3. The numbered groups (1, 2, 3, 4) work together to become experts in their particular jump using the task cards given by the teacher with pictures and skill cues.

4. Once the numbered groups feel confident in their specific jumps, students return to their Learning Teams.

5. The expert in each group then demonstrates their jump to the other members of their Learning Team and then gives encouragement and feedback while the other members perform the jump.

circle to discuss the lesson in a Group Processing session. She wanted Group Processing to be a student-centered activity so she tried to ask questions that required students to think about what the learning intentions were for the day, how they have met their learning intentions, and what changes they would make for the next lesson: 'What did you see that showed you met your learning intentions today?' or 'What do you think we should change in the next lesson?' Jacquie wanted the students to engage at their level and be 'creative thinkers', which she believes might motivate them to participate actively in their Physical Education lessons.

Learning Teams

The structure *Learning Teams* has evolved into a complex Cooperative Learning Structure. In *Learning Teams* students are divided into small groups and everyone has an assigned role designed to help students complete the task in their Base Cooperative Groups. For example the roles could be: coach, equipment person, recorder, and encourager. Each learning team decides on a team name with their teacher's guidance. Students share responsibility through roles. The teacher tries to act as a facilitator, explaining and demonstrating a skill and then expecting the students to 'give it a go'. The teacher describes group outcomes and goals (the recorder must record this). Each student has an explicit role assignment to carry out but all students are expected to perform the task. As a coach you will find that the Cooperative Learning Structure of *Learning Teams* works well in lead-up games for any team sport activity. Teachers should choose different roles to suit the students, the task, and the context.

An example of *Learning Teams* that has been used as an introduction to Cooperative Learning is Triangle Ball. Triangle Ball is an activity to develop physically accurate passes and support play. Each member of the group is assigned a specific role: coach, equipment person, recorder, or encourager. When learning to use Cooperative Learning Structures choose one role and practice that with the students. Then add on the other roles progressively and scaffold them into future activities. We suggest one at a time depending on how well the students are learning the roles and your experience with teaching students about the roles. Generally, we start with the role of coach, then equipment person, then encourager, and then recorder. But you decide. It depends on you and your students and your context. The recorder has to write down what the teammates are doing and for most students writing in Physical Education or community sport is a novel task. That is, most students are not used to writing during such lessons and therefore the teacher or coach should introduce this in a progressive manner; one writing task at a time. An example of a Learning Task sheet appears in Figure 3.1.

Triangle Ball

Cooperative Learning Structure: Learning Teams
Physical task: Accurate passes and support
Cognitive task: Understand support play
Social task: Give feedback and receive feedback appropriately

Triangle Ball task sheet

1 Four players in a square, three v. one; three players work on the corners and sides of the square.
2 One of the four players works in the middle area and tries to intercept the ball as the other three pass it around.
3 Players with the ball can only pass and run along the perimeter lines of the square.
4 No diagonal passes. Passive defender first – focus on offense = good accurate pass.
5 When a player has possession of the ball they cannot move.

```
∧  O1 o _____ >∧  O2              _____    ball movement
                                        -----    movement of support player
            D 4
∧  O3 ------------------->∧
```

Task 1:
Play Triangle Ball and support the ball carrier on both sides with accurate passes.
1 Passive defender first – focus on offense = good accurate pass.

Task 2:
What went well? What do you need to work on? (**Rally Team CL Structure**).

Task 3: Modify Triangle Ball:
Discuss modifications to Triangle Ball to suit your group. **CL Structure Numbered Heads Together**.
Then play Triangle Ball again.
Chosen modifications could focus on:
➡ Success criteria = support play, i.e. moving to ball
➡ Triangle Ball – no defender
➡ Students come up with a modification and everyone in the group can tell the teacher what those agreed modifications are (**CL Structure Numbered Heads Together = strategizing**).

Learning cues / success criteria:
1 Call name and make eye contact
2 Reach for ball – show a target
3 Move into a supporting position
4 Give appropriate feedback
5 Accept feedback appropriately
6 Accurate pass/catch

When you all feel ready, complete the form below, rating each player's performance with each skill.
Use the CL Structure **Pair-Check-Perform**:
1 A assesses B, while C assesses D.
2 B assesses A, while D assesses C.
3 Pairs of students now move to assess other students. The teacher can randomly assess any pair.

Awesome – uses the cues every time
Good – uses the cues most of the time
Needs Work – rarely uses the cues

Names	Call name	Reaches for ball	Support – move to ball	Give feedback	Receive feedback	Accurate pass/catch

Task 4: Try to assess other players
Create a strategy to use this rubric for assessing each other. **CL Structure Numbered Heads Together**.
Perhaps use one or two cues from the assessment rubric.

Group processing
What happened?
So what?
Now what?

FIGURE 3.1 Learning activity – Triangle Ball

Collective Group Score

In *Collective Group Score* teammates add up the scores from all team members to create a collective group score for an activity. Collective Group Score encourages students to try their best to complete an activity or perform a number of repetitions, since everyone's score is important for the total score.

As an example, students in their groups of four perform as many repetitions of an exercise in a given period of time as they can, and then add the repetitions together to create a 'Collective Group Score' (see example in Figure 3.2). For the next class, students set a specific target group goal for the number of repetitions they hope to perform. You can also have *Whole Class Collective Score* – each group's score is added together to make a class total Collective Group Score, which the class could try to beat the next time they perform a task. A detailed example of Group Score appears in Chapter 5, Figure 5.5.

Self-processing / A time to reflect

Self-processing questions

1   What is your prior experience with Cooperative Learning Structures?
2   Do you think Cooperative Learning Structures can work in your Physical Education, coaching Outdoor Education, or community program?
3   What Cooperative Learning Structures appeal to you?
4   What are some of your questions, issues, and/or concerns regarding Cooperative Learning Structures?

Our reflections

Ben

When observing teachers first trying to use Cooperative Learning Structures I have seen a huge range of results. Ideally we would like to see students working with each other, listening to each other, cheering for each other, and laughing loudly with each other. But that is not always the case when trying a new pedagogical approach like Cooperative Learning. When you first use Cooperative Learning Structures the students might be confused, or they might not have enough information, so they are off task; they might be disturbing other classmates, and reducing the potential learning. We understand that this is an investment of time and energy to use Cooperative Learning Structures to create a positive learning environment but you need to be persistent with your trial and error. This is a normal learning process for any of us if we want to accept the challenge; good teaching requires time, effort, persistence, and critical reflection. We hope that some of these Cooperative Learning Structures are interesting to you. We trust that you will allocate some time in your teaching or coaching to test out some of the Cooperative Learning Structures and then contact us (Ash and Ben) about your

Physical activity circuit

The coach: _____
provides feedback to the group members to improve their performance.

The reader/ The recorder: _____
reads and records the task and makes sure all group members understand it – gets clipboard.

The organizer: _____
organizes equipment for next group – puts equipment away at the end of class.

The encourager: _____
encourages group members to be involved and provides positive comments to all group members.

Physical activity circuit – Recorder sheet

Activity:	Group member 1	Group member 2	Group member 3	Group member 4	**Collective Group Score**	Goal for next lesson
1. Padded tennis						
2. Triceps dips						
3. Pacer run						
4. Sit-ups						
5. Step ups						
6. Jump rope						
7. Hula hoop						
8. Phantom chair						
9. Choice…						
10. Choice…						

Learning Activity 1:
Work in your group to complete the activities on the task sheet.

Learning Activity 2:
Briefly explain activities created by your group for activities 9 and 10:
For example, crab walk, horizontal jump, hopping, shuttle run, and so on.

Learning Activity 3 – Group processing:
Students' questions:
➡ What station went well for you as a group? What station did you have trouble with?
➡ Did you see Positive Interdependence? Did you see Individual Accountability?

Teacher's questions:
➡ What were the: physical task/s, cognitive task/s, and/or social task/s?
➡ How would you teach a Cooperative Learning activity?

Learning activity 4 – Overall group processing questions:

What happened?
So what?
Now what?
➡ Can you try Cooperative Learning in a lesson next week?
➡ Questions? Issues? Concerns?

FIGURE 3.2   Collective Group Score task sheet

experience. We are always interested to hear how Cooperative Learning is going in your program.

Ash

As we say throughout this book (indeed, see Chapter 4), it takes time to learn to teach in a new way and it takes time for your students to learn to learn in a new way. You will all make mistakes and it might be a little frustrating, but when isn't teaching a little frustrating? A friend of mine used to say (with regards to skiing) that if you're not falling over then you're not trying hard enough and I always use the same analogy with my teaching. Falling over isn't a problem, it's not standing back up that is. Remember what Thomas Edison said, 'I have not failed. I've just found 10,000 ways that won't work.' In finding your ways that work you need to be prepared to find a few that don't.

References

Aronson, E. (Ed.). (1978). *The jigsaw classroom*. Beverly Hills, CA: Sage.

Cohen, E. G. (1994). Restructuring the classroom: Conditions for productive small groups. *Review of Educational Research, 64*(1), 1–35. http://doi.org/10.3102/00346543064001001

Dyson, B. & Grineski, S. (2001). Using cooperative learning structures in physical education. *Journal of Physical Education, Recreation & Dance, 72*(2), 28–31. http://doi.org/10.1080/07303084.2001.10605831

Dyson, B. & Casey, A. (2012). *Cooperative learning in physical education: A research-based approach*. London: Routledge.

Gillies, R. M. & Boyle, M. (2011). Teachers' reflections of cooperative learning (CL): A two-year follow-up. *Teaching Education, 22*(1), 63–78. http://doi.org/10.1080/104762 10.2010.538045

Grineski, S. (1996). *Cooperative learning in physical education*. Champaign, IL: Human Kinetics.

Hattie, J. (2012). *Visible learning for teachers: Maximizing impact on learning*. New York: Routledge.

Johnson, D. W. & Johnson, R. T. (1999). Making cooperative learning work. *Theory Into Practice, 38*(2), 67–73. http://doi.org/10.1080/00405849909543834

Johnson, D. W. & Johnson, R. T. (2009). An educational psychology success story: Social interdependence theory and cooperative learning. *Educational Researcher, 38*(5), 365–379. http://doi.org/10.3102/0013189X09339057

Kagan, S. (1989). The structural approach to cooperative learning. *Educational Leadership, 47*(7), 12–15.

Kagan, S. (1994). *Cooperative learning*. San Juan Capistrano, CA: Kagan Cooperative Learning.

Kagan, S. & Kagan, M. (2009). *Kagan cooperative learning*. San Clemente, CA: Kagan.

Mosston, M. (1981). *Teaching physical education* (2nd ed.). Columbus, OH: Merill.

Mosston, M. & Ashworth, S. (2008). *Teaching physical education* (5th ed.). San Francisco, CA: Cummings.

Palinscar, A. S. & Brown, A. L. (1984). Reciprocal teaching of comprehension-fostering and comprehension-monitoring activities. *Cognition and Instruction, 1*(2), 117–175. http://doi.org/10.1207/s1532690xci0102_1

Sharan, Y. (2010). Cooperative learning for academic and social gains: Valued pedagogy, problematic practice. *European Journal of Education*, *45*(2), 300–313.

Slavin, R. E. (1996). Research for the future on cooperative learning and achievement: What we know, what we need to know. *Contemporary Educational Psychology*, *69*(1), 43–69. http://doi.org/http://dx.doi.org/10.1006/ceps.1996.0004

4

THE ROLE OF THE TEACHER OR COACH IN CREATING A POSITIVE COOPERATIVE LEARNING ENVIRONMENT

Chapter overview

One of the differences between a Cooperative Learning classroom and a traditional classroom is the role and positioning of the teacher or coach. Cooperative Learning relies on the teacher or coach being the 'guide on the side' rather than the 'sage on the stage' and this chapter explores strategies that teachers can use to help them learn how to develop this aspect of their teaching. This role is often new for the students themselves and this chapter offers practical examples of how this role reversal can be successfully engendered and how the teacher or coach can position him/herself to facilitate the learning of all students in their classrooms, regardless of prior expectations. It takes time for teachers and students to understand their new roles and this chapter provides real world examples and strategies for making this change manageable, productive, and fun.

We believe that

1. It takes time to change the way that you teach and it takes time to change the way we coach.
2. It takes time for children to 'learn to learn' in a new way. We are taught how to learn (i.e. sit silently and listen to the teacher) and we have a role to play (i.e. sit silently and listen to the teacher). Cooperative Learning disrupts this, and one of your roles is to help students to understand how learning now occurs in your sessions.
3. Developing a positive learning environment through the use of Cooperative Learning is something that needs to be built and sustained.
4. The time you invest in developing a positive learning environment will pay

you back many times over the course of a lesson, a unit, a season, a year, and even the duration of a student's time in your school.

5. Mistakes are inevitable. Indeed, as the old adage goes, 'you can't make an omelet without breaking some eggs'.
6. Learning from mistakes and getting better is part of a good pedagogy.
7. It is important to listen to your students and understand that they will also find change a difficult thing to come to terms with.

Imagine the scene

You've made the decision to adopt a Cooperative Learning approach in your work as a practitioner, but what now? Previously you felt comfortable with your role but now you have made a conscious decision to change it – your role – for this session at least. That doesn't mean that your responsibilities have changed, far from it, but it does mean that the way you act has changed. Previously, and in varying degrees, you've been in control of what you do and what your students do but now you're not feeling so much in control. In fact you're feeling uncertain and don't know what you need/want to do.

You've started with the best of intentions; your first session is intricately planned and the students have started well. They're in their groups and are excited about what they're doing. You're using one of the structures that we wrote about in Chapter 3 and you've even had a chance to walk around the periphery of the session and help some of your students individually and in their groups.

However, and just as your confidence is growing, out of the corner of your eye you see a dispute beginning. Luke, a normally quiet boy who keeps himself to himself, has thrown your worksheet on the floor and has walked away from his group in tears. Jemma, your normally reliable soccer captain, is giggling while the others in the group stand around and stare – some group members smirk and some look concerned. The noise has caught the attention of the other groups in the class and you get the sense that the session is in danger of breaking down. You see that other groups have discarded the sheet as well and that they're not quite doing what you had hoped. What do you do?

In another lesson you'd know exactly what to do but now you're unsure. You could stop the whole class, but until this breakdown things seemed to be going well. You could tell them what to do, you could see if they can resolve the situation themselves, or … what? The seconds are ticking and you're not sure how to intervene while still maintaining a positive Cooperative Learning environment.

Introduction

This chapter looks at the initial stages of creating a positive Cooperative Learning classroom and its aim is to help you get to a position where you can take your first steps in using the model with your students. By the end of the chapter you should have a better understanding of the approach and feel confident to give Cooperative Learning a go. By using the step-by-step tasks we have presented or by teaching through one of the five lessons plans we have prepared we hope that you will be in a position to say that you have tried Cooperative Learning.

In the rest of the chapter, we begin by exploring some of the difficulties you might encounter in beginning to teach through Cooperative Learning. But rest assured these should, perhaps, be likened to teething problems. That is, difficult at the time but leading to the development of your Cooperative Learning 'teeth'. That said, we will also explain why we feel that change is a naturally demanding process and aim to show that by taking your time and introducing the approach slowly and carefully it will be much easier for you and your students. Later in this chapter we do this by introducing some clear indicators that you are beginning to use Cooperative Learning, what we called 'additional procedures' (Goodyear, 2015) in Chapter 2, that sit alongside the five elements (see Chapter 1). We will also share some strategies for adopting the model and provide you with some pre-written lesson plans. It's our hope that these challenging steps will be made much easier through these examples and that you can begin to see how to develop your new Cooperative Learning pedagogy.

Learning to teach in a new way

The situation described at the beginning of the chapter is normal and is one that many practitioners face on a regular basis. How many times have you seen a beginning teacher caught in a moment – a lesson even – of indecision and how many times have you simply wanted to step in and save them? In turn, how many times have you wanted the floor to open up and swallow you when something has gone wrong? It's a different situation, however, when you know what to do and can react immediately and instinctively rather than one where you have to think through a problem before you can respond. That moment of uncertainty or indecision can be telling and is often very uncomfortable, especially for an experienced practitioner, and yet it might well be one you experience as you start to get to grips with the Cooperative Learning approach.

Pedagogy – as we explained in Chapter 1 – is a blend of teaching, learning, and curriculum. It is the interplay of these three aspects of education that define good pedagogy, and yet when you change one element of this trio then the pedagogical process also changes. A, B, and C might still equal D but the balance has shifted. But that 'recalculation' is what you've decided to do. You've moved away from a familiar and comfortable approach to your teaching and challenged yourself to do something different – better we'd say – for the benefit of your students. But the decision to shift is the easy bit (so to speak). Now you need to follow through with it, which is where this book comes in, of course.

Pedagogical change could be likened to learning a new language or a new skill. It might be a related skill or a similar language but the 'rules' aren't the same. English, for example, shares something like 2,000 words with Spanish and yet speaking one language doesn't mean that you can automatically speak the other – no matter how many words they have in common. Taking a sporting example, the skills of cricket and baseball might be similar – they are both striking and fielding games – but no one would expect an international cricketer to simply transfer to a major league baseball team, at least not without some time in the minors.

It's the same with learning a new pedagogical approach. Many of the interactions will be familiar – just as the interplay between two friends who meet for coffee in Spain is familiar to an English speaker – but the nuances of the interactions between teacher and learner are different. If we take the example at the start of the chapter, how would you have instinctively reacted? Both of us think we'd have stopped the lesson (before our Cooperative Learning days) and brought everyone in to reiterate the aims and roles inherent in the lesson, in the unit, indeed in the model. Even so, that reaction goes against the fundamental ideas of the Cooperative Learning.

Students (and in this case teachers and coaches) can learn as much from getting it wrong as getting it right – after all, we are supposed to learn from our mistakes. Remember the words from the quote of American inventor Thomas Edison from the last chapter, 'I haven't failed. I've just found 10,000 ways that won't work'. This is, to us, one of the key messages in Cooperative Learning. Finding ways that don't work is fine as long as participants learn from the experience. That said, in the example above, we would have encouraged the other groups to return to their own group's work and brought Jemma and Luke's group together. Using a structure like 'I do – We do' (Velazquez-Callado, 2012) or Think-Share-Perform (Grineski, 1996) we might have asked the group to consider why they had acted as they had. This could be called Group Processing. We might get them to think, firstly individually ('I') and then as a group (We), why the altercation had occurred. Why were the face-to-face interactions no longer promotive? Where had the small group and interpersonal skills broken down?

Such an approach is not as straightforward as stopping and talking to the whole class (and is certainly more time consuming) but in our experience and the experiences of others reported in the literature, teaching students how to resolve their own conflicts can have huge benefits. It has been suggested that traditional approaches to teaching – ones that position the teacher as the 'sage on the stage' – make students too dependent on the teacher. In other words, students feel that they don't have to be responsible for their own actions because the teacher will act as the arbitrator of acceptable behavior and tell them when they've overstepped the mark.

That's not the Cooperative Learning way, so to speak, and we want students to understand that they have an equally important role to play in the ways in which they work with and for their peers as they do in how they personally develop. One of the fundamental ideas associated with Cooperative Learning is that students *sink or swim together*. This is more than just a saying. It underpins the whole pedagogical approach of Cooperative Learning and is something that, as practitioners, we should be constantly aspiring to. In the next section we will start to look at strategies that might be employed to help you start to create a truly cooperative classroom.

Creating a positive Cooperative Learning environment

The first thing to acknowledge is that simply placing students in groups will not mean that they will automatically cooperate. The requirement for group work does not equate automatically to cooperation. The second thing to acknowledge is that this will take time – just refer to Edison's 10,000 ways that won't work – but the effort made at the start will pay dividends in the not too distant future. You don't pick up a Spanish phrase book and immediately start a fluent conversation. Instead you learn the basics. A few phrases that make up the basics of the language: please and thank you; my name is; Please can I?; Where can I?; How can I?; and so on. Fluency takes time – years in most cases (especially when it comes to a language) – but there are simple ideas you can implement to get yourself started: (a) start small, (b) use lesson zero, (c) understand the Cooperative Learning model one or two elements or additional procedures at a time and then begin to bring them together, and (d) learn to teach in a new way. Don't forget that while you're learning to teach in a new way the students are also learning to learn in a new way.

But how do you know you're getting it right? There are the elements to consider, but these are contained in another set of indictors – the additional procedures (see Figure 4.1) – that help you to see if you are teaching through Cooperative Learning. They are called additional procedures not because you have to use them to help your students work cooperatively but because they have been strongly associated with the Cooperative Learning model. If these additional procedures (five of which are the fundamental elements; see Chapter 1) are evident then you have taken a big step toward using Cooperative Learning in your teaching.

FIGURE 4.1 Additional procedures

The first additional procedure is the use of mixed ability groups (which might be learning teams of four or five and/or gender pairs or teams for the duration of a unit). Such combinations are inherent in the idea that groups in Cooperative Learning are heterogeneous (i.e. diverse). The second additional procedure is that, as a teacher, you adopt the role of facilitator and encourage the students, through open questioning and the use of high-quality resources, to depend on each other as much (if not more) than on you. The role of facilitator in education is discussed in detail by Goodyear and Dudley (2015) and in Cooperative Learning as Dyson et al. (2004) suggested, 'The teacher shifts from director ... to the facilitator of learning activities' (p. 238). The third additional procedure is that there is a group goal that students work together to achieve. The fourth and final non-element additional procedure is that you use a Cooperative Learning Structure. As you have already learned, there are literally hundreds of these and in the first instance (that is not say that you might not eventually create your own structures) the use of a structure helps you to implement Cooperative Learning as best you can.

Start small

Rome, as they say, wasn't built in a day, and neither is a new pedagogical approach. Start small. Don't jump in at the deep end but choose something manageable. In learning to use Cooperative Learning we both followed this adage but did it differently and advise you to do the same. Find your own way. Ash started with a single unit of work and one Cooperative Learning Structure, i.e. Jigsaw (Casey, 2004), while Ben started by teaching the students how to cooperate (Dyson, 2001) through the use of cooperative games. Either way, the key is to not bite off more than you can chew.

The keys are *you* and *yours*. You know *yourself* and you know *your* students. Find what you think works for them and give it a go. If it's too hard then scale it back. If it's too simple then ramp it up. Don't worry about taking one step forwards and then two back again. Don't worry about setting off in one direction and then having to do an about-turn and going somewhere completely different. What worked for us won't necessarily work for you − not 100 per cent anyway − and it will need to be tweaked at best and abandoned at worst. Both of us have done both (and still do), as it is dependent on us and ours and not some existing plan. Fundamentally, however, you are going to have to teach your students how to learn through Cooperative Learning and this means not just jumping in at the deep end. Ash coined a phrase that we have used for a while now − 'lesson zero'.

Teaching lesson zero

What is lesson zero? Lesson zero is the time − prior to the start of your Cooperative Learning lesson/unit − where you tell your students about the approach. For students to be able to learn from, rather than alongside, each other they need to be prepared to start thinking of learning in a different way. Knowledge and understanding is no longer just going to flow from you – the teacher – but will come from many different locations: primarily from their interactions with each other and the tasks. To do this they need to understand the purposes of learning through and in a Cooperative Learning classroom and they need to be given the opportunity to understand how lessons will be structured. They need to understand their roles and how they will be provided with opportunities to participate in activities that develop them across many domains – psychomotor, cognitive, social, and affective (Casey & Goodyear, 2015) – and not just develop their skills. How might this look?

1. The teacher discusses with the class the social and academic goals of the unit, e.g. to help each other to learn and to improve the ability to use tactical plays.
2. The teacher emphasizes that students are dependent on each other rather than him/her. They must use the worksheets provided and organize the tasks and learning themselves.
3. The teacher discusses and/or demonstrates the structure of the lessons, e.g. 'You will work in small teams of four or five. At the beginning of the lesson you get changed, collect your team worksheet, and work out as a team the goals of the lesson and what each student in the team needs to do. You organize the tasks as a team and progress through these. At the end of the lesson you answer the two questions at the bottom of your sheet about what went well in group work and what your group needs to improve on.'
4. Time is allocated for students to become acquainted with their team.
5. Teams look through the worksheets or their team folder.
6. The team plans how they will work together and discuss what they have been told by the teacher.
7. Time is allocated for a class discussion and students are given the opportunity to ask questions.
8. Time is allocated for Group Processing.

One or two elements and/or additional procedures at a time

Once you have 'taught' lesson zero then it is time to give Cooperative Learning a go. However, remember, you wouldn't try and teach or learn anything in its entirety on the first attempt. You would modify the game or look at one aspect at a time. Do the same with Cooperative Learning. By all means decide to teach a unit of work but focus on some of the key ideas. Choose an element or additional procedure (or two or three) and start from there. In some of the work we've done in our broader research teams we have encouraged teachers to monitor and evaluate their use of the elements and additional procedures. But how will you recognize them? Table 4.1 should help you to recognize and achieve them.

Recognizing the elements and additional procedures is one thing. Starting to use them is another. The key, as we have said, is that every student feels that they have a part to play in the group. They need to genuinely feel that their opinion and

TABLE 4.1 The Additional Procedures and how they might be achieved (Goodyear, 2015)

Additional Procedures	How to achieve
Group goal; students work in pairs or small groups to achieve a group goal.	Goals of the lesson are defined on the student worksheets.
Teacher facilitator: students learn from each other rather than the teacher.	Students use the task sheets to set up the learning activities themselves. The teacher uses open questioning.
Positive interdependence: students are dependent on each member of their group to be able to complete the goal.	Students are assigned a role on a rota each week which is in their team folders.
Individual accountability: students are assessed on their contribution to group work and their performance.	Task sheets have tick boxes for the recorder to assess whether each team member and the team has achieved the learning cues.
Promotive face-to-face interaction: students have positive interactions with members of their group.	The teacher encourages students to listen to each of their team members during discussions and positively reinforce each other's performance.
Group processing: the group reflects on what they have learned and how they can improve their ability to work as a group.	At the end of each lesson the team answers questions, e.g. What went well in group work? What does your group need to work on?
Cooperative Learning Structure	The structure for this unit is, for example, Learning Teams.
Small-group and interpersonal skills	Free and easy communication between group mates.

actions count equally to everyone else's and for that to be recognized they need a voice. Ironically, children don't always have a voice and Group Processing is one element that allows them, their group mates, and you to discover their voice. It is also a great way to understand what your students have learned as a result of your combined efforts.

Group Processing example

At an appropriate juncture, stop the groups and ask them to sit close together, i.e. toe-to-toe, knee-to-knee, face-to-face, and reflect on what they have done. In the first instance ask them to think (but not out loud and not with one another) about three questions before getting them to talk as a group (this helps every student to have a voice and something to say):

1. What happened? – This question focuses on the session and what the students actually did. The key is not to tell them what they did but let them think about it and recall the significant moments; you'll be surprised what they think is important and/or memorable.
2. So what? – This question is designed to get the students to think not just about what happened but the significance of it to them and their group. What do they say? Don't be surprised if they don't express what you wanted them or expected them to say. This, in our experience, is often when your hopes for their learning take a bit of a knock and something you thought was significant is forgotten and a throwaway line or unplanned for 'teaching moment' is the focus of their learning.
3. Now what? – This question is designed to help them (and you) think about what they need/want to learn next. This question is a great catalyst for forward thinking, planning, and doing. It challenges the students to think about what they need, as learners, to progress and it requires them to think of the group's needs as well as their own. This is a 'we' question but is one that is informed by each individual 'I'.

These three questions, described by Ben in 2002 – simple as they are – get the students thinking about what they have got out of the session and what they need next. The 'next' might mean you need to tweak your plans a little on the one hand or throw out the whole next session and start again on another plan. That said, it is about the learner. The teacher needs to focus in on what the students need and not on what the teacher has planned, and it is both challenging and refreshing to start our pedagogical thinking from that perspective.

Learning to learn in a new way

Finally, remember that while it is uncomfortable for you it is also uncomfortable for your students. They have spent years 'learning' how to be a student and have been rewarded for sitting quietly and following instructions, for dressing out (wearing the right clothing), and looking active, and now, in changing your expectations, they have to change the perceived benefit of their established responses, i.e. sitting quietly is no longer always a good thing. Be aware of these difficulties and help them to understand what is now expected of them (see 'lesson zero').

Give it a go!

In the following five examples we've designed standalone lessons or activities that you can use that focus on some but not all of the elements and additional procedures of Cooperative Learning (we have highlighted the elements we think are significant at the top of the worksheet). They are designed to help you develop your understanding of Cooperative Learning in action. Each uses a structure, mixed teams, and expects you to act as a facilitator.

WORKSHEET 4.1 Creating a dance/gymnastics sequence or routine using a Jigsaw classroom

Individual accountability	Positive interdependence	Interpersonal and small group skills	Face-to-face interaction	Group processing
Learning objective	Students contribute equally to the creation of a group routine using the Jigsaw classroom (see Chapter 9).			
Students' role within the task	Students are split into groups of four or five and each group is given the same number of cards (see pictures below). Each card shows a start and finish position. The student's job is to create an individual and short routine/ sequence that starts and finishes in their group allocated position (i.e. start at 2 and end at 3). Students then teach each other their routine and the whole group should create a whole routine that they can then perform together.			
Equipment/ pre-lesson tasks	Start and finish shape cards are needed. You will need a set of four or five cards per group and space to create the routine and then perform as a group.			
Task	Student 1 – starts from position 1 and creates a short (i.e. 10 seconds) routine or sequence and ends in position 2. Student 2 – uses positions 2 and 3. Student 3 – uses positions 3 and 4. Student 4 – uses position 4 and either position 1 or 5. Once each individual has developed, rehearsed, and remembered their routine then they must teach their group mates the routine. The end product is a group performance that works all the way through the sequence.			
Your reflection (3 Whats)	What happened? (Describe the learning.): So what? (How does this move your aims forward?): Now what? (How do you adjust your teaching for the next lesson?):			

WORKSHEET 4.2 Peer assessment in swimming: using student expertise to enhance learning

Individual accountability	Positive interdependence	Interpersonal and small group skills	Face-to-face interaction	Group processing
Learning objective	Students engage in peer assessment to develop and enhance performance in swimming (see Chapter 8).			
Students' role within the task	Split the students into pairs and then put two pairs together to form a group. If this is not possible then use groups of three as well (this is a pair-check-perform). Ask the students to peer assess one another in relation to the learning cues provided. Once the initial peer assessment has been completed within the pairs, the pairs are then pair checked by their peers (thus the name pair check).			
Equipment/ pre-lesson tasks	Worksheets – laminated for use in the pool Waterproof pens or wax pencils for writing on the worksheets Floats etc. for use in the water			
Task	**(This initial task works on body position but similar work could be done on arms, legs, and whole stroke)** 1. Hold onto the side with both hands and with the soles of both feet against the sidewall. 2. Let go with your hands and duck under the water. 3. Arms are brought above your head so that your upper arms cover your ears and your palms touch in a 'spear' point. 4. Drive legs and push through the spear point and 'rocket' off the wall. 5. Maintain body position until you stop moving. (Try and beat your best drive across multiple attempts.) **Teaching points:** 1. Feet on the wall 2. Duck completely under 3. Hands in spear point and rocket			
Your reflection (3 Whats)	What happened? (Describe the learning.): So what? (How does this move your aims forward?): Now what? (How do you adjust your teaching for the next lesson?):			

WORKSHEET 4.3 Discovering the key aspects of throwing in Track and Field in Learning Teams

Individual accountability	Positive interdependence	Interpersonal and small group skills	Face-to-face interaction	Group processing
Learning objective	Students are to understand the key similarities and differences between different types of throws in Track and Field athletics (pull, push, sling, and heave).			
Students' role within the task	In their Learning Teams students set up a number of markers at 2, 6, 10, 14, 16 meters, and maximally (i.e. how far they think their best throw might be).			
	Students to throw to each marker in turn (i.e. 2 meters, 6 meters, etc.) while a peer observes them. Students note what they do on each throw and what changes. Note: on the shortest throw they will just use their arms and increasingly more parts of their bodies will become involved as they throw further.			
	Students can coach one another to aid in understanding (try tip, tip, coach).			
	After each type of throw students engage in a discussion.			
Equipment/ pre-lesson tasks	Clipboards, results tables, pencils			
	Balls for throwing			
	Tape measure			
Task	Using a table containing different throws and some writing space to record their observations, ask students to throw the various sized balls (i.e. tennis ball, soft ball, soccer ball, basketball) each of the required distances.			
	With each throw students need to record what parts of their body they use, how they use them and the effort they exert.			
	One of the throws needs to be a maximal throw to show the full throw and highlight what is required to throw their furthest distances.			
	Groups are asked to give feedback to their peers on the requirements of each throw.			
	Groups are to create some learning outcomes and a throwing practice to improve their collective efforts.			
	A Team Game Tournament or Student Teams Assessment Division (see Chapter 8) could be used as a structure for this lesson (see Chapter 10)			
Your reflection (3 Whats)	What happened? (Describe the learning.):			
	So what? (How does this move your aims forward?):			
	Now what? (How do you adjust your teaching for the next lesson?):			

WORKSHEET 4.4 Creating and explaining restarts in team games using Numbered Heads Together

Individual accountability	Positive interdependence	Interpersonal and small group skills	Face-to-face interaction	Group processing
Learning objective	Student Learning Teams (see Chapters 3 and 10) are to create a restart in a team game. All students must understand the tactical and strategic importance of the restart.			
Students' role within the task	Students will contribute to the development of a restart, e.g. a sideline ball in basketball, a throw-in in soccer. Students need to work together to devise the restart, thinking of player movement, the weight of the pass, etc. One student will be selected at random using Numbered Heads Together (see Chapter 3) and asked to describe the restart and all its component parts to the rest of the class.			
Equipment/ pre-lesson tasks	Equipment for the game(s) selected, e.g. balls Cones to mark out the playing area for each group			
Task	Using an assigned area – maybe 20m by 20m – students, in small groups of four or five, devise a restart for a game. The restart should involve one fewer player than there are in the teams, i.e. for a group of four a two-v.-one would be practiced. This creates an extra player who will describe the restart to the rest of the class while the others perform. All players should understand the 'language' of the restart, e.g. fake, v. cut, roll. All players should understand the tactics of the restart, e.g. short pass to bring the defender forward and create a two-v.-one with the receiver and the restarting player. Picking a number in each group randomly, the groups perform the restart and the chosen player explains the movements and tactics to the rest of the class.			
Your reflection (3 Whats)	What happened? (Describe the learning.): So what? (How does this move your aims forward?): Now what? (How do you adjust your teaching for the next lesson?):			

WORKSHEET 4.5   River crossing challenge using I do – We do

Individual accountability	Positive interdependence	Interpersonal and small group skills	Face-to-face interaction	Group processing
Learning objective	To develop an approach to problem solving that includes the thoughts and ideas of all individuals.			
Students' role within the task	Work in learning teams (see Chapter 3) that contain no more than five students.			
	At the start of the task each student is provided with the instructions for completing the task			
	Students must try and solve the problem on their own for the first five minutes (I do) before coming together to discuss a group solution (We do). Use a structure like Think, Pair, Explain, Perform (see Chapter 5).			
	Each player must describe their solution to the group from their written notes and the overall group solution is only devised once a group discussion has occurred.			
Equipment/ pre-lesson tasks	Cones to mark out two 2m-by-2m squares – position these squares 5m apart.			
	One big ball, one medium-sized ball and one small ball			
	One bat or racket			
Task	**The problem:** You come to a river that is 100m across carrying a boat (the bat or racket), a sack of grain (the big ball), a fox (the medium ball), and a chicken (the small ball). The boat is only big enough for one person and one item. However, if the fox and the chicken are left together then the fox will eat the chicken. Also, if the chicken is left with the grain then the chicken will eat the grain. How do you get everything safely to the far bank of the river?			
	I do: Individual students are given five minutes to try and plan a way across the river with their cargo. They make notes using the paper provided.			
	We do: The groups come together to discuss their individual solutions and then a group solution is discussed. This must also be written down.			
	Solution (for your eyes only): Take the chicken over the river first and come back with an empty boat. Take the fox over and bring the chicken back. Take the grain over and come back with an empty boat. Now take the chicken over.			
Your reflection (3 Whats)	What happened? (Describe the learning.):			
	So what? (How does this move your aims forward?):			
	Now what? (How do you adjust your teaching for the next lesson?):			

Self-processing / A time to reflect

Self-processing questions

1. Is it worth the effort? With so many things to do in your working day do you have time to make such changes?
2. What elements and/or additional procedures do you think it will be easiest/hardest to implement?
3. How did your first attempt go? What things did you (all of you) learn and how might it change your work?
4. What happened? So what? Now what? – Can you apply these questions to this chapter?

Our reflections

Ben

We are challenging you here to make a change in your pedagogical practice and we realize that this is not comfortable for you. You have to move outside your comfort zone. Many times in our research over the last 20 years we have noticed, as Andy Sparkes reminded us many years ago, that there is often *innovation without change* (Sparkes, 1991). Cooperative Learning is not an easy way out of teaching; it requires time, effort, persistence, reflection, and patience, but we believe the rewards outweigh the perspiration.

Ash

Change is a hard thing. It requires a starting point but it also requires a sense of what the destination is and why you might want to get there. The saying goes 'every journey begins with a single step', which is true, but the very notion of 'journey' speaks of an end point. To me the desired end point in Cooperative Learning is a widening of the learning that occurs in my sessions. It is fluency with the model that allows me to look at more than just skill development. It's a sense of sharing the learning process with the students and making them an integral part of everything that happens.

References

Casey, A. (2004). Piece-by-piece cooperation: Pedagogical change and jigsaw learning. *The British Journal of Teaching Physical Education, 35*(4), 11–12.

Casey, A. & Goodyear, V. (2015). Can cooperative learning achieve the four learning outcomes of physical education? A review of literature. *Quest, 67*(1), 56–72. http://doi.org/10.1080/00336297.2014.984733

Dyson, B. (2001). Cooperative learning in an elementary physical education program. *Journal of Teaching in Physical Education, 20*(August 2015), 264–281. http://doi.org/10.1080/07303084.2003.10608363

Dyson, B., Griffin, L. L., & Hastie, P. (2004). Sport education, tactical games, and cooperative learning: Theoretical and pedagogical considerations. *Quest, 56*(2), 226–240.

Goodyear, V. (2015). Developing students' promotive interactions over time: Teachers' adaptions to and interactions within the cooperative learning model. AIESEP international conference. July, 2015, Madrid, Spain.

Goodyear, V. & Dudley, D. (2015). 'I'm a facilitator of learning!' Understanding what teachers and students do within student-centered physical education models. *Quest, 67*(3), 274–289. http://doi.org/10.1080/00336297.2015.1051236

Grineski, S. (1996). *Cooperative learning in physical education.* Champaign, IL: Human Kinetics.

Sparkes, A. (1991). Curriculum change: On gaining a sense of perspective. In A. Sparkes & N. Armstrong (Eds.). *Issues in Physical Education* (pp. 1–19). London: Cassell Educational Limited.

Velazquez-Callado, C. (2012). Cooperative Learning and physical activity into practice with primary students. In B. Dyson & A. Casey (Eds.). *Cooperative learning in physical education: A research-based approach* (pp. 59–74). London: Routledge.

5

HOW TO IMPLEMENT COOPERATIVE LEARNING IN PHYSICAL EDUCATION AT THE ELEMENTARY OR PRIMARY SCHOOL LEVEL

Chapter overview

Many elementary school teachers use Cooperative Learning in their classrooms. However, most teachers do not think of using Cooperative Learning in their Physical Education classes (Colby, 2014; Dyson et al., 2014). In addition, there is research to suggest that many teachers use group work, but do not necessarily use a defined Cooperative Learning Structure or the elements of Cooperative Learning when they are teaching (Antil et al., 1998; Dyson, et al., 2004; Dyson et al., 2010). In this chapter we provide practical examples of using Cooperative Learning Structures at the elementary level (primary school level) incorporating the main elements of Cooperative Learning: teaching Interpersonal Skills, Face-to-Face Promotive Interaction, Positive Interdependence, Individual Accountability, and Group Processing. We discuss the design of lesson plans, creative task sheets, and reflection on this innovative pedagogical practice. Furthermore, we will explore how the implementation of Cooperative Learning might, for example, successfully achieve the new National Standards in Physical Education in the US and the National Curriculum in the UK, New Zealand, and Australia.

We believe that

1. Elementary students can learn the five elements of Cooperative Learning.
2. Elementary students can learn Cooperative Learning Structures.
3. Effective communication with peers is difficult for many students. The elementary years are an appropriate time for students to learn Interpersonal and Small Group Skills.
4. Teachers need to teach students interpersonal skills – it's just as important as subject matter knowledge.

5. It is valuable for students to learn different roles that can support group work and help learning.
6. Physical activity (PA) may be worthwhile but it does not equate to a quality Physical Education program.

Imagine the scene

At Finlandus Elementary School, grade 5 (year 6), Andreas enters the gym and begins his workout. Based on his test results Andreas and his teacher Ms. Romar have created a personalized physical activity program including ten selected aerobic activities. For example: three sets of 5 dips, two sets of 15 crunches, and shooting the basket into the hoop. This is the warm-up that Andreas devised and it includes what he felt were important and fun things to do.

As soon as Andreas and his classmates complete their warm up they move to the stations that are set up around the gym. The students are in small groups organized in the Pair-Check-Perform (for an example and definition see Chapter 3) Cooperative Learning Structure (Box 3.1). Each of these stations provides instructions for practicing skills associated with the game of volleyball. Each station has a task sheet that lists three learning cues for each specific skill.

Andreas and his partner are working at the bump station (the volleyball forearm pass station). First they practice bumping to each other. His partner, Jo, tosses the ball six times to Andreas and then they switch. Andreas and Jo remember when they had practiced tossing the ball to each other. Ms. Romar was very particular. The volleyball had to be tossed like a rainbow, that is, high in the air with a good arch and easily caught by the partner.

Next the students practice bumping balls that are thrown to the right and to the left so that Andreas has to move to the ball. Next, soft volleyballs are thrown in the air in either direction.

As their skill level increases the balls are thrown faster and higher.

Andreas feels confident practicing this skill because he remembers the many times Jo has encouraged him even when he had a bad hit. He remembers yesterday when she reminded him to keep a low center of gravity and wide base of support and to watch the ball, which would help him volley the ball more successfully.

It really helped when Jo showed him what she meant and then watched him perform that task to make sure he understood it. Another thing that helped him learn was partner-checking using the Cooperative Learning structure of Pair-Check-Perform. All the students would watch their partners and then check off on a task sheet the parts of the skill they performed correctly and then give each other help on parts that needed extra practice. Jo wasn't always great at this but she has learned, as they all have, how to observe, and now has the confidence to give good feedback.

Using the task sheets and partner-checking really helped Andreas learn. He also liked helping Jo learn. As Andreas was leaving PE class he thought about how much he had learned and he liked that.

Introduction

As we have mentioned earlier, Cooperative Learning challenges students to work closely with one another to accomplish tasks. When implementing Cooperative Learning at the elementary level (or primary school level), start gradually with one task at a time and begin with a class group that you think will cooperate. At the elementary level students need explicit guidance to begin to learn Cooperative Learning. Many of the teachers we have worked with over the years suggest that starting small increases the likelihood that you will be successful. This chapter will be helpful as it presents Reciprocal Teaching strategies that can be used at any level but should be used with elementary children, especially when you begin Cooperative Learning.

Research, ours and others, suggests that before implementing Cooperative Learning it can be helpful to spend time engaging the students in activities that promote positive social skills or interpersonal skills (Dyson et al., 2010). In Physical Education, sport, and PA settings we are familiar with 'ice-breaker' activities or different forms of team building. For example, a good way to start is a name game. A common name game is 'Your Name and Your Move'. Students stand in a circle and each student says their name and performs a movement. For example: My name is Ben and I like to give high fives. Ben moves into the center of the circle and says: 'My name is Ben and I like to give high fives' and he gives a high five in the air and everyone follows Ben's lead. Then the next person, Javier, starts: 'His name is Ben and he likes high fives. My name is Javier and I like to jog.' And Javier jogs on the spot; everyone follows the lead of Javier and jogs on the spot. And following Javier everyone follows the lead of the next person until everyone in the group has said their name and performed their move. Another activity is *Find Someone Else Who Can*. Students can move around the gym seeking out other students who can perform or who have learned to perform different physical tasks. For example, find someone who can kayak, find someone who can ride a skateboard, find someone who can hip-hop dance, and so on.

Depending on your students you might introduce two or three team building activities (for more on team building activities see Sutherland, 2012). For many students, beginning to learn positive social skills or interpersonal skills is one of the most important requirements for introducing Cooperative Learning in your coaching or teaching setting. We suggest that you might consider teaching a full unit of work on team building before you start using Cooperative Learning Structures.

In this chapter we focus on Interpersonal and Small Group Skills development, Group Processing, and Positive Interdependence. These are three of the key elements to Cooperative Learning. Although all of the elements will be covered in the text, this chapter asks you to start small and be purposeful and progressive with your students and focus on these Cooperative Learning elements initially when implementing Cooperative Learning.

Interpersonal and Small Group Skills

Once you have taught several lessons or a unit on team building we suggest that you review your students' social skills and Small Group Skills. Many students find it difficult to effectively communicate with peers. Our experience has taught us that merely placing students in groups will not automatically result in cooperation. We have all seen examples of dysfunctional groups at schools, universities, or in the community. Therefore, students need to be explicitly taught social skills (Dyson & Dryden, 2014; Sapon-Shevin, 2010). Learning interpersonal skills has been advocated specifically by National Standards five and six in the US (NASPE, 2013), the key competency of 'Relating to Others' in the New Zealand curriculum (MOE, 2007), and the requirement in the UK national curriculum that pupils should engage in 'co-operative physical activities' (Department for Education, 2014).

Several years ago Johnson and Johnson (1990) created guidelines to help teachers and coaches develop social skills with their students:

1. Students must learn what an appropriate social skill is and the timing of when to use it.
2. Students need to *'buy into'* the social skill and understand why they are using it.
3. Students should role play the social skill, for example, making sure students are listening to others.
4. Students must learn the social skill in a number of different situations and subject areas, not just Physical Education.
5. Discuss the social skill in the Group Processing sessions. For example, you could discuss the way we give and receive feedback: 'Did we give and receive feedback appropriately today?'

We've found that elementary students can learn the major concepts of social skills, for example: listening to each other and working as a team (Dyson & Casey, 2012). We have some students' comments to support the value of social skills. A year 5 (grade 4) student, Chris, suggested that Cooperative Learning encouraged his class 'to listen and to talk. So you have to give everyone else a chance but you can have a chance as well so everyone gets a go.' And Allison, a year 6 (grade 5) student, commented, 'We learn how to work together and listen to each other and listen to the teacher or whoever's taking us for PE. Listen to our teammates and all that and if they're talking cooperate with them'.

Returning to the Johnson and Johnson (1990) guidelines above it becomes clearer that it is important to explicitly teach rather than simply assume that students can develop appropriate social skills. Personally, we've found that one of the most beneficial strategies is to provide 'student talk time' in the form of Group Processing during each lesson (Sutherland et al., 2014).

Group Processing

One way for students to improve their Interpersonal and Small Group Skills is Group Processing. For elementary-aged students the Cooperative Learning element of Group Processing might be foreign to them. To recall for the reader, our definition of Group Processing is: a verbal reflection that serves as an opportunity for the students to express their thoughts, feelings, and ideas and for the teacher to guide feedback as a facilitator to the students. In a Group Processing session we suggest that you discuss:

- What went well for you as a group?
- What did you have trouble with?
- What do you need to work on?

Students have commented that the Group Processing time they have is important (Dyson et al., 2010). This can be a valuable teaching and learning tool that is often overlooked or neglected due to an over-crowded curriculum and time constraints. It is also often overlooked or ignored because it is seen as downtime and therefore not physically active enough. Research has repeatedly shown (see Darnis & Lafont, 2013) that learning is enhanced when young people get a chance to talk about what they have done, and yet this is repeatedly overlooked in physical activity settings.

Try to build time into your lessons, either during or at the end, to discuss issues or process what happened in the lesson. Because of time considerations with your teaching, Group Processing has to be kept brief initially; we recommend five minutes (Dyson, 1994). The teacher facilitates the discussion by asking questions like: 'Give me an example of how your group worked today?' 'How did you solve problems that arose?' 'What did your team or partner do well?' or 'What is something you or your team need to work on?' It is imperative that the students take turns responding and providing the class/group their comments. Often we might start the discussions in their base groups and then, using a structure like *Numbered Heads Together*, ask one student to summarize the group's discussions. Therefore, the teacher or coach needs to develop a strategy to ensure each student in the class contributes to the Group Processing at some time during each unit – indeed, that they contribute to all aspects of the lesson (but that's a bigger point). There will always be some students who try to dominate the discussion, but just like all parts of Cooperative Learning we develop more completely if all students contribute to Group Processing; it is, after all, sink or swim together.

Group Processing can be an effective teaching strategy for several reasons. For example, teachers can use it to gain information and feedback from the students. Students are able to develop solutions to problems, obtain feedback on their performance, and share successes with their class. The teacher and students can use information obtained during Group Processing sessions when planning and participating in future lessons. A major limitation is that it is hard to find time to fit Group Processing into each lesson. Indeed, in Ash's early work he deliberately missed this element. Looking back on this it was an easy solution to the problem and hindsight tells him that his students missed out. Indeed, while others may not agree, Ash would now position Group Processing as a vital part of Cooperative Learning as a pedagogical model. That said, it isn't easy to include and initially it needs to be planned into your lessons after a specific task or at the end. As your experience with Cooperative Learning grows, however, we hope you will see the benefit of Group Processing and, like Ash, allocate more time to it as you become more confident implementing Cooperative Learning.

One Cooperative Learning Structure that we have found very useful to help teach students Group Processing is *Inside-Outside-Circle Reflection*. This structure is modified from another of Kagan and Kagan's (2009) structures, Inside-Outside-Circle. Inside-Outside-Circle Reflection organizes students in two circles, one on the inside (tighter together or in a smaller space on the inside of the circle) and one on the outside, further apart in distance. The teacher or coach can pose a question, for example, 'Why did your team work well today?' or 'Why did your team not work well today?' or 'Positively critique your team's performance today.' Students rotate to face new partners every 30 seconds to discuss the issue, concern, or problem posed by the teacher (in a five-minute period students can talk to ten different students).

Positive Interdependence

To encourage Positive Interdependence, Bertucci et al. (2012) suggested assigning each group member complementary and interconnected roles, such as reader, recorder, coach, facilitator, encourager of participation, and checker for understanding. Student roles are an important part or characteristic of many Cooperative Learning tasks or lessons. Working with students to develop roles takes time and patience. However, when students understand their roles they are able to make decisions and solve problems on their own. Students will often need help to understand and become familiar with their roles. As the teacher or coach you need to choose roles that will best fit your content, your students, and/or your setting. On many of the task sheets or in our lesson plans we have included student roles.

Examples of these roles are:

- Coach – provides feedback to group members, makes sure everyone is on task.
- Encourager – provides positive specific comments to all group members.
- Recorder – reads the task and records any comments, answers, etc.
- Equipment manager – initially organizes equipment and gathers and then puts away equipment. In addition, makes sure equipment is respected and used appropriately.

At Campus School in Memphis, USA, Suzanne Griffin used roles to encourage students in a Language Arts task; students were asked to learn a specific set of vocabulary words or grammar concepts (see Figure 5.1). This could be adapted for PE by changing the roles to suit the PE content.

Lesson planning

In the next section we will explore different Cooperative Learning Structures and tasks and guidelines for lesson planning. This section is designed as a guide for a teacher or coach wanting to implement Cooperative Learning Structures into their pedagogical work.

Summarizer/Proofreader

Name: _____ Date: _____

Your job is very important! You are in charge of writing the information your team discovers. You will be in charge of writing the information on your poster in a neat and creative fashion. Spelling counts!

Word Wizard

Name: _____ Date: _____

Your job is very important! You are in charge of looking up the vocabulary words in the science book. You will read important findings aloud to your group. You will take any needed notes to help the summarizer and other team members plan your poster.

Illuminator

Name: _____ Date: _____

Your job is also very important! You are the illustrator for your team. You will be responsible for the creative design and actual illustrations on your poster.

Motivator/Supply Organizer

Name: _____ Date: _____

Your job is equally important! You are to help keep your team positive and motivated. You are to redirect your team members if they get "off track." If disagreements arise, help talk out the situation at hand. You are also in charge of team supplies. Keep them organized and return when task is completed.

** Note: Though each person has a specific role to complete, it is important to share ideas and plan together. You may provide advice to each other in terms of the different roles.

FIGURE 5.1   Student roles for Language Arts

Lesson plan design

There are many ways to design an effective lesson plan. Johnson, Johnson, and Holubec (1994) have been publishing Cooperative Learning lesson plan designs for 30 years. Below we provide a modified example of a Johnson, Johnson, and Holubec (1987) lesson plan. In this design we include what you would normally expect in a lesson plan and then we have added sections to the lesson plan that you could use in a Cooperative Learning lesson. We have highlighted these additions with an asterisk (*) in Figure 5.2.

An example of a lesson plan by Rachel Colby, Maine, USA, was used in a Jumping and Landing unit for year 3 and 4 (8- to 9-year-old) students (Figure 5.3). In this lesson plan Rachel presents both *Jigsaw* and *Think-Pair-Share* Cooperative Learning Structures.

Lesson title: _____

Teacher: _____

Subject: _____

Instructional objectives: (Learning intentions) _____   Grade level:

Resources required: _____

* Assignment to groups: _____   Group size:

* Roles: _____

Lesson format:

Tasks: * How do I ensure Interpersonal Skills
                                                     and Small Group Skills?:
_____
                                                     _____
_____
                                                     _____
_____

* How do I ensure Positive Interdependence?:   * Social skills taught:

_____   _____

_____   * Defined as:

* How do I ensure Individual Accountability?:   _____

_____   * Phrases that encourage explicit social skill:

_____   _____

* How do I ensure Promotive Face-to-Face Interaction?:   * Use of rewards/motivators:

_____   _____

_____
                                                     * Monitoring and interaction:
* Criteria for success:
                                                     _____
_____

_____   * Monitoring by: Teacher : _____

* Expected behaviors: Student: _____ Other: _____

_____   * How do I ensure Group Processing?:

_____   _____

FIGURE 5.2 Cooperative Learning lesson plan format

Unit: Locomotor Movement (Jumping and Landing)
Achievement level: 3

Class level: Year 3 & 4
Learning environment: Gym or outside court

Duration: 60 minutes
Number of Ss: 24

Pedagogical model(s): Cooperative Learning, Skill Theme Approach
Key focus for lesson: Students will master 4 jumps: 2 feet–1 foot; 1 foot–2 feet; height; distance

Equipment needed: Task cards, pencils, hula hoops (2/group), jump ropes (2/group), poly spots (4/group)

Learning Intention(s):
- Students will move and control different parts of their bodies simultaneously.
- Students will understand how their bodies need to move for different types of jumps.
- Students will give/accept specific feedback to/from teammates.

Key competencies:
- T = Thinking
- MS = Managing self
- RO = Relating to others
- PC = Participating and contributing
- U = Using language, symbols and texts

Time	Activities	Teaching points	Differentiation	Teaching as inquiry	Key competencies
5 min	Introduction to lesson: Review Roles of Group Learning Teams (LT): Think of a sports team you have been on. Everyone has an assigned role. The idea is that you develop team cohesion and each individual has a role. Each learning team decides on a name with teachers' guidance. Share responsibility through roles. Divide into groups of four. Teacher describes group outcomes and goals (recorder may record this). Teams work to play game or complete task.	• Coach (C)– makes sure group knows what they are doing and stays on task • Encourager (E)– gives positive specific feedback to team members • Recorder (R)– Fills out task sheets • Equip. manager (M)– gathers and puts back equipment, makes sure it's used appropriately	Have cue cards with descriptions of roles	What is your role?	T, MS, RO, PC, U
	Social Skill of the Day Think-Pair-Share: First Think by yourself, then talk in a Pair, then Share ideas with class.	• Today we will be giving and accepting specific feedback. • Ss in LT's answer question and report back to class • What does specific mean?	Give guiding sentences: Specific means using cues like....	What does specific mean?	

FIGURE 5.3 Physical Education lesson plan

Time	Activities	Teaching points	Differentiation	Teaching as inquiry	Key competencies

10 min	<u>Warm up:</u>
	Fit Friends
	Jigsaw:
	Each student is responsible for learning a portion of content. Then teach to other members of their group. Teacher assigns task to group, divided into four separate parts. Each member takes one part and learns it, then teaches it to group.
	Number students in Learning Teams 1–4. All 1s go together, all 2s go together and so on. Divide students into four groups. Each group learns a skill, learning cue or part of the movement. Then original learning teams combine, and each student takes it in turns to teach their part of the skill or movement to rest of the group.
		• Each role comes together to figure out solution for their specific part of the fitness routine (see task cards)
		  • C – Arm exercise
		  • E – Leg exercise
		  • R – Full body exercise
		  • M – Lap movement
		• Roles go back into their LTs and teach rest of group their part of fitness routine
		• LTs perform full routine as a group
			Task cards have ideas to help Ss with exercises.
			
			Ss can modify exercises to their level, i.e. push-ups can be knee push-ups
				How do we perform and teach the exercise?	T, MS, PC, U

20 min	<u>Skill activity:</u>
	Jumping Jack Flash
	(Jigsaw)
		• Each role comes together to be an expert for their specific jump (see task cards)
		  • C – Take-off 2 feet, land 1 foot
		  • E – Take-off 1 foot, land 2 feet
		  • R – Jump for height
		  • M – Jump for distance
		• Roles go back into their LTs and teach rest of group their jump. Give each member of their group positive and corrective feedback for the jumping cues
		• R records progress on task cards
		• Each expert asks group:
		  • What helps us stay standing when we land?
			Have cues written on task cards
			
			Have pictures depicting the types of jumps on task cards
			
			T demonstrates jumps to different expert groups
				What are the jumping cues?
				
				What helps us stay standing when we land?
					T, MS, RO, PC, U

FIGURE 5.3   (cont'd)

Time	Activities	Teaching points	Differentiation	Teaching as inquiry	Key competencies

20 min	Challenge Activity: Jump On It! *(Jigsaw)*	• Each role comes together to build a part of the jumping obstacle course with given equipment (see task cards)
		  • C – Hula hoops
		  • E – Jump ropes
		  • R – Poly spots
		  • M – Lines on ground
		• Roles go back into their LTs and teach rest of group their part of the obstacle course
		• LT goes through entire obstacle course together
			Change height/distance of obstacles based on the Ss need	How do we move our bodies to cross the obstacle?	T, MS, PC, U

10 min	Group Processing: *Think-Pair-Share*
	
	Numbered Heads:
	Teammates put their heads together to reach consensus. Teacher poses problems, students have own time (teacher choice as to how long) to think about/answer question, students stand up and put heads together in group sharing answers, discussing and teaching. Students sit down when everyone knows answer. Teacher calls a number, students answer using: answer board, choral practice, finger responses, response cards, manipulative, chalkboard responses, demonstrations, explanations.
		• In LTs, Ss answer following questions. Use Numbered Heads to report answers back to class. C leads discussion:
		  • What did your group do well today with jumping?
		  • What specific feedback did your group give?
		• Have R write down answer to next question on reflection task sheet
		  • What did your LT do well today to work together?
		  • What teamwork goal will you have for next class?
			Have cue cards to help guide discussion	What did our group do well today with jumping?
				
				What specific feedback did we give?
				
				What did our group do well today to work together?
				
				What is our teamwork goal for next class?
					T, MS, RO, PC, U

FIGURE 5.3 (cont'd)

Fit Friends Task Cards

C Arm Exercise	E Leg Exercise
• Push-Ups • Wall Pushes • Shoulder Taps • Reach & Pulls	• Ski Jumps • Squats • Lunges
R Full Body Exercise	M Lap Movement
• Star Jumps • Fluffy Stars • Inch Worm	• Jog • Skip • Gallop • Slide

Jump On It Task Cards

C Hula Hoops	E Jump Ropes
R Poly Spots	M Lines

Jumping Jack Flash Task Cards

C Take-Off 2 Feet Land 1 Foot	E Take-Off 1 Foot Land 2 Feet
• Bend Knees • Use Arms • Balance • Bend Knee	• Bend Knee • Use Arms • Balance • Bend Knees
R Jump for Height	M Jump for Distance
• Bend Knees • Push Arms Up • Stretch Body • Bend Knees	• Bend Knees • Push Arms Out • Bend Knees • Stay Standing

Group Processing Cue Cards

Our group did well with the jumping cue of….	Our group gave specific feedback when…. We said….
Our group did well working as a team when we….	Next class we will work on …. to improve our teamwork.

FIGURE 5.3   (cont'd)

Cooperative Learning Structures

As discussed in Chapter 3, Spencer Kagan is the most well known proponent of Cooperative Learning structures. If you google Spencer or go to Kagan's website (http://www.kaganonline.com/free_articles/research_and_rationale/increase_achievement.php) you will see a large number of structures and suggestions, literature, and school-based research to support the Cooperative Learning Structures and your use of them.

Structures for the elementary level

Here we will present structures that we think are most useful at the elementary or primary level. As Chapter 3 suggests, the intention of these Cooperative Learning structures is to provide a way of organizing the interaction of individuals in a classroom. Cooperative Learning Structures have step-by-step procedures that are used to present, practice, and review a task or problem. The Cooperative Learning Structures we present can help to increase the interactions between pairs or within members of a team (Kagan & Kagan, 2009). Cooperative Learning Structures also help teachers incorporate the main elements of Cooperative Learning, i.e. teaching Interpersonal Skills, Face-to-Face Promotive Interaction, Positive Interdependence, Individual Accountability, and Group Processing, in an explicit manner into a lesson. However, when learning how to use Cooperative Learning Structures in your class we suggest emphasizing three elements at the beginning: Interpersonal and Small Group Skills, Positive Interdependence, and Group Processing (Dyson et al., 2010; Dyson & Rubin, 2003) and building from there. As we have mentioned earlier, when implementing Cooperative Learning, start progressively with one task at a time and initiate your Cooperative Learning experience with a class that you think will be open to a new pedagogical practice. At the elementary level students need explicit guidance to begin to learn Cooperative Learning. We suggest you start with lesson zero and we have outlined a progressive teaching style for this in Chapter 4 (Figure 4.1).

Many classroom primary teachers use Cooperative Learning Structures in their classes, so they have many ideas on how to use Cooperative Learning in Math, Science, or Language Arts content. However, most classroom teachers do not think of using Cooperative Learning as a pedagogy in their PE classes (Dyson et al., 2014). An English and a Science example follows, which could be modified to be used in Physical Education. A Physical Education example of *Numbered Heads Together* can be found in Chapter 3.

Numbered Heads Together

A typical Cooperative Learning Structure example used by Greg Norman at Papatoetoe South School, New Zealand for his grade 5 (year 6) English students is *Numbered Heads Together*.

The specific task is for students to learn how to spell words together. The wider learning intention is for students to learn to read, write, and spell words with their teammates. This could be easily adapted for Physical Education by asking students to spell words that are specific to Physical Education content. For example, spell the major bones in your body (for example: Arm: ulna, radius; Legs: femur, tibia, fibula; Spine: vertebrae, lumbar, thoracic).

The task: the teacher poses a problem, 'How do you spell bones in your body? The challenge will be for you all to spell four bones from your body.' Each student thinks about bones in their body and offers suggestions of how to spell them in their groups. Then the teammates put their heads together to reach consensus about how to spell four bones. That is, the students use the Cooperative Learning Structure *Numbered Heads Together* in their group, sharing their suggestions and discussing. Students sit down when everyone knows how to spell four bones and checks that all students in their team have a number one through four. The teacher calls a number, and that numbered student goes to the whiteboard to write up the agreed spelling of their four bones.

Word Webbing

A typical Science example using a Cooperative Learning structure used by Wendy Poole at Wakaaranga Primary School is Word Webbing. Word Webbing is modified from a Kagan Cooperative Learning Structure and can be used in Science or other content areas (S. Kagan, 2007). Word Webbing could be modified for Physical Education or coaching. The task could be to word web the best strategies to defend your goal in hockey.

Topics for Word Webbing can be as simple as *phases of matter*: gas → liquid → solid, or as complicated as: *the scientific method*: Determine the problem or question, gather information/research information, form a hypothesis, observe, gather data, discuss findings, make conclusion, present implications.

The task: the teacher gives the students a concept, topic, or idea. Students write the main idea in the center of their team paper. Then in the team's unique color each student in the team writes one idea related to the central concept/topic/idea and connects it with a line or arrow to that topic. They then add as many ideas and details to their team word web as they can. Students can use words, symbols, arrows, and simple illustrations to best represent the main ideas of the topic and the connection to its parts.

Challenge-Challenge-Trade

A Cooperative Learning Structure that may interest you is *Challenge-Challenge-Trade*. This version was adapted and used by Rachel Colby, Maine, USA (Figure 5.4). This activity is an adaption of Kagan's Cooperative Learning Structure, 'Quiz–Quiz–Trade'.

- Teacher makes challenge cards that focus on the skills learned in the unit, fitness skills, or other PE skills that can be reviewed (balance on one hand, do ten jumping jacks, skip in a circle, etc.).
- Each student is given a challenge card and puts one hand up.
- Students pair up by high fives and challenge each other to do the challenge on the cards, then trade cards.
- Students then find another student with a hand up to challenge-challenge-trade with.

FIGURE 5.4 Challenge–Challenge–Trade

Partner Cards

Partner Cards is another modification of Quiz-Quiz-Trade. Many of you may have used this task in your teaching and yet not given the same name to it. In Partner Cards the goal is to collectively perform the prescribed skill or activity with a partner. Cards that have a task or skill that needs to be performed are scattered on the floor. Pairs will pick a card at random and then work together to understand how to perform that task. Once they have succeeded at that task they show the teacher, who will then let them pick another card. Rewards are given to students who successfully perform the skill. This activity could be modified to be specific in a certain area or sport. For example, all cards could have netball-related tasks or skills that need to be coached and learned, e.g. learn how to chest pass to a partner. 'Remember, hold the ball on the sides up to your chest, and push it to the floor close to your partner so it bounces up to their hands'. This could also be very broad at the end of a unit to encompass all of the areas that have been learned about.

Think, Pair, Explain, Perform

Think, Pair, Explain, Perform is a Cooperative Learning Structure that has been adapted from general education. The teacher poses a question to the class and asks the students to 'think' about their response. Then students are asked to 'pair' up and talk to a partner about their ideas. Next, students are asked to 'explain' and then 'perform' their activity idea/solution to the class.

An example could be: 'Think what the learning cues are for a forearm pass in volleyball' (knees bent, body low to the ground, forearms straight, and move to the ball).

Collective Group Score

In *Collective Group Score* teammates add up all the scores from all team members to create a collective group score for an activity. Collective Group Score encourages students to try their best to complete an activity or perform a number of repetitions since everyone's score is important for the total score. As an example, students in their groups perform as many repetitions of an exercise as they can in a given period of time, and then add the repetitions together to create a collective group score. For the next class students set a target group goal for the number of repetitions they hope to perform. This can be divided up any way they choose and allows them to self-differentiate (so to speak). You can also have Whole Class Collective Score – each group's score is added together to make a class total Collective Group Score, which the class could try to beat the next time they perform a task or which you could use in an interclass competition. An example of Collective Group Score appears in Figure 5.5.

For the lower elementary level, students can use the *Collective Group Score*; for upper elementary students *Collective Activity Score* can be used; these are modifications of a structure presented by Steve Grineski (1996). The task is for students in their groups to perform as many repetitions of an activity as they can during a physical activity circuit in a PE lesson, for example jump rope, shots into the basket, step-ups on a bench, badminton volleys, etc. After three to four station rotations the students set a goal for their future performance. Then each group's target goal can be added to the class total. This collective activity could be modified to reinforce any activity that the teachers want students to learn, for example class routines, class rules, or appropriate student behaviors.

Another less complicated form of the Cooperative Learning Structure *Collective Group Score* is the activity *Tossing into the hoop*. The aim of this activity is to score

---

Task 1:
Learning intention: fun and pleasure in moving – students' choice of activity
Cooperative Learning Structure: Collective Group Score

The coach: _____

provides feedback to the group members to improve their performance.

The reader: _____

reads the task and makes sure all group members understand it – gets clipboard.

The recorder: _____

records each student's performance – totals group score.

The organizer: _____

organizes equipment for next group – puts equipment away at the end of class.

The encourager: _____

encourages group members to be involved and provides positive comments to all group members.

FIGURE 5.5   Task sheet: Collective Group Score – physical activity circuit

Circuit Recorder sheet

Activity:	Group member 1:	Group member 2:	Group member 3:	Group member 4:	**Collective Group Score:**	Goal for next lesson:
1. Group juggle						
2. B-ball pass						
3. Shuttle run						
4. Ski jumps						
5. Jump rope						
6. Hula hoop						
7. Badminton rally						
8. Group choice						
9. Group choice						

FIGURE 5.5 (cont'd)

Task 2:
Students in their teams create their own activity for the circuit.

Activities 8 & 9:
Briefly explain activities created by your group:

Task 3 – Group Processing:
Student questions:
➡ What station went well for you as a group? What station did you have trouble with?
➡ Did you see Positive Interdependence? Did you see Individual Accountability?

Additional teacher questions:
What were the:
Physical task/s; Cognitive task/s; and Social task/s:

FIGURE 5.5   (cont'd)

as many points as possible by throwing the ball through the hoop, and the other two in your group of three move the hoop to help the throwing be successful. Once you have thrown the ball five times you trade places with your partners. This activity can improve students' manipulative skills, tracking, refines spatial awareness, and refines effort awareness. When the activity is completed the students can add up their Collective Group Score. This could be modified by having four members in a team. Two of the members of the team are shooting. That way there is a greater opportunity to participate for the time allocation. This could be used for different ball sports, such as rugby, softball, European handball, basketball, and so on, so that different skills and techniques could be used with different balls.

A less complicated form of the Cooperative Learning Structure *Learning Teams* is *Objective Juggle*, which is a modification of Grineski's (1996) 'Sportball Juggle'. The aim of this structure is to successfully move a maximum number of different objects (cones, jump ropes, spikey balls, etc.) or sports balls (soccer balls, tennis balls, rugby balls) in sequence within a team. Students in a Learning Team stand approximately 6 feet apart in a square formation and attempt to move the different objects or balls simultaneously around their square. Students decide on the types of skills, the types of different objects or balls, and the different levels for each object or ball. The teacher or coach could get all children to chest pass, and the focus could be: making eye contact before throwing, timing so it does not hit another ball, and throwing accurately so that the object gets to the other student. This activity could be modified by adding different objects or balls in when the students become proficient or are successful at the passing/catching. You could also mix this up with different requirements. For example, the red ball could mean chest pass, blue ball could mean bounce pass, etc., or you could concentrate on a specific sport, e.g. in a basketball unit you could have different types of basketball passes, or at the end of the unit you could have soccer ball passes, or rugby ball lateral passes, and so on.

Task sheets

We have found that creating quality task sheets or task cards is an important skill to learn for teachers or coaches. Their development and implementation is problematic at times. For example, the task sheets can be too simple for year 6 but might be more appropriate for year 3 or year 4 (Figure 5.6 Basic task card for exercises) and not challenge the students enough or be too complicated and frustrate or confuse the students. We hope that Figure 5.7 is a useful example for you of a learning activity for learning how to juggle a soccer ball. What we want is to create task sheets that offer differentiation but also challenge the students wherever they are in their developmental level of learning. In Chapter 2

10 Push Ups	10 Sit Ups
10 Jumping Jacks	5 Squats
5 Lunges	10 Ski Jumps
10 Shoulder Taps	10 Mountain Climbs
5 Left Hops	5 Right Hops

FIGURE 5.6 Basic task card for exercises

Learning intentions:
1. Physical: Students will learn how to soccer juggle the ball in a group of four.
2. Social: learner provides appropriate feedback and support for other learners.
3. Cognitive: Understand the learning skills for the soccer juggle.
4. Can meet the key competencies of the New Zealand curriculum: relating to others, active participation, managing self, language symbols and text, and thinking (MOE, 2007).

Decisions:
Group size: four
Roles: lace kicker, header, kneer, instepper
Materials: Soccer balls (20), cones
Cooperative Learning Structure: Jigsaw

Task 1: Learn how to soccer juggle the ball in a group of four
Organization: Leader of each skill teaches group following cues for each skill.

Learning cues:
1. lace kicker: contact made on inside line of laces, ankle held firm with toes up for self-control and pointed for pass, don't kick too high;
2. header: contact made on forehead, use arms for balance and to provide accuracy, arch back to provide power;
3. kneer: contact made on flat surface/knee comes up high, contact made just behind knee, lead body back slightly to keep out of the way;
4. instepper: contact made on arch of foot, contact made in front of body, best pass to sole-side of foot.

Task 2: Competing against other teams to soccer juggle the ball in a group of four

Learning cues:
1. lace kicker, header, kneer, instepper
2. move into a supporting position
3. call name communicate

When you all feel that you are ready, complete the form below, rating each player's performance with each skill.
   Awesome – uses the cues every time
   Good – uses the cues most of the time
   Needs Work – rarely uses the cues

Tasks	Complete Y/N	Number of attempts	Issues encountered
All laces			
All headers			
All knees			
All instep			

Task 3:
Create your own soccer juggle modified game or routine.

Group Processing:
What happened? So What? Now What?
➡ What went well for you as a group?
➡ What did you have trouble with?
➡ What do you need to work on?

FIGURE 5.7 Learning activity for learning how to juggle a soccer ball

we discussed the contribution that Lev Vygotsky (1978) has made to our under-standing of how students learn. Vygotsky (1978) presented his *zone of proximal development*. This is the concept of creating the appropriate task and positive learning environment, where the child can be successful only if their teammates or their teacher capably assist the student.

Self-processing / A time to reflect

Self-processing questions

1. What have you learned from your experience with Cooperative Learning at the elementary or primary level?
2. What Cooperative Learning Structures, Cooperative Learning elements or Cooperative Learning tasks appeal to you?
3. What is difficult for you and your experience with Cooperative Learning in your elementary or primary program?
4. What are some of your questions, issues, and/or concerns about using Cooperative Learning in your elementary or primary program?

Our reflections

Ben

We have enjoyed watching teachers use Cooperative Learning at the elementary level. We believe that if students can learn how to communicate and cooperate with each other (i.e. working together, really listening to each other, cheering each other on, and laughing out loud) at the elementary level then hopefully they will take those valuable skills on to high school. However, any new pedagogical approach like Cooperative Learning often has a steep learning curve. We have found that there are early adopters and late adopters with Cooperative Learning. For many teachers Cooperative Learning can be too difficult and confusing and you may not have the time or resources needed to teach Cooperative Learning. We understand that there is a huge investment of time and energy required in order to use Cooperative Learning. We hope that some of these Cooperative Learning elements, Cooperative Learning Structures or Cooperative Learning tasks have interested you. We hope that you will persist with your attempts at Cooperative Learning. It does require a rearrangement of the way you allocate your time in your teaching, but we believe that it is worth the effort and perspiration. We encourage you to try it at the elementary level as a teacher, coach, or community worker and then let us know how it goes. Even better, look for some friends or colleagues to try Cooperative Learning together and compare and contrast your experiences.

Ash

In my experience there is often an assumption that children can't do something without help. Yes, they need to learn how to interact and, as Ben says 'communicate and cooperate with each other', but they also need to be trusted. We often take a 'can't' rather than a 'can' and assume that things need to be fixed. Children are seen (as we will discuss in Chapters 7 and 11) as lacking something or in need of help and yet our collective experiences of using Cooperative Learning have been (more frequently than not) a 'wow' rather than an 'argh' experience. If you trust your children then they will pay you back with wow moments of your own, but if you expect arghs then you will probably get them.

References

Antil, L. R., Jenkins, J. R., Wayne, S. K., & Vadasy, P. F. (1998). Cooperative learning: Prevalence, conceptualizations, and the relation between research and practice. *American Educational Research Journal, 35*(3), 419–454. http://doi.org/10.3102/00028312035003419

Bertucci, A., Johnson, D. W., Johnson, R. T., & Conte, S. (2012). Influence of group processing on achievement and perception of social and academic support in elementary inexperienced cooperative learning groups. *The Journal of Educational Research, 105*(5), 329–335. http://doi.org/10.1080/00220671.2011.627396

Colby, R. (2014). Cooperative Learning in primary physical education in Aotearoa/New Zealand: The challenges of change. A dissertation submitted for partial fulfillment of the requirements for the degree of Masters of Professional Studies in Education. Unpublished dissertation, The University of Auckland.

Darnis, F. & Lafont, L. (2013). Cooperative learning and dyadic interactions: Two modes of knowledge construction in socio-constructivist settings for team-sport teaching. *Physical Education & Sport Pedagogy, 20*(5), 459–473. http://doi.org/10.1080/17408989.2013.8 03528

Department of Education. (2014). National Curriculum in England for physical education. Retrieved May 8, 2015, from https://www.gov.uk/government/publications/ national-curriculum-in-england-physical-education-programmes-of-study/ national-curriculum-in-england-physical-education-programmes-of-study

Dyson, B. (1994). Student views of an alternative physical education program. *Research Quarterly for Exercise & Sport, 65*(1), A–68. Retrieved from http://proxy.binghamton. edu/login?url=http://search.ebscohost.com/login.aspx?direct=true&db=a9h&AN=95 02070769&site=ehost-live

Dyson, B. & Rubin, A. (2003). implementing cooperative learning in elementary physical education. *Journal of Physical Education, Recreation & Dance, 74*(1), 48–55. http://doi. org/10.1080/07303084.2003.10608363

Dyson, B. & Casey, A. (2012). *Cooperative learning in physical education: A research-based approach.* London: Routledge.

Dyson, B. & Dryden, C. (2014). Cooperative learning: Social skill development in physical education. *ACHPER Active and Healthy Magazine, 21*(2/3), 6–11.

Dyson, B., Griffin, L. L., & Hastie, P. (2004). Sport education, tactical games, and cooperative learning: theoretical and pedagogical considerations. *Quest, 56*(2), 226–240.

Dyson, B., Linehan, N. R., & Hastie, P. A. (2010). The ecology of cooperative learning in elementary physical education classes. *Journal of Teaching in Physical Education, 29,* 113–130.

Dyson, B., Barratt, M., Berry, S., Colby, R., & Dryden, C. (2014). Cooperative learning as models based practice: Pedagogy of the possible. Paper presented at Physical Education New Zealand Conference, Christchurch, New Zealand.

Grineski, S. (1996). *Cooperative learning in physical education*. Champaign, IL: Human Kinetics.

Johnson, D. W. & Johnson, R. T. (1990). Social skills for successful group work. *Educational Leadership, 47*(4), 29–33.

Johnson, D. W., Johnson, R. T., & Holubec, E. (1987). *Structuring cooperative learning: Lesson plans for teachers*. Edina, MN: Interaction Book.

Johnson, D. W., Johnson, R. T., & Holubec, E. (1994). *Cooperative learning in the classroom*. Alexndria, VA: ASCD.

Kagan, S. (2007). (Ed.) *Cooperative learning*. (Rev. Austr). Heatherton, Vic.: Hawker Brownlow Education.

Kagan, S. & Kagan, M. (2009). *Kagan cooperative learning*. San Clemente, CA: Kagan.

MOE. (2007). *The New Zealand Curriculum*. Wellington, New Zealand: Learning Media.

NASPE. (2013). *National standards & grade-level outcomes for K-12 physical education*. Champaign, IL: Human Kinetics.

Sapon-Shevin, M. (2010). *Because we can change the world: A practical guide to building cooperative, inclusive classroom communities* (2nd ed.). Thousand Oaks, CA: Corwin.

Sutherland, S. (2012). Borrowing strategies from adventure-based learning to enhance group processing in cooperative learning. In B. Dyson & A. Casey (Eds.). *Cooperative learning in physical education: A research-based approach* (pp. 103–118). London: Routledge.

Sutherland, S., Stuhr, P., & Ressler, J. (2014). Group processing in cooperative learning: Using the Sunday afternoon drive debrief model. *Australian Council for Health Physical Education and Recreation, 21*, 12–15.

Vygotsky, L. S. (1978). *Mind in society*. Cambridge, MA: Harvard University Press.

6

RECIPROCAL TEACHING IN PHYSICAL EDUCATION, COACHING, AND PHYSICAL ACTIVITY SETTINGS

Chapter overview

This chapter provides real-world examples of how teachers and coaches can use their strategies and Cooperative Learning Structures in their programs. Drawing on the work of a number of elementary, middle level, and high school teachers, we use examples and provide resources that we hope will help you to effectively use and begin to master the reciprocal and peer teaching strategies. Mosston (1981) presented Reciprocal Teaching as part of his 'Teaching Styles'. We present Reciprocal Teaching as a starting point for teaching Cooperative Learning as a pedagogical practice. Teaching and coaching examples are given from the elementary level upwards. Additionally, the chapter provides developmentally appropriate steps and methods to help you introduce, progress, and then move beyond these strategies and begin to use an increasing range of Cooperative Learning Structures.

We believe that

1. Reciprocal Teaching can be used effectively in Physical Education classes and in community and coaching settings.
2. Many teachers and coaches already use Reciprocal Teaching strategies.
3. Teachers and students can learn a number of Reciprocal Teaching strategies that help the development of students' social skills (interpersonal skills).
4. Teachers and students can learn how Reciprocal Teaching can make an important contribution to their teaching and learning.
5. Learning to use Reciprocal Teaching strategies takes time with *ongoing practice* in your gymnasium or educational setting.

6. It is difficult to learn Reciprocal Teaching strategies without guidance and support, but educators can learn and experiment with Reciprocal Teaching.
7. By using Reciprocal Teaching tasks you are starting to use some of the critical elements of Cooperative Learning, including Interpersonal Skills, Positive Interdependence, and Face-to-Face Promotive Interaction.

Imagine the scene

We are at Campus School in Memphis, Tennessee. Mrs. Diane Coleman, an expert teacher and veteran of 30 years of teaching, has previously taught her students how to climb. The school is fortunate to have a horizontal climbing wall. The wall is 35 feet long and called a 'traverse wall', and the highest climbing grip hold is 3 feet from the ground. It has a 3-foot red relief line all the way across it. The students cannot put their feet above this line, so the students are never more than 3 feet off the floor.

Students are paired with buddy partners that have been chosen earlier in the unit by Mrs. Coleman. The idea of a buddy partner is that they work to help each other to be successful.

Luke and Brennan are buddy partners. Luke is a bit cautious because he has only been on the climbing wall twice. Brennan has been on the climbing wall more and he climbed it with his dad at a parent night at Campus School. Sean and Josh are also buddy partners. Sean is short for his age and Josh is the same size – they have the same reach (i.e. arm span), so they can aim for the climbing holds positioned at a similar distance.

Mrs. Coleman has focused on the basic learning cues of using their feet, keeping their body close to the wall, and using the foot-holds and hand-holds when climbing. She tells the kids to 'keep your body close to the wall like Spiderman'. This seems to help them remember what to do. Mrs. Coleman tells the students to 'use one foot and one hand on the wall at all times so you move your hands and feet alternately'. She reminds them that there should be 'No crossing of the hands and feet to move across the wall, this turns your body away from the wall', and 'Keep your hands above the shoulders.' The students use arm muscles to help pull and keep them on the wall. Using arm strength and leg strength together to navigate the wall makes it easier to move across it.

On the horizontal climbing wall the partners work together to traverse the wall, one partner at a time while the other partner spots the climber and offers feedback (see the spotting described in Box 6.1). Brennan starts the traverse wall and Luke moves with him just in case he slips with his feet and/or hands. Brennan moves quickly and his body is not close to the wall. Luke yells, 'Body close to wall, Spiderman.' Immediately Brennan's body moves closer to the wall. Luke comments, 'Good job.' Brennan jumps off at the end of the wall looking happy with himself.

Luke has to wait for his turn as Sean is climbing with Josh spotting for him. Luke is a little more cautious than Brennan as he begins his climb. He begins but his body is pushed back from the wall because he has crossed hands. Brennan says, 'No crossing your hands and feet' and 'Don't look at me, face the wall.' Luke turns back to the wall, stops for a minute and makes sure his next hand and foot placements are not crossing. Brennan watches Luke carefully and says, 'Good, good, yes.' Brennan then yells to Luke who is halfway across the wall, 'Keep your hands high.'... 'Yeah, above your shoulders' ... 'Way to go Spiderman.'

BOX 6.1: TEACHING SPOTTING

When a teacher asks one student to spot another, this can be an example of Reciprocal Teaching. Please refer back to the scenario above, which portrays an example of Reciprocal Teaching using a partner/buddy spotter on a horizontal climbing wall. Spotting is defined as a partner assisting another to complete a task. In climbing, 'belaying' is a technique used so that one partner can assist another to complete the climb or part of a climb. It could be a vertical or horizontal climbing wall at your school or community center or camp. Essentially, it allows one partner to climb while the other partner belays them. In climbing spotting is used to spot anyone who is ascending or descending, or moving along a cable reverse element. It is the 'basic' spotting strategy used often for any situation in which a participant may be unstable. Buddy spotters are used in both ways. Technically, the buddy spotter monitors the communication system on behalf of the participant doing an activity when there is more than one spotter. Supportively, the buddy spotter encourages, communicates, and engages in an experience with a participant doing an activity from start to finish. When a climber touches the ground, the buddy spotter is there to provide a steady hand, celebrate success, and help with equipment. In Reciprocal Teaching, participants are spotters and climbers – each student gets the opportunity to climb and to spot. Spotting is a learned skill, that is, it describes a set of technical skills that are taught before participants are responsible for spotting each other off the ground.

Luke jumps down at the end of the wall and puts his hands in the air, 'I am Spiderman!'
Luke and Brennan laugh.

Introduction

The form of Reciprocal Teaching presented in the teaching scenario above is similar to peer tutoring, where one of the pair acts as a tutor and the other as a learner. In this case the coach is the spotter and the climber is the learner. Unlike a tutoring role, where one student teaches the other, in our Cooperative Learning version of Reciprocal Teaching the spotter and the climber roles change after a predetermined amount of time so that both students have a turn at climbing. Our goal in the end would be for both learners to reach a level of ability so that they were skillful enough to teach and climb with others. One constant learning intention, in each Reciprocal Teaching lesson, would be that the 'teacher' provides appropriate feedback to their partner.

Each pair should make adjustments to their feedback based on the learning cues and different activities practiced so that they both become better climbers.

There is a great deal of research to support Reciprocal Teaching from general education and there are several forms of it in education (Alton-Lee et al., 2012; Ayvazo & Ward, 2009; Hattie, 2012). This chapter seeks to offer a much broader perspective on how students can work together for their mutual benefit. This is similar to the concept found in ecological sciences of 'mutualism'. For example, the sea anemone and the clown fish have a mutual relationship with each other, where both species benefit from the association. There are many examples from the natural sciences of what we are trying to achieve in education. Thanks to Science teacher Elizabeth Howe from Onehunga High School in Auckland, NZ, for bringing the term mutualism to Ben's attention recently in a postgraduate class. Mutualism is an example of reciprocal giving and taking. Getting back to the concept of a reciprocal style of teaching, in this chapter we hope to present a number of several reciprocal structures that you can test out in your own teaching context.

In this chapter first we will discuss the value of social skills for children. After arguing for the relevance of social skills to be taught explicitly by teachers, coaches, and community workers we then explain Reciprocal Teaching.

The importance of social skills development for kids

Over the years we have seen a growing need for Interpersonal and Small Group Skills to be taught to students. If students at the elementary level can learn strong and resilient interpersonal skills then this will assist them throughout their schooling (Dyson & Dryden, 2014). However, young students cannot be thrown in the 'deep end' of the complicated classroom social environment. Therefore we suggest that by working in pairs or in a positive Reciprocal Teaching partnership students can learn the interpersonal skills to be successful with their social interactions. When the groups get larger than two, students are expected to interact appropriately with their peers in a classroom setting. To become a group member students need differentiated tasks that provide learning at their level in a progressive manner.

In a typical class setting most students today do not have the ability to accurately assess or 'read' a social situation, self-evaluate, self-monitor, and adjust as necessary (Sapon-Shevin, 2010). These skills must be taught directly to your students (Sharan, 2010). One way to help these kids is to provide immediate and frequent feedback about inappropriate behavior or social miscues, and positive feedback when they interact appropriately. Role-playing can be very helpful to teach, model, and practice positive social skills, as well as ways to respond to challenging situations like teasing. Focus on one or two areas that are most difficult for your students, so that the learning process doesn't become too overwhelming and so that your students are more likely to experience successes. Many kids these days struggle to start and maintain a conversation or interact with another person in a reciprocal manner (for example, listening, asking about the other student's ideas or feelings, taking turns in the conversation, or showing interest in the other student), negotiating and resolving conflicts as they arise, sharing, maintaining personal space, and even speaking in a normal tone of voice that isn't too loud. We have all observed this in early childhood education but somehow we expect that when students go to elementary school or high school they will exhibit higher levels of social skills. The teacher, coach, or community must clearly identify and give information to their students about social rules and the behaviors that they want to see. Reciprocal Teaching and Cooperative Learning allow the teacher or coach to set up learning situations that practice these pro-social skills again and again.

A Reciprocal Teaching task for helping students track a ball is Towel Ball (Box 6.2). In this example students need to talk and interact with each other to track a ball or object that they project off a towel. This simple Reciprocal Teaching task is designed with the learning intentions of improving hand-eye coordination (physical skills) and interpersonal skills (social skills).

Developmental psychologists suggest that as a child gets older peer relationships and friendships are often more complicated, but it is equally important for teachers, coaches, community workers, and parents to continue to be involved and to facilitate positive peer interactions (Ladd, 1999). The middle school and high school years can be difficult for a child who struggles socially. Even if a child remains unaccepted by the peer group at large, having at least one good friend during these years can often protect the child from the negative impact of snubbing by their peer group. Pairing all students up with an empathetic 'buddy' in a Reciprocal Teaching activity within the classroom can facilitate social acceptance (Dowler, 2012). Support for social skills development for students comes from developmental psychologist Vygotsky (1978). Vygotsky (1978) highlights that importance of social interaction in learning. He argues that the assistance of a partner who has more knowledge can assist the learner towards greater knowledge gains. Vygotsky (1978) is well known for his notion of the 'zone of proximal development' or ZPD, which he suggests can help the learner reach their full potential. That is, with the help of another person (teacher or tutor) a child has the capability

---

BOX 6.2: TOWEL BALL

Learning intention: To improve hand-eye coordination and tracking skills (physical skills) and develop interpersonal skills (social skills).

To toss a ball or object into the air so that it is jointly caught by two students holding a towel. This activity helps children with timing of tossing the ball and tracking the ball in the air. This activity can improve students' manipulative skills and tracking and it refines spatial awareness and effort awareness. There are many variations on this skill, for example, letting the ball bounce before catching it, bouncing it off a wall, and tossing the ball to another team so they can catch the ball and then switching roles.

to improve their developmental abilities and therefore reach closer to their full potential or capability.

The amount of social skills development

Teachers in today's schools often feel pressure from their principal, board of governors, superintendent, parents, and/or the media with the need to make sure their students excel in Math and Literacy. This has been presented as No Child Left Behind (NCLB) in the US, the standards based movement in NZ, and the National Curriculum in the UK. Teachers often feel that they have to focus on these core key academic areas of learning and this is foregrounded in their instruction. In Physical Education we have a similar emerging focus on physical activity (McKenzie & Lounsbery, 2013). So how much time should the Physical Education teacher, coach, or community worker spend on social skill development compared to students being physically active?

We have noticed that many of the students who come into our classroom will not have appropriate Interpersonal and Small Group Skills (Dyson & Dryden, 2014). Social skills are not only useful for helping your class run smoothly but are also relevant for life and work outside the classroom (Sharan, 2010). Students need to be taught social skills, and US National Standards 5 and 6 relate directly to social skill development (NASPE, 2013) and in the purpose of study, in the UK National Curriculum (i.e. 'build character and help to embed values such as fairness and respect' (Department for Education, 2013). Similarly, in New Zealand one of the five Key Competencies is 'Relating to Others' (MOE, 2007).

As teachers and coaches, we often assume that if we teach a cooperative activity or a cooperative game then students will automatically learn Interpersonal and Small Group Skills. This is a huge assumption. Do students learn how to listen to each other, share ideas, take responsibility, work together, make shared decisions, and respect each other in a cooperative game? In practice we have found that it requires a concentrated effort, with explicit learning intentions, to help students learn appropriate interpersonal or social skills even in a pair. As we have stated earlier in the book, our suggestion is to start implementing Cooperative Learning gradually with one task at a time and begin with one class that you think will cooperate (Sapon-Shevin, 2010). That is, assume that this is going to take time and perspiration, so try to reduce some of that stress on yourself. One strategy that Physical Educators and Coaches have used for years is the Reciprocal Teaching style. Mosston (1981) presented Reciprocal Teaching as part of his 'Teaching Styles'. We describe Reciprocal Teaching as students working in pairs: 'you teach, now I teach'. As physical educators, Outdoor Education instructors, dancers, coaches, drama teachers, and community workers we have often used Reciprocal Teaching, pair teaching strategies, or partner work in our teaching and learning settings. Teaching swimming skills with partners is a good example of the buddy system in Reciprocal Teaching. Of course, in a swimming setting the teacher, coach, or instructor is responsible for the safety of all their students but having students organized into manageable pairs helps with management, behavior, and instruction of students.

Many swimming programs develop swimmers' confidence and skills by working in partners, based on the 'reciprocal style' of teaching (Mosston, 1981). In swimming this technique can be based on observation assessment, and providing partner or swimming buddy feedback. One partner swims while the other partner observes and tries to determine errors in the swimming technique. The swimmers talk about the movements observed and provide feedback to each other. The teacher or instructor observes the class with knowledgeable (swimming content knowledge) volunteers (teachers' assistants, parents, or older students). For this to work more effectively swimmers need to be taught the basic learning framework most useful in swimming technique (Water safety NZ: http://www.swimmingnz. org.nz/education/). In New Zealand the 'FLAB' acronym is used to remind partners what to concentrate on in a sequential manner. Since swimming is such a complex task and often difficult to observe accurately we start with Floating, then move to Leg work, then Arms, and then Breathing (= FLAB). For a swimmer to improve they need to see the whole stroke, but this is a differentiated approach, recognizing that there will be a wide range of abilities when we teach swimming. This Reciprocal Teaching technique also forces the swimmers to cognitively engage in the learning process, that is, forces them to think about their floating, their leg work, their arms, and/or their breathing. Reciprocal Teaching can be a welcome break for teachers and their students from the monotonous drills and direct style of teaching that is often observed in Physical Education or 'learn to swim' sessions.

How to implement Reciprocal Teaching

Initially, when you start to implement Cooperative Learning, we suggest that you start with only two roles: coach and performer/player. Reciprocal Teaching provides the opportunity to learn social skills when only having to deal with one other person. This strategy is less complex to organize than groups of four or five and each student gets a chance to try both roles. Reciprocal Teaching can help teach social skills to encourage students to get ready for using Cooperative Learning structures. In Mosston's (1981) reciprocal style of teaching students are assigned to work in pairs, with each student given responsibility as either a coach or performer. In this case the coach is responsible for providing specific feedback to a partner about his/her performance and the performer is allowed many opportunities to practice. For example, when teaching kicking and punting, Pat Yeaton has designed a specific task sheet (Figure 6.1). Pat is an expert physical educator at North Hampton Elementary, New Hampshire, USA. The coach has only one person to focus on and can provide his/her partner/the player with specific feedback while the player has plenty of opportunities to practice.

In this Reciprocal Teaching situation Pat acts in the role of facilitator. To remind the reader, when the teacher or coach acts in the role of facilitator they are guiding and supporting student engagement and continually moving around the teaching environment, actively monitoring and interacting with their students. This is not an opportunity for the teacher to perform non-teaching tasks; for example, managing and organizing equipment; this is the 'teacher as activator' as described by Hattie (2012). When facilitating learning the teacher has a specific role, for example, if the teacher observes 'good form' or 'appropriate technique' by the students then the teacher is able to move to a student and provide appropriate required support and guidance.

To start using Reciprocal Teaching successfully a dedicated amount of planning is required. For Pat to introduce a task it takes time and is a little trial and error. Student pairing needs to be thought out carefully so that students can start to work with a partner. Pat will initially match some students together, that is, preferably not friends, students who are more tolerant with a student with disabilities, and she is careful not to match a potential bully with a student who is not socially

---

Recorder's name: _____   Team color: _____

Goal for the day: You should be able to run and kick a ball that is moving slowly toward you or away from you, using the laces of your foot.

___1. Stretches

___2. Class will review laces kick with the teacher

___3. Cues for kicking with the laces:
  Kick underneath the ball, connect with your laces
  Toes follow through to target

___4. **Forceball**. One partner is the roller, the other is the kicker. Partner rolls the ball from 10 feet away and moves back to get the ball as it is kicked. Use the laces kick 5 times each.
  Roller rolls ball to kicker

___5. Have your partner watch you and your partner play Forceball. They will give you a check if you use the cue and a minus if you don't.

Name	kick under the ball	use laces	follow through
_____			
_____			

___6. **Rogueball**. Roll ball away from you and then run up and kick it using the laces. Your partner will get the ball for you and throw it back. Take 5 turns and switch. Give your partner corrective feedback.

___7. **Kicking to targets**. With a partner, practice kicking to a target. Use the instep kick and switch after 5 turns. Sign below when you feel you are all good at kicking using the instep.

FIGURE 6.1 Grade 3 kicking and punting lesson 4 task sheet

confident. The equipment for the activity needs to be pre-planned. In this case a ball between every two students, cones to mark out areas, a target set out as one of the stations, and all the task sheets printed (one per pair). We have found task sheets or task cards to be useful since the tasks can be scaffolded into the learning environment by the teacher. In Figure 6.1 Pat uses three tasks: Forceball, Rogueball, and Kicking to targets. Each of these tasks need to be taught explicitly to students before this Kicking and Punting lesson can be successful. That is, the kids need to know what is expected of them, but they also have to learn some of the learning cues. In this lesson Pat reviews the learning cues with the students before the tasks begin.

For Reciprocal Teaching to be successful it must be presented in a respectful manner; start with positive comments and frequent reinforcement of appropriate behaviors. The teacher really does need to be 'out and about' and visible to the students, and there is much research to support this teaching strategy of the teacher as activator (Hattie, 2012). We want students to learn how to listen to each other, share ideas, take responsibility, work together, make shared decisions, interact in a positive manner, and respect each other in a Reciprocal Teaching environment.

Self-processing / A time to reflect

Self-processing questions

1. What Reciprocal Teaching tasks do you use when you teach or coach?
2. Can you see how Reciprocal Teaching could be a starting point for implementing Cooperative Learning?
3. How can Reciprocal Teaching develop a student's social skills?
4. When you start using the Reciprocal Teaching strategy what content do you prefer to teach/coach?

Our reflections

Ben

Many teachers that I have observed over the years have used the Reciprocal Teaching style of teaching. There are now a huge number of studies to support the use of Reciprocal Teaching in general education. I know that we as teachers, coaches, and community workers have utilized many forms of Reciprocal Teaching in our teaching, coaching, and learning experiences in Physical Education and out-of-doors experiences. I challenge you to send us some of your ideas or publish your ideas in a professional journal or online. We have a great deal to teach general education about the use of the Reciprocal Teaching and unfortunately most general education folks don't even know who Muska Mosston (1981) was and what a great contribution he made to education.

Ash

Just working together is not enough to make this relationship reciprocal. Students are taught from an early age that school is about competition. They cover their work up so others can't copy. They are often punished when they work together and silence is often the preferred state of 'being' in many classrooms. We believe that noise and collaboration are good things. After all, how many offices or workplaces have you been in that are silent and discourage collaboration? We are rarely tested as individuals and yet we don't mirror this system in schools. Reciprocal Teaching is a great way of starting to change the way your classrooms work.

References

Alton-Lee, A., Westera, R., & Pulegatoa-Diggina, C. (2012). *Quality teaching for diverse (all) learners in schooling/he ako reikura (te katoa): hei kete raukura (BES) exemplar 4: Reciprocol teaching.* Wellington, New Zealand. Retrieved from https://www.educationcounts.govt.nz/goto/BES.

Ayvazo, S. & Ward, P. (2009). Effects of classwide peer tutoring on the performance of sixth grade students during a volleyball unit. (Report). *Physical Educator, 66*(1), 12–22.

Department for Education (2013). National curriculum in England: PE programmes of study. Retrieved from https://www.gov.uk/government/publications/national-curriculum-in-england-physical-education-programmes-of-study

Dowler, W. (2012). Cooperative learning and interactions in inclusive secondary school physical education classes in Australia. In B. Dyson & A. Casey (Eds.). *Cooperative learning in physical education: A research-based approach* (pp. 159–165). London: Routledge.

Dyson, B. & Dryden, C. (2014). Cooperative learning: social skill development in physical education. *ACHPER Active and Healthy Magazine, 21*(2/3), 6–11.

Hattie, J. (2012). *Visible learning for teachers: Maximizing impact on learning.* (I. ebrary, Ed.). New York: Routledge.

Ladd, G. W. (1999). Peer relationships and social competence during early and middle childhood. *Annual Review of Psychology, 333.*

McKenzie, T. L. & Lounsbery, M. A. F. (2013). Physical education teacher effectiveness in a public health context. *Research Quarterly for Exercise and Sport, 84,* 419–430. http://doi.org/10.1080/02701367.2013.844025

MOE. (2007). *The New Zealand Curriculum.* Wellington, New Zealand: Learning Media.

Mosston, M. (1981). *Teaching physical education* (2nd ed.). Columbus, OH: Merrill.

NASPE. (2013). *National standards & grade-level outcomes for K–12 physical education.* Champaign, IL: Human Kinetics.

Sapon-Shevin, M. (2010). *Because we can change the world: A practical guide to building cooperative, inclusive classroom communities* (2nd ed.). Thousand Oaks, CA: Corwin.

Sharan, Y. (2010). Cooperative learning for academic and social gains: Valued pedagogy, problematic practice. *European Journal of Education, 45*(2), 300–313.

Vygotsky, L. S. (1978). *Mind in society.* Cambridge, MA: Harvard University Press.

7

HOW COOPERATIVE LEARNING IS RELATED TO THE DIFFERENT CONTEXTS FOR LEARNING: WORKING WITH PERSONS WITH DISABILITIES AT THE ELEMENTARY LEVEL

Chapter overview

One of the increasingly common aspects of any educational setting is our enhanced understanding and appreciation of children and young people who come to our classrooms with physical and/or learning disabilities and exceptional needs (Grenier & Yeaton, 2012). Drawing on the experiences of Physical Education teachers and research, this chapter presents school-based examples and resources that will help readers to plan and teach Cooperative Learning lessons that are both inclusive and developmentally appropriate for all learners in their classes, but most particularly in this chapter, those persons with disabilities (Grenier, Dyson, & Yeaton, 2005; Grenier & Yeaton, 2012; Grenier, 2006; Yeaton, 2015).

We believe that

1. Cooperative Learning can be an inclusive pedagogical practice in Physical Education and physical activity settings.
2. Many teachers and coaches struggle to be inclusive of all students or players.
3. Teachers and students can learn how to include persons with disabilities and exceptional learners.
4. Positive Interdependence is a key Cooperative Learning element to enable the inclusion of all students in the pedagogical practice.
5. To modify and adapt practice to meet the needs of *all* learners is a challenge for all educators.
6. Trial and error with guidance will create a more supportive and inclusive learning environment.

7. Students can learn to be proactive so that they can reduce exclusion and segregation.
8. Students should be provided with many opportunities to play, interact, make decisions, solve problems, and positively support and encourage each other.

Imagine the scene

We are in the school hall at Papatoetoe South School in Auckland, New Zealand, watching a Physical Education class. Moana has suffered from cerebral palsy since she was born and is now in year 5 and is 10 years old. Moana is not excluded or segregated from her class but fully integrated into the program. In fact, she is a key contributor and the teacher relies on her to be role model for the other students.

The students huddle in their Learning Teams and Moana reads the task: 'Use all group members to form a pyramid.' The students think for a moment and then Tipi says 'How do we include Moana?' There are nods from the other two group members, MacKenzie and Sam. Moana isn't embarrassed because she is used to this question; she seems to appreciate that her group wants her to be a part of their balance routine. Moana scoots, pulling her body along the floor with her strong arms. She moves to the center of the mat. 'OK, how about I be on the bottom with Sam and Kenzie since we are the biggest.' The other kids nod. Moana, Sam, and Kenzie form the base of the human pyramid and then Tipi, a small Filipina girl, moves cautiously onto the top of their pyramid. Then Moana says, 'That's good but let's find another kid to be on top.' Moana looks around the hall and sees Kairyn. Kairyn, a boy who has been diagnosed with autism, and who often does not fully participate in Physical Education, has none of his group there today. He is sitting in the corner of the hall, not disturbing anyone but not participating either. Moana scoots over to him, moving her body with her arms as her legs don't function. Moana asks Kairyn to join in. He puts a smile on his face and says, 'What do you want me to do?' Moana says, 'We want you to be king of our pyramid, on top with Tipi.' Kairyn hesitates because he doesn't really know Tipi, who is a new girl in their class. Moana reassures Kairyn and says, 'It will be fun.' He reluctantly walks over while Moana tries to keep up with him as she scoots across the floor again. Moana gets back to her group and says excitedly, 'Look who's going to join our pyramid.' Sam and MacKenzie nod but Tipi doesn't respond. Moana, Sam, and MacKenzie get themselves organized on the base of their group pyramid and Tipi moves up between Moana and Sam, her hands on their shoulders, her knees on their hips. Then Kairyn moves up between Sam and MacKenzie and then he starts smiling – he likes being up high above most of his classmates and he is happy to be part of the group. (In talking with Sue Berry, the Deputy Principal at Moana's school, she talks about Moana and calls her a gift. 'We are not doing these kids a favor, … we receive much more than we give. It is a gift of empathy and understanding.')

Why use Cooperative Learning as a pedagogical practice when trying to include and engage *all* students in the learning process?

We believe that Cooperative Learning can provide a positive pedagogical framework that invites persons with disabilities into your classrooms or community settings. We agree with Adrienne Alton-Lee that Cooperative Learning is an equity pedagogy (Alton-Lee, 2011). That is, an engaging pedagogy that is both purposeful and meaningful (Dyson, 2014) and which has the potential to include *all* children. Research has demonstrated over the last 20 years that all students required quality pedagogy and typically the characteristics of such teaching are: it is student-centered, the teacher is responsive to the needs of the students, and there is active engagement – and this is intended for *all* students (Hattie, 2012). In fact, Hattie (2012) argues that Peer Tutoring and Cooperative Learning are two of the most effective strategies that teachers can use.

In New Zealand, Mitchell (2014) has been a strong advocate for Cooperative Learning as the most effective strategy for including persons with disabilities into teaching and learning. Mitchell (2014) suggests that Cooperative Learning teaches through empathy and cohesive pedagogical strategies that can develop a positive classroom climate. In this inclusive classroom, the practice of fairness, tolerance, teamwork, understanding, and respect for different points of view can exist. As students learn to work together the classroom becomes an inclusive community, not one of division. In the US Grenier and Yeaton (2012) have argued that Cooperative Learning is a critical pedagogy for students with disabilities.

We should never stop exploring the ways to further include kids in Physical Education, physical activity, and outdoor activities. But, what does *inclusion* mean to us? Mara Sapon-Shevin (2010) provides a useful definition: 'Inclusion means we all belong. Inclusion means not having to fight for a chance to be part of a classroom or school community. Inclusion means that all children are accepted' (p. 9). What gets in the way of our inclusivity? Regrettably, in our typical institutions of education we are systematically taught patterns of exclusion and at times we have even come to accept exclusion as inevitable. Sadly, often we do not even notice the lack of inclusion. Growing up, we were taught that there simply are not enough resources, there is not enough time, or equipment, or space for everyone and that some people have to be excluded. Sapon-Shevin (2000) has suggested that these messages, once internalized as we grow up in a *normal* world, can be difficult to counteract. Unfortunately, we are often in danger of failing to teach children what Sapon-Shevin (2010) refers to as 'an inclusive response to difference' (p. 11). Nonetheless, in this text we are unashamedly supportive of many different kinds of students learning to work and play together – learning to be positively interdependent on one another – *all* of us together. Remember in Cooperative Learning *we sink or swim together*. Grenier (2006) also suggests that we should include the notion of equity – not only is it inclusive, but *all* students are *contributing* members.

This inclusive response cannot be overstated and in education should never be in question. Inappropriately, our institutions of school, sports clubs, community, and/or outdoors experiences often focus our attention on what children cannot do, on their weaknesses or areas of need. This focus keeps us from seeing the *whole* child and narrows our appreciation for difference. As Sapon-Shevin (2010) has reflected: 'Are differences seen as something to be avoided, ignored, worked around, and minimized? Or as characteristics to be understood, valued, appreciated, supported, and celebrated?' (p. 13).

What would it be like if classrooms, the community, and the outdoors were based on elements of Cooperative Learning?

So, what would it really be like if classrooms, the community, and outdoor experiences for children were based on elements of Cooperative Learning? We would see with Positive Interdependence *all* students working together to complete a shared task; with Promotive Face-to-Face Interaction, *all* students in close proximity to each other supporting and encouraging; with Individual Accountability, *all group members* doing their part of the task or enabling others to complete the task; and with Group Processing, *all group members* critically reflecting about how *all* students were encouraged to participate in the task, talking openly and honestly about how *all* students felt when they *all tried* to complete the task.

We need to attend to many parts of the learning environment: what is taught, how the room is arranged, what kinds of Cooperative Learning structure/s are going to be used, how the groups are organized, and what kinds of assessment are going to be used to indicate that there has been progress for students.

Strategies for inclusive practices

Heterogeneous groups

One of the premises (or additional procedures) of Cooperative Learning is heterogeneous groups (Goodyear, 2015). This vision of heterogeneity flies in the face of the reality of many of our schools as we often segregate students by ability, gender, and race without even realizing that we are setting a *non-inclusive* learning environment (Ball, 2012). Sapon-Shevin (2010) suggested that there are a number of research studies to suggest that ability groupings did not consistently outperform mixed ability classrooms and students did not learn more than in mixed ability groupings. More specifically, Oakes (2005) suggested that schools continue to replicate inequities along lines of race and social economic status, and this perpetuates inequity. Sapon-Shevin (2010) reported that students with high-ability/high-achieving schoolmates were more likely to do well at school and highlighted that social backgrounds had a strong impact on student achievement (Ball, 2012). While ability grouping does have an impact on student self-worth and their opportunities for relationships across groups (Oakes, 2005), gifted and exceptional students also are teased and ridiculed and no one wants to be labeled as a 'nerd'. Sapon-Shevin (2010) suggested that grouping students according to test scores creates distance and that such ability groupings can result in an overemphasis on differences.

Sapon-Shevin (2000) points out that organizing students in Cooperative Learning heterogeneous groups does involve different kinds of planning and preparation. However, we have found that many teachers report increased student enthusiasm, better outcomes, and higher engagement with a diverse range of students working together. We now present some strategies that we have found useful to create a positive and inclusive learning environment. That is, *Group Processing, the Full Value Contract, thinking outside the box, Individualized Educational Program, and social skill development.*

Group Processing

The teacher or instructor needs to help students learn how to figure out ways to include their classmates on the team or in the game or on a visit to a boat club. In Cooperative Learning it's been found (Sutherland et al., 2014; Sutherland, 2012) that the strategy of Group Processing can be useful to talk about important issues in the classroom, gymnasium, or camp. By talking to each other, Grenier and Yeaton (2012) noticed that students modify and adapt after Group Processing. For example, during a creative movement class, group mates modified the task down by using paper spread out on the floor to show Sammy (a disabled student) where he should move.

Full Value Contract

For students to be fully engaged in the learning experiences they must feel physically, socially, and emotionally safe. Our friends and colleagues in Outdoor Education or Adventure-Based Learning (Sutherland et al., 2014; Sutherland, 2012) have been reminding us of inclusive practices for many years. In Ben's early work with Project Adventure schools in Columbus, Ohio, we learned about the Full Value Contract (FVC) (Dyson, 1994). The FVC asks each student to write a contract at the beginning of the lesson. That is, each child comes up with a physical goal and a social goal or personal goal (emotional goal) at the beginning of the unit and these goals are discussed by the teacher and students frequently during the unit (Dyson & Sutherland, 2015).

Thinking outside the box

In Columbus, Ohio, at Devonshire Elementary, they have taken on and practice Project Adventure in an effort to engage in 'thinking outside the box'. Pat Price, the principal, is very proud of their achievements over the years and this school is another example of demonstrating inclusive practices. At Devonshire (a K–6 school) all students go on a camp which, in fairness, may not be that unique. However, at Devonshire they have modified the high ropes course at a local Outdoor Education center (Camp Mary Orton) to include two groups of students who might not normally be involved in a challenging high ropes course, that is, kindergarten and grade 1 children (5- to 7-year-olds) and persons with disabilities. You can picture the sense of achievement when students working in their Adventure Group are able to navigate a challenge course. Alone, this would be difficult for any of the students to complete, but in their Cooperative Learning groups they are able to help each other balancing on the beams, crossing the stream, climbing over tree stump obstacles, or walking along a narrow shaky bridge made from wooden slats.

Individualized Educational Program

Many students who are evaluated as persons with disabilities in the US and New Zealand are required to have an Individualized Educational Program (IEP). The IEP is much more successful if it is set with the student and their parents in mind. Moving beyond the notion of the IEP we can define inclusion more broadly to welcome students into our classrooms. This process should be about 'acknowledging the many differences students bring to the classroom (not just characteristics labeled as disabilities) and accommodating all those differences in a shared community. Addressing student differences related to race, class, gender, ethnicity, language, family background and religion are all part of creating an inclusive classroom' (Sapon-Shevin, 2010, p. 90). 'The goal should be to notice, understand, respond, and connect' (p. 91). Utilizing Cooperative Learning Structures we can create a positive learning environment where *all* students feel that they belong to the group and can contribute to completing the task. Connected to the IEP is the utilizing of related service providers as support people (educational psychologists, occupational therapists, physical therapists, etc.) in the education process with explicit Cooperative Learning intentions.

Social skill development

As some readers will be aware, an Individualized Educational Program (IEP) should have a social component. As educators we need to help kids to be comfortable with interacting and socializing with different students, that is, students labeled as able-bodied, and those with physical, social, cognitive, or other disabilities. We have found that Cooperative Learning Structures can provide a useful way to work on students' social interactions and their differences. Cooperative Learning focuses on pedagogy that is respectful and sensitive and that allows students to develop strategies for understanding someone else's perspective. We will now talk about the social skill development of students through Cooperative Learning, particularly for those students who struggle with acceptance. Wendy Dowler (Dowler, 2012, 2014), from Australia, has carried out research to demonstrate that students with disabilities can learn social skills. Grenier and Yeaton (2012) have also argued that social skill development using a Cooperative Learning pedagogy is particularly helpful for those who struggle with acceptance. By learning appropriate social skills these students can be integrated into the general Physical Education class. As educators, there is much we can do with technology that encourages communication with *all* students (Grenier et al., 2005)

A case study for an inclusive Physical Education program

The next section presents Pat Yeaton and her teaching as an example of an inclusive Physical Education practice. Pat teaches at North Hampton Elementary in New Hampshire and she has created a truly inclusive and welcoming Physical Education program. In Physical Education we have a great opportunity to include students with disabilities, students who have exceptional needs, and students who are different. Pat has been the subject of close study and analysis and the subject of many papers and presentations over the years (Grenier et al., 2005; Grenier & Yeaton, 2012; Grenier, 2006).

One of Pat's strategies is the preview. Pat uses the preview to meet the needs of *all* students at her school (see Figure 7.1).

At the SHAPE conference in Seattle, Pat (Yeaton 2015) suggested that Cooperative Learning allows for 'unveiling' Physical Education. Pat stated that 'PE is not a Secret!', meaning that Cooperative Learning can help take the mystery out of what is happening in the gymnasium, particularly for the students who have disabilities. She suggested that Cooperative Learning can create a positive learning environment and that it provides 'natural supports' for the teaching of Physical Education. We all know that we need to have the equipment organized in Physical Education and Pat has some specific suggestions for us. For example, hoops are out with all the necessary equipment for each group ready before the class starts, folders

---

Which students are you trying to reach with the preview? What are their disabilities? Which strategies of teaching (e.g. visual, modeling, verbal) work best for them?

1. Identify outcome(s) for PE class for that particular unit/lesson.
2. Decide what activities you will do during class to meet those outcomes.
3. Create the lesson to meet the outcomes.
4. Create a visual lesson plan to 'show' what you are doing in class.
5. Does the student see the occupational therapist (OT)? If yes, share the visual plan with the OT so they can preview with the student as well.
6. Does the student have an aide? If yes, share the visual plan with the aide so they can preview with the student just before they come to class.
7. Set up a time that is convenient for both you and the classroom teacher to come and preview with the class the lesson for the day.
8. Preview the lesson with the whole class. Give cues, model skills, ask questions, etc.
9. Leave behind the visual plan so that it can be posted and students can check it on their own.

FIGURE 7.1   Previewing *with* students their disabilities

for each group help keep their task sheets, and an equipment manager retrieves and puts back the equipment. The role of the equipment manager is to help and support the flow of equipment in and out of the group. Pat is a proponent of using poly spots for allowing students to create personal space but in their Cooperative Learning Learning Teams Pat she encourages students to work in 'face-to-face contact'. That is, they are 'knee-to-knee, toe-to-toe' most of the time.

In Pat's classroom social skills are modeled, practiced, and learned through the Cooperative Learning Model. Verbal skills are an important part of the social skill process. Tone and volume of voice and the words that are used when working with others are all verbal skills that are necessary for students to be successful. These skills are used as part of communicating with others. In Cooperative Learning students all have jobs that they need to perform. The coach previews the necessary new skill with the teacher and then models for the teacher so that they understand and can teach the skill. The coach then returns to the group and models/teaches the group the new skill. Through this process students learn to effectively communicate within their group. The teacher can observe and interact with students so as to facilitate and help the coach along so that the group can complete the task. The encourager has the job of encouraging others on their team. Pat uses posters in her gymnasium with words and visual gestures that students have created in brainstorming sessions. Students can refer to their own comments when they are in the encourager's role. This is an ongoing process and a form of positive communication that students learn to use with one another. For example, Figure 7.2 shows a picture of an encourager poster used by Pat.

In the inclusive classroom, Positive Interdependence and positive reinforcement are often demonstrated by Pat and by her students. Positive Interdependence is observed when students try to work together to solve a problem or complete a task. The tasks are complex and they require all group members to be successful to complete the task. Grenier and Yeaton (2012) have argued that Cooperative Learning fosters 'true' inclusivity given its inherent foundational practice of

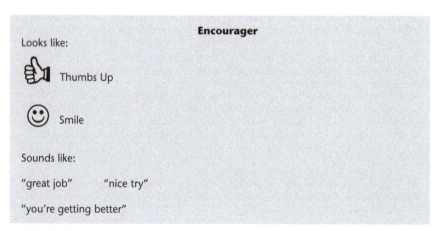

FIGURE 7.2 Encourager poster

equal Positive Interdependence. Reinforcement of developmentally appropriate behaviors is a common occurrence in the inclusive classroom or gymnasium Pat creates. Students praise their group members when they are successful and Pat provides positive specific feedback to guide her students' activities.

Visual supports (text and video)

In the students' group folder there is a page that provides a description of each role with a photograph as a visual cue. An example of the role of coach appears in Figure 7.3.

Skill acquisition is an important part of Pat's Physical Education program. She suggests that the iPad allows students to view the skill being performed. For example, in her classes, students use the video model for learning basketball skills, allowing them to digitally record the skills performed in the lesson. The use of a visual device allows the student to modify and adapt their movement and this challenges the student at their own level; that is, it allows for differentiated instruction. There are endless possibilities for the use of technology, but to be effective it needs to be embedded into the lesson with specific examples, including video modeling, iPad scripts, and social stories. In Pat's classes the students with cerebral palsy, autism, and other developmental disabilities have liked the responsibility and responded more favorably to visual tasks.

During or after the lesson there is a debrief or Group Processing session of what has happened during the lesson. Using the video model for helping students learn basketball assists this learning process. A picture of a camera appears in Figure 7.4.

- Leads the team in stretches.
- Teaches the team new skills.
- Keeps the team on task.
- Starts and stops activity.

FIGURE 7.3   The role of the coach

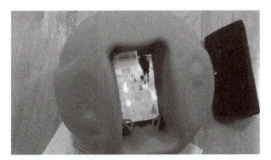

FIGURE 7.4   Video model for basketball

Michelle and Pat draw on student case studies from a number of their research projects to provide examples of how Cooperative Learning has been utilized to facilitate inclusion in Physical Education (Grenier et al., 2005; Grenier & Yeaton, 2012; Grenier, 2006). They suggest that Cooperative Learning is appropriate for developing students' cognitive and social skills and they also argue that it is an approach that helps to promote equitable peer relationships through Positive Interdependence and shared responsibility for learning. Furthermore, the experience of Pat, a Physical Education specialist at the elementary level, shows how Cooperative Learning can be used as a catalyst for reducing barriers and prejudice against students with disabilities. Michelle and Pat have often drawn our attention to case studies of students with cerebral palsy, autism, and developmental disabilities to illustrate how students with disabilities can be integrated into an inclusive Physical Education classroom. Through adaption and the careful grouping of children using Cooperative Learning strategies Michelle and Pat have shown how students who were previously marginalized and excluded – despite the teacher's best intentions – are included and find a place to flourish in a Cooperative Learning gymnasium.

When teaching, Pat defines the space so that it is not overwhelming for students; after all, there are lots of distractions in the gymnasium. She has found that when students are accountable to their group members they are more likely to stay on task. The practice of giving stickers to students who support, encourage, work as a team or complete the task has been useful for Pat. In addition, Michelle (working with Pat) has utilized Cooperative Learning as a critical pedagogy for students with disabilities. Cooperative Learning can help create a learning environment that allows persons with disabilities to be part of a positive learning environment with equal peer relations facilitated by the use of Positive Interdependence and individual and group accountability for learning (Cohen & Lotan, 2004; Grenier & Yeaton, 2012; Grenier, 2006). Pat argues that students can learn social interaction and they can learn to work with students that they normally wouldn't work with. She reflected:

> I have the students working in small groups of four usually. Kids learn to work with kids who they would normally not work with. They might say at the start of the unit I can't work with Johnny or Suzie, but at the end of the unit they are working together. These are valuable life lessons for the kids.

When it comes to her role in the classroom Pat feels that:

> Cooperative Learning provides a format for student-centred, self-directed learning. It is really their responsibility to try it or not. My role is more of a facilitator than teacher. I am more of a guide, helping them in their learning and giving them ideas. Students read, record, and discuss skills with classmates in their learning groups or in a debrief at the end of class with all students. Generally, I believe they do try it.

Initially, using Cooperative Learning was an adjustment for Pat in her teaching and a big adjustment for students: 'I had to bargain with the students, hey, you don't have to listen to me anymore. You can be responsible and move through the task sheets on your own at your own pace'. Pat is now experienced in teaching students Cooperative Learning roles, such as coach, equipment person, encourager, and checker. She chooses roles that are useful for her students and the content being taught. She takes time to have students learn their roles. Pat has developed lesson plans that guide the students to progressively learn their roles. She has now worked with Cooperative Learning for a decade and argues that consistent routines motivate students to follow the task.

Self-processing / A time to reflect

Self-processing questions

1. Does your school, community, or sport club have a mission statement that refers explicitly to welcoming diversity and including all? Are your learning areas physically accessible to every student?
2. Do all children have access to extracurricular activities including dance, sports, music, drama, Adventure Education, and art programs?
3. Do your students engage in inclusive thinking: 'How can we get Moana's wheelchair on the bus to go on the field trip? What kinds of snacks and drinks can we have at the celebration that everyone can enjoy without harm? How can we figure out positions in the game so that everyone can participate at their level?
4. Do students know about and appreciate one another's uniqueness and respect this in a positive learning environment?
5. How can we create learning environments where children learn to value and appreciate everyone?
6. How do the lessons our students learn about inclusion in our schools, community, sports clubs, and outdoor experiences help develop an understanding and interest in addressing issues of exclusion and/or segregation?

Our Reflections

Ben

Teachers, coaches, and community workers need support. We need to be conscious of the huge demands placed on teachers today, particularly with regards to core subjects like Science, Math, and Literacy. They all need planning and collaboration time to plan, observe, and critically reflect on their practice. They need to have appropriate administrative support and emotional supports to be effective in the twenty-first century. Disguising disabilities is not the answer and if we ignore disabilities they won't go away. Children are very perceptive; they know who is good at spelling, they know who is gifted at baseball, they know who is overweight. Students are already well aware of differences in their classroom. We need to acknowledge these differences and work against exclusion. We must take on an advocacy role when confronting examples of elitism and exclusion in our classroom and in our teaching and learning experiences in Physical Education, the community, sports clubs, and out-of-doors experiences. The placement of segregated special education classrooms isolated from other students should not be tolerated in our education systems of the twenty-first century.

Ash

There are many things we wouldn't tolerate in our lives and yet we inadvertently allow them to occur in our lessons. In a recent practitioner response to my blog (www.peprn.com) Patty Kestell from Cedarburg, WI (the 2013 National Elementary Physical Education Teacher of the Year) borrowed the words of Lieutenant General David Morrison, Australian Chief of Army, to say 'the standard you walk past is the standard you accept'. When it comes to inclusion I feel we walk past too many unacceptable standards but in doing so we endorse them on our way. That needs to change.

References

Alton-Lee, A. (2011). (Using) evidence for educational improvement. *Cambridge Journal of Education*, *41*(3), 303–329. http://doi.org/10.1080/0305764X.2011.607150

Ball, A. F. (2012). To know is not enough: Knowledge, power, and the zone of generativity. *Educational Researcher*, *41*(8), 283–293. http://doi.org/10.3102/0013189X12465334

Cohen, E. G. & Lotan, R. A. (2004). Equity in heterogeneous classrooms. In J. Banks & C. McGee Banks (Eds.). *Handbook of Research on Multicultural Education* (2nd ed., pp. 736–749). San Francisco, CA: Jossey-Bass.

Dowler, W. (2012). Cooperative learning and interactions in inclusive secondary school physical education classes in Australia. In B. Dyson & A. Casey (Eds.). *Cooperative learning in physical education: A research-based approach* (pp. 159–165). London: Routledge.

Dowler, W. (2014). Cooperative learning as a promising approach for the inclusion of students with disabilities. *ACHPER Active and Healthy Magazine*, *21*(2), 19–24.

Dyson, B. (1994). Student views of an alternative physical education program. *Research Quarterly for Exercise & Sport*, *65*(1), A–68. Retrieved from http://proxy.binghamton.edu/login?url=http://search.ebscohost.com/login.aspx?direct=true&db=a9h&AN=9502070769&site=ehost-live

Dyson, B. (2014). Quality physical education: A commentary on effective physical education teaching. *Research Quarterly for Exercise and Sport*, *85*(2), 144–152. http://doi.org/10.1080/02701367.2014.904155

Dyson, B. & Sutherland, S. (2015). Adventure based learning. In J. Lund & D. Tannehill (Eds.). *Standards-based curriculum development* (3rd ed., pp. 56–68). Boston, MA: Jones Bartlett.

Goodyear, V. (2015). Developing students' promotive interactions over time: Teachers' adaptions to and interactions within the cooperative learning model. AIESEP International Conference. July 2015, Madrid, Spain.

Grenier, M. (2006). A social constructionist perspective of teaching and learning in inclusive physical education. *Adapted Physical Activity Quarterly*, *23*(3), 245–260.

Grenier, M. & Yeaton, P. (2012). Cooperative learning as an inclusive pedagogical practice in physical education. In B. Dyson & A. Casey (Eds.). *Cooperative learning in physical education: A research-based approach* (pp. 119–135). London: Routledge.

Grenier, M., Dyson, B., & Yeaton, P. (2005). Cooperative learning that includes students with disabilities. *Journal of Physical Education, Recreation & Dance, 76*(6), 29–35. Retrieved from http://www.tandfonline.com/doi/abs/10.1080/07303084.2005.10608264

Hattie, J. (2012). *Visible learning for teachers: Maximizing impact on learning.* (I. ebrary, Ed.). New York: Routledge.

Mitchell, D. (2014). *What really works in special and inclusive education: Using evidence-based teaching strategies* (2nd ed.). New York: Routledge.

Oakes, J. (2005). *Keeping track: How schools structure inequality* (2nd ed.). New Haven, CT: Yale University Press.

Sapon-Shevin, M. (2000). Schools fit for all. *Educational Leadership, 58*(4), 34. Retrieved from http://search.ebscohost.com/login.aspx?direct=true&db=aph&AN=4024157&site=eds-live\nhttp://libproxy.nnmc.edu:2077/ContentServer.asp?T=P&P=AN&K=4024157&S=R&D=aph&EbscoContent=dGJyMNLe80SeqLc4v+vlOLCmr0uep69Ssay4SLOWxWXS&ContentCustomer=dGJyMPGttU6upq9Rue

Sapon-Shevin, M. (2010). *Because we can change the world: A practical guide to building cooperative, inclusive classroom communities* (2nd ed.). Thousand Oaks, CA: Corwin.

Sutherland, S. (2012). Borrowing strategies from adventure-based learning to enhance group processing in cooperative learning. In B. Dyson & A. Casey (Eds.). *Cooperative learning in physical education: A research-based approach* (pp. 103–118). London: Routledge.

Sutherland, S., Stuhr, P., & Ressler, J. (2014). Group processing in cooperative learning: Using the Sunday afternoon drive debrief model. *Australian Council for Health Physical Education and Recreation, 21,* 12–15.

Yeaton, P. (2015). Essential inclusive practices. The SHAPE National US Conference, April, Seattle.

8

HOW TO IMPLEMENT COOPERATIVE LEARNING IN PHYSICAL EDUCATION AT MIDDLE AND HIGH SCHOOL LEVEL

Chapter overview

While it is hoped that students will experience high-quality Physical Education throughout their school careers, this is not always the case. This chapter is designed to help teachers and coaches to introduce Cooperative Learning to older students who may have little or no experience of learning together in school. As with all the chapters it draws on real-world examples and shows – across multiple activity areas – how different structures and approaches to teaching through Cooperative Learning can be used. It examines the factors in schools that might help or hinder the use of innovative pedagogical approaches and shows how teachers and coaches might introduce the five key elements of Cooperative Learning to their classrooms. It provides sample lessons that focus on the different elements and Cooperative Learning Structures and demonstrates how they can be used in different settings. Specific tasks are presented that guide teachers and coaches to encourage students to be independent enquirers, creative thinkers, reflective learners, team workers, self-managers, and participants who contribute to the completion of the task.

We believe that

1. Trust is a key facet of successful change in education – trust in yourself, trust in your students, and trust in your curriculum.
2. As Confucius said, 'The man who moves a mountain begins by carrying away small stones' and therefore, while it takes time, the mountain (or in this case the pedagogy) gets moved.
3. If we take on the idea (and the challenge) of moving small stones then we need to find small things to change rather than trying to shift our whole pedagogical approach.

4. By taking on personal responsibility for what happens in our own classrooms we stand a better chance of positioning learning and learners as the central facet of our work. When we do this we move away from tradition and expectation and focus on each individual.

5. When we decide to change, it is a progressive process. We are making the change because we fundamentally believe things need to change. That belief doesn't alter even if the first, second, tenth, or one-hundredth attempt to change fails.

6. Learning is a building process. If we set out to move the mountain then we are committing to put it somewhere else and we are committing to make it stable. To do that we need to build carefully and continually strive for a better future.

7. Before you start a unit of work you will have to, as suggested previously in this book, try to use each of the five elements in your teaching to get a 'feel for' them. It is only by trying things out and getting comfortable with them that you will feel comfortable to try the whole model with a class across a whole unit of work.

Imagine the scene

Mrs. Bailey hears the bell and she sees her class hurrying down the corridor to get to her lesson. Jane smiles as she passes her teacher and instead of asking the expected question 'What are we doing this week?' she simply says, 'I'm the encourager this week and we're going to be the best group ever.' The rest of the class follows on quickly behind and the talk in the changing room is not about the weekend or their science lesson or what so and so said. It's about the lesson to come. Mrs. Bailey hasn't had to utter a word or clarify the content because the students already know what is expected of them – at least at the start of the lesson.

The group is quickly out and they enter the gym. The equipment manager takes care of the group's needs and while the warm-up manager begins to get everyone prepared for the lesson, the encourager (Jane included) is heard and seen giving praise (verbal and otherwise) to his or her teammates. At a given signal each coach moves away from their respective team and they quickly congregate around Mrs. Bailey. She asks Kyle what the first task in the lesson is and he confirms that his team is already reviewing the last lesson as they do their warm-up and think that they need to develop their defensive play. Suzie suggests that they are doing likewise and asks if Mrs. Bailey could help out. She agrees but waits to see what the others are planning. Patrick and Teresa say that their groups, respectively and independently, felt that they need more time in the small-sided game they developed last week as they didn't quite master the concepts as they had hoped. Jack has been looking on the Internet and has found a conceptual game that he thinks will help his group with restarts and they want to try that.

Mrs. Bailey agrees, and having allowed the others to go back to their groups, starts to talk Kyle and Suzie through a small-sided modified game that will help them to develop their group's defensive understanding. While the basic structure is laid out Mrs. Bailey uses mainly questions to challenge the two students to come up with some answers, rules, and modifications of their own before returning to their group. Even though the two coaches have been away for a few minutes the groups have not been idle and have engaged in a small-sided game to work on closing down space and denying their partner a chance to get towards a designated target.

Scanning the room, Mrs. Bailey knows that everyone is on task (not her task but their own) and engaged. Her job is to prepare them for the next progression. She doesn't do it simultaneously and on no occasion does she stop the whole class for a conversation. She moves the groups along as and when they need it and she tries to do this based on the students' needs and expectations and not her own. She has resources on hand that are differentiated for the individual learners in her class and she is always encouraging the students to develop both individually and collectively. You could argue that nothing is coordinated, but in the organized chaos that appears to ensue everyone has a place and learning and learners form the heart of the experience.

Introduction

Every school, community, or sports club is different. Between us (Ben and Ash) we have been in maybe a hundred and they all have different advantages and disadvantages. If we take 'the school' as our example we see that, as a concept, it is very homogeneous. People see it as a standardized, uniform, consistent, and habitual 'place' where standardized, uniform, consistent, and habitual things happen. The sports club could be viewed as similarly homogeneous. Practices in Physical Education and sports coaching are seen in the same way and we get a sense of what does or doesn't happen in the subject or field. While that idea suits the needs of many people – from politicians to researchers and teachers/coaches to parents – it is not necessarily the case and it doesn't help individual practitioners or departments make changes. Yes, the similarities often outweigh the differences, but the differences are important too. The length of lessons/sessions has an impact on what can or cannot be achieved, the distances from one lesson to another (or indeed from home to the club), the traditional successes and routines in the department, the relative expertise of the staff, and the expectations of the parents all play their part in what you, as a practitioner, face on a daily basis, and it is against these dominant ideas that you present your new pedagogical ideas and aspirations.

Never, in any of our collective experiences, have the dominant ideas simply been brushed aside. Change requires negotiation and should be considered as a journey and not as an end point. They (changes) are considered (and expected in many cases) simply to work and to keep on working. After all, when you try something new you judge it on its ability to make things better. Impulse purchases often, but not always, sit idly in a cupboard alongside the unwanted or unused presents that someone else thought were a good idea at the time. The same can be said of the new ideas that come from professional development/learning events or from staff training days or from social media platforms such as Twitter. They look like great ideas but when the euphoria slips away and the realities of your site of practice are considered, they are simply too difficult to instigate. The resources are set at a level that make them useful in an ideal situation but they were not developed to be used over time and nor were they flexible enough to use as you want. One of the reasons for this – in the same way that deciding to lose weight or get stronger or get fitter is not the same as actually achieving any or all of these things – is that good ideas take time to instigate and develop. Like flat-packed furniture, buying it and getting it home is the easy part. Building it and putting it in place is the real task. The same goes for new pedagogies. Buying or borrowing this book was a good first step but now you have to build a new way of teaching and learning.

In the remains of this chapter (and throughout the whole of the book) our aim is to help you to implement Cooperative Learning in your middle and high school Physical Education curriculum, community, or sports club. This starts with lesson zero and ends, we propose, when both you and your students are comfortable with the interrelationship between the five elements, the additional procedures, the pedagogical goals, and, fundamentally, the way that teaching, learning, and curriculum (i.e. pedagogy) look and feel in your lessons.

Lesson zero

At its heart, lesson zero is your chance to explain what is about to happen and prepare your students for what they are going to experience in the lessons that follow. Aspirationally we would like to hope that this is a personal journey (for you and for your students) that will last throughout your respective time at the school (it certainly did for Ash and his students – see the example in Box 8.1) but even if it is just for one unit of work, they need to know that the rules have changed.

In a traditional Physical Education classroom or coaching session (and as we have explained earlier on in the book) you wouldn't expect Mrs. Bailey's class (in the scenario above) to take place. It is not 'normal'. We have examples of this happening (Casey, 2014; Dyson et al., 2010; Goodyear & Casey, 2015) but only after a lot of practice on the behalf of the teachers and the students. Our most comprehensive example comes from the work of Vicky Goodyear, who has worked with one department for more than four years (see Chapter 13 for more details) and helped them to create learning environments like Mrs. Bailey's. However, they all started with a lesson zero and an acknowledgement that both they (as teachers) and their students needed to relearn what it meant to be in Physical Education. In many respects it was a 'heads-up' that change was coming and a decision to bring the students in on it from lesson zero.

But what might this look like? In the example that follows we draw on one of Ash's units of work around Track and Field athletics. He was working with a group of 11- to 12-year students on the first day of their new (to them) unit of work. Prior experience (see Casey & Dyson, 2009) had already told him that it was not (a) fair or (b) conducive to learning to try and start a unit of work in a new approach without helping the students to understand what was expected of them. In the long term he saved himself time and his students apprehension by taking a lesson zero to explain what was to come.

BOX 8.1: AN EXAMPLE OF LESSON ZERO

Ash was using the Learning Teams approach and prior to the lesson he published the team sheets on his Cooperative Learning noticeboard. The teams had been selected heterogeneously (i.e. so that they were mixed ability, gender, ethnicity, race, socio-economic background, and they didn't include friends or rivals in the same group). He also wrote and printed materials for the team folders. These contained the following: a summary sheet which gave an overview of the Cooperative Learning approach and how it would change the way the lessons would run; a team sheet; a lesson timetable showing what they would do each week; lesson plans/task sheets for each lesson in the unit; a matrix showing what roles students would take in each lesson; sheets that gave an overview of each of the roles; a warm-up sheet; the final team sheet (blank) for the culminating event (an Olympic competition); a team contract; a list of Ash's expectations of the students; and a list of what the students could expect of him in return. Each team had their own folder and these were to be kept in the PE department and would be distributed at the start of each lesson.

The pupils entered the gym and sat in their teams. They were then 'walked' through the folder. The ethos and mechanics of Cooperative Learning were explained and the structure of each of the lessons was explored. Team roles were examined and the students were free to ask questions and discuss different ideas and concepts. All of the five elements were used in the session so that the students got used to what it meant to be individually accountable or to engage in Group Processing. The students were then asked to democratically choose a team name and an emblem (these ranged in this example from the Bacon Sandwiches to the White Roses). Once everything had been explored they signed their team contracts and Ash signed his teacher's contract and the lesson ended.

After the lesson Ash reworked the team sheets and the folders to represent the student-selected teams and emblems and updated the Cooperative Learning noticeboard. Experience told him that there would still be teething problems and while he had a good understanding of what was to follow, the students would need lots of support and encouragement to take on their new roles and meet fully with Ash's aspirations for the unit.

Different structures and approaches

It is beyond the scope of this book to provide examples of what might be used in any and every lesson. However, in what follows it is our hope to provide a few real-world examples of what you might be able to achieve using different structures or approaches to teaching through and with a Cooperative Learning approach. We use three main examples here: Student Teams–Achievement Divisions (STAD), Think-Pair-Share or Pair-Check-Perform, and Learning Teams, while at the same time being aware that the next chapter examines the Jigsaw classroom structure specifically.

Student Teams–Achievement Divisions (STAD)

STADs were developed at Johns Hopkins University by Robert Slavin and colleagues and 'are based on the idea of having students work in Cooperative Learning teams to learn academic objectives' (Slavin, 1996). At its heart (as with all Cooperative Learning approaches) the focus is on students working together to learn together and therefore students are individually responsible for their own and their peers' learning. It is not enough to say 'I get it'. The focus is, instead, on the idea that 'we get it' is more important.

While all five elements would be considered as being important, Slavin felt that the specific focus on *team rewards*, *Individual Accountability* and *equal opportunities for success* separated STAD from other approaches. Importantly, STAD is not a competitive structure – indeed all, some, or no teams might achieve a designated criterion in a lesson and this would have no impact on the rest of the student Learning Teams. Success is defined by team learning and not on an individual or a 'versus' basis.

STADs are the most extensively researched of all Cooperative Learning methods; they have been used in lots of different subject areas and are very adaptable. The main idea behind STAD is to help and encourage students to help and encourage others to master skills presented by the teacher. However, while the groups learn together, assessment is undertaken on an individual basis (at which time students can't help one another). The results of these assessments are averaged and then measured against previous results. Rewards are gained when the new average exceeds either a team's previous average or the criteria for the task. The whole cycle of activity usually takes between three and five lessons and is best used when teaching well-defined objectives.

At the heart of STAD is the idea of motivating students through the use of team rewards. By encouraging and helping their teammates to do their best, and by acknowledging that learning should be important, valuable, and fun, students learn to help each other overcome difficulties and potential roadblocks. Furthermore, they learn to assess their respective strengths and weaknesses and they come to understand that anyone can be a 'team star' in a given week if they score above their personal average.

So how does it work?

STAD is made up of five main components: class presentation, teams, quizzes, individual improvement scores, and team recognition (Slavin, 1996).

Class presentation

The unit is presented to the class at the start of the unit. Often, in traditional Physical Education classrooms, the students get an overview but they are left to discover more about their learning as they move through the unit. Using the idea of *lesson zero*, STAD encourages students to focus carefully on what they will be expected to do and how their quiz score will impact on the team score.

Teams

Teams will contain four or five students and will be selected heterogeneously. This will ensure that each group represents a cross-section of the class in terms of academic performance (which in Physical Education is their ability), sex, and race or ethnicity. The main aim of the team is to ensure that everyone does well in terms of their learning. After you, as the teacher or coach, present the materials for the unit, the teams meet to prepare for the task(s) ahead. Teams are important and at every juncture emphasis is placed on teams and their members doing their best for the team, and on the team doing its best for its members. The teams provide peer support, mutual concern, and respect for everyone – they look after their own. In the words of the Musketeers, it is a case of 'all for one, and one for all'.

Quizzes

The idea of quizzes shows the roots of STAD in subjects like Math and Science, but these can be adapted easily for a Physical Education classroom. Let's imagine that your lesson is focused on dance or gymnastics and you have been working on some key aspects of transition or symmetry or asymmetry. The quiz would take the form of a short routine that the team felt exemplified these aspects. This routine (maybe ten seconds long) could be repeated (one after the other) by each member of the team. If this was recorded on an iPad an assessment could be made, individually, and an average awarded for the team. Such a quiz would ensure that every student is individually responsible for knowing the material while also giving teams an idea of what individuals needed to improve – both in terms of understanding and performance. These quizzes could be taken at the start of the unit and then at different stages through the unit as a means of showing understanding and performance levels.

Individual improvement scores

Individual improvement scores give each student a performance goal that is achievable only if he or she works hard and performs better than in the past. It is focused on self-improvement and is not dependent on the approach of any other student. Any student can contribute to the team's success but only if they show definite improvement over past performance. They are given a base score and then judged against the margins against which they improve this score.

Team recognition

The idea of a team average allows the team to develop and gain recognition if their average score improves. This means that, while they will be rewarded if everyone succeeds, they can also gain recognition if they improve as a team. This system acknowledges that while the idea of doing well as a team is important, students cannot be held solely responsible for the development of their peers. That is your responsibility, and we all know that sometimes kids have 'off-days' or are affected by things outside of our control. Sometimes kids reach their full potential in an activity and specialist knowledge and time is needed to help them move forwards – things that their peers (no matter how good or dedicated they are) cannot help them with.

Summary

STAD, like many Cooperative Learning Structures, is a new way of structuring the classroom. The emphasis is on individual and team learning but not on competition. The differences in quiz scores is unimportant; the focus is on improvement. What matters is the development that each student undergoes. But this is not just about academic learning – which in the case of Physical Education is often considered to be, well, physical. It is also about the other learning domains that we

Team Lightening's summary sheet				Date: 3rd April	
Team members	Base score	Quiz score 1	Improvement points	Quiz score 2	Improvement points
Sarah G	30	33	3		
Rich M	25	27	2		
Jamie B	20	18	0		
Tamsin C	25	32	7		
Team score	100	112	12		
Team average	25	28	3		
Team award	Bronze	Bronze Plus	Lesser Bronze		

FIGURE 8.1   Team summary sheet

have previously discussed – the cognitive, social, and affective domains (see Casey & Goodyear, 2015).

The most straightforward way of using STAD might be in a traditional skills-based lesson where you have set outcomes such as learning the set shot in basketball. While both of us would advocate for a more student-focused and progressive curriculum, one that moves away from the dominant focus on skills, you need to start somewhere that is comfortable. Try STAD in a short unit of basketball and look for ways to measure improvement and learning. Once you understand the structure and the ways of using STAD then you can experiment with changing other parts of your teaching. It is important that you not try and change too many things at once in your lessons because to learn to teach and learn in a new way takes time.

Pair-Check-Perform

When asking students to work together in pairs we are often faced with a concern about the quality and accuracy of the feedback. Consequently, we often go to each of the groups in turn to 'double check' the student interactions and in the process we negate the whole purpose of the exercise, i.e. to encourage students to take responsibility for their own and others' learning. Pair-Check-Perform, as discussed in Chapter 3, is a Cooperative Learning Structure that does the double-checking for us.

In Pair-Check-Perform students are, in an ideal world, in groups of four. Schools, unfortunately, don't operate in ideal worlds (much as teachers might like them to) and therefore class numbers are rarely divisible by four. Even if they are, someone is sure to be away from school at least once during your unit and therefore you will need a plan B. In our experience, this means you have two potential groupings, and experience tells us that groups of three and/or four work. While this changes the dynamics a little, it does mean that different peers observe each student. As each grouping requires a different set-up we will explain each one in turn.

Group of four

This is the classic Pair-Check-Perform and it works as follows. The students are divided into groups of four and then again into pairs. Student A works with student B and simultaneously student C works with student D. One student takes on the role of the performer while the other takes on the role of coach/observer. In the example we use below (and have used in the past in our teaching) the topic is swimming and the students are working on their arms in breaststroke (see Figure 8.2).

The worksheets are double laminated (in an effort to keep them waterproof) and the students use chinagraph (wax) pencils to mark the sheets. In the first cycle, A and C (respectively) take on the role of coach while B and D swim. Once the learning cues have been addressed, and when the students are ready, they swap

The coaches are given the following instructions:

Ask your partner to pull with breaststroke arms.

1. Using a float between your legs, push off the wall in flat position – one pull underwater.
2. Turn your palms outward and pull with both hands out and around in a circular motion to shoulder height.
3. Use the pull of your hands to pull your head up and out of the water to take a breath.
4. As your head comes down, your arms extend back out ready for the next stroke.
5. As your hands reach the extended position, glide for the count of two before taking the next stroke.
6. Repeat a minimum of four times before swapping roles.

Students (in their role of coach) are asked to watch and assess how their partners achieve the following three learning cues (LC):

- LC1. Palms out and pull with both <u>hands to shoulder height</u>.
- LC2. <u>Use pull to lift head</u> and take a breath, extending arms when head goes back down.
- LC3. <u>Glide for a count of two</u> before taking the next stroke.

FIGURE 8.2 Swimming sheet

FIGURE 8.3 A group of four *Pair-Check-Perform* assessment matrix

FIGURE 8.4 A group of three *Pair-Check-Perform* assessment matrix

roles. This is the pair work that we are all familiar with. However, in Pair–Check–Perform there is an additional element (see Figure 8.3).

Once both cycles have been undertaken, a third rotation occurs – the Pair–Check–Perform. In an effort to hold the students individually accountable – both as performers and coaches – the third cycle involves A and B observing and assessing C and D in relation to the three LCs before the roles are once again reversed and C and D observe and assess A and B. The key here is that the students act as a second and third pair of eyes respectively and allow you, as the teacher, to play a broader role. It is important, though, that you don't override the coaches, or they are disempowered and the approach breaks down. Therefore it is vital that you don't challenge the coaches directly (unless they are being unsafe) and that you don't talk to the swimmers. Instead, through questions and guidance your role is to help the coaches to help their performers.

Group of three

In this grouping (and in order to maximize engagement) it is necessary to stagger the performances (see Figure 8.4). Following the same set of instructions as for the group of four, the coach asks his or her first swimmer to perform one length/width and assess them before asking the second swimmer to perform. The coach repeats the staggered swim until he or she is happy that the learning cues have been assessed. Once student A has assessed students B and C then he or she swaps with B and the cycle is repeated. In this way A assesses B and C, B assesses A and C, and C assess A and B, and consequently each coach is 'checked' by one of their peers.

Summary

We have used Pair–Check–Perform for whole units of work and seen some massive improvements in our students. It is a great, and safe, way of supporting your students as they start to move away from you and branch out on their own. It is important that you help them move away and support them as they learn to help one another. We might use the analogy of 'sink or swim together' but this is not a case of throwing them in at the deep end and hoping they can stay afloat. Take it slowly but, importantly, don't directly undermine them as this will not help them in either the short or the long term. Ensure you talk to the coach and not the performer and help them to settle into their role. This is important in all Cooperative Learning approaches as it is the bedrock of what you are trying to achieve: confident, self-sufficient, independent learners.

Help or hinder

As we have mentioned before, schools, communities, and sports clubs are not homogeneous places where standardized, uniform, consistent, and habitual things happen. They are each unique in their own way and that is what makes you, as practitioners, experts in your own context. That said, these are some ideas, in many cases learned the hard way, that might help you to avoid and/or overcome what we think are common obstacles.

BOX 8.2: SMALL STONES COME FIRST

1. Move small stones first: Research suggests that change is evidence based (Casey, 2014). Teachers want to see how it works before committing to using it. This is certainly one of the core reasons that we have structured the book as we have and have sought to give you real-world examples and sample lessons to help you make the decision to change. The same rule applies with your colleagues (both inside and outside Physical Education). They want to see the results of change before signing up for change. You will need to prove that it works, and that means starting small. Take one class and try it with them. Be comfortable yourself in what you are doing before you try it with multiple classes and year groups. People are more likely to allow you to make small changes with one class than they are to commit to wholesale changes based on our belief that this really works. If you can provide evidence that it works then, in all probability, they will be prepared to allow the changes to escalate.

2. If it's worth doing it's worth doing well: Commit to change and put it on paper. We have talked before about gaining fluency in Cooperative Learning in just the same way as you gain fluency in a new language. It takes time and until you are even 'conversationally' fluent then you need the phrasebook at hand. The reason why Ash planned out his whole unit in the example above is because it scaffolded and supported his teaching until such time as his competence and confidence grew. The folders also served as a crutch of sorts that supported everyone as they negotiated this new pedagogical approach. While, now, both of us could (if needed) create a lesson that incorporates the key elements of Cooperative Learning at very short notice (although they wouldn't be our best work) and adapt existing lessons to bring them more inline with the tenets of the model, this wasn't always the case. So don't do things from memory, but invest in them. This might mean acquiring some noticeboard space and purchasing some new equipment but if it is worth doing then it is worth that investment.

3. Finding time: We'd like to suggest that you can immediately find a longer unit or create a longer unit to base your Cooperative Learning aspirations on, but be realistic. You are changing the way you teach and the way your students learn and this should not be a quick process. Experience tells us that going too fast can spell the end for any curriculum change. Learn to walk before you try to run.

Self-processing / A time to reflect

Self-processing questions

1. Think of a class to start with. That's how we started, one group at a time and one lesson at a time. Who will you start with?
2. You are changing the way that children learn so be clear in your head what you want to do. Plan it out. But where will you start? Lesson zero?
3. Be clear what you want to achieve and write it down. When things get difficult or don't quite work, go back to this and remind yourself why you decided to invest in your teaching and your students' learning in this way.

Our Reflections

Ben

My first experience with Cooperative Learning at the high school level was with a teacher and students in Montreal, Canada. The teacher used Learning Teams and it was very effective to plan and organize students into Cooperative Learning Groups. But as Ash states, this is not business as usual. For you to take on Cooperative Learning as a pedagogical practice you need to make a conceptual shift in your approach to teaching. It is important to use lots of extension tasks and be progressive. You may need to have more than one lesson zero to help your students start to learn some of the essential elements of Cooperative Learning: Group Processing, Interpersonal and Small Group Skills, and Positive Interdependence.

Ash

I have used both STAD and Pair-Check-Perform in my teaching (and still do) and have found them great ways of structuring the classroom. That said, I started my first unit as a novice like everyone else and took it slowly. Yes, there were times when I went too fast and I ended up re-starting units or re-teaching lessons because I got it wrong. This is when I came up with the idea of lesson zero. Things were so new to the kids that they just didn't understand what was expected of them. Cooperative Learning changes the way they learn and you need to acknowledge that and help them to learn to learn in a new way. It's worth it.

References

Casey, A. (2014). Models-based practice: Great white hope or white elephant? *Physical Education and Sport Pedagogy*, *19*(1), 18–34. http://doi.org/10.1080/17408989.2012.726977

Casey, A. & Dyson, B. (2009). The implementation of models-based practice in physical education through action research. *European Physical Education Review*, *15*(2), 175–199.

Casey, A. & Goodyear, V. (2015). Can cooperative learning achieve the four learning outcomes of physical education? A review of literature. *Quest*, *67*(1), 56–72. http://doi.org/10.1080/00336297.2014.984733

Dyson, B., Linehan, N. R., & Hastie, P. A. (2010). The ecology of cooperative learning in elementary physical education classes. *Journal of Teaching in Physical Education*, *29*, 113–130.

Goodyear, V. & Casey, A. (2015). Innovation with change: Developing a community of practice to help teachers move beyond the 'honeymoon' of pedagogical renovation. *Physical Education & Sport Pedagogy*, *20*(2), 186–203.

Slavin, R. E. (1996). Research for the future on on cooperative learning and achievement: What we know, what we need to know. *Contemporary Educational Psychology*, *69*(1), 43–69. http://doi.org/http://dx.doi.org/10.1006/ceps.1996.0004

9

THE JIGSAW CLASSROOM – PUTTING THE PIECES OF COOPERATIVE LEARNING TOGETHER

Chapter overview

This chapter explores the Cooperative Learning Structure 'Jigsaw' and demonstrates the Jigsaw classroom. Included in this chapter are a number of examples and classroom resources to aid you to be a competent user of this approach inside one lesson. Specifically, this chapter gives numerous examples of how the Cooperative Learning Structure 'Jigsaw' works and how it is able to use the five elements of Cooperative Learning. In a step-by-step approach it shows how practitioners can implement and understand the five elements. For example, in using groups of students as the pieces of a puzzle in learning, this chapter shows how a lesson can be taken apart and then put together in numerous ways to aid the students in learning about and through physical activity. It shows how the students become Individually Accountable for their piece of the jigsaw and how they are also responsible to one another (or Positively Interdependent) for their piece – for without it, the picture (or in this case the learning) is incomplete. The chapter shows how students can use Jigsaw to develop their Face-to-Face Interactions and learn about working cooperatively in small groups. Finally, it demonstrates the importance of Group Processing in the co-construction of knowledge.

We believe that

1. Classrooms can be structured to position the students as key knowledge brokers.
2. Children are great judges of how to explain things that they (and therefore their peers) will understand.
3. If you trust students they will pay you back many times over.

4. Trust has to be gained by the teacher or coach as much as it needs to be earned by the students.
5. Mistrust shouldn't be the default position that it has become.
6. Kids trust the systems they know and, as pedagogues, we need to help them embrace the changes that we want and help them to understand why such changes will be better for them in the long run.

Imagine the scene

The class is noisy. They always are. But this is not the noise of inane chatter, but of children working together. Your role has been to watch Mrs. Scott teach and if you didn't know better you'd think that the children were the teachers. In fact they are, but only because they have been empowered to be so.

Walking around the gym, you find children engaged in informed discussions. Their small group and interpersonal skills are excellent; and not just those you'd expect. You taught this class a year ago and you know that they were never this cooperative or supportive when you had them. Yet, here's Jasmine working with her group and she is the one with the knowledge. No one else is interjecting and stating their opinion. They don't know what she knows and they want to. Moving on, you find three other students working in their own way with the same knowledge. It is clear that they (the student teachers) have gained something or learned something that only they know.

Mrs. Scott isn't idle either. Relieved of the need to tell the students what they are learning today (she helped the students understand that knowledge in the weeks that preceded this lesson), she is able to talk to her students and help them on an individual basis. Her interactions are facilitatory and she watches and asks questions of those in her charge. There are 'incidents' but the children play as much of role in moving beyond these as Mrs. Scott. Her role is to ask questions and she is always on hand to help the student expert, but she doesn't override them or question their judgment. She asks them questions and helps them to see the next step(s) but never in a way that undermines them. They are the experts and her role is to help and not hinder them in the new role/responsibility.

Introduction

Google defines the word jigsaw as 'a puzzle consisting of a picture printed on cardboard or wood and cut into various pieces of different shapes that have to be fitted together'. Using this idea as an analogy, and positioning the various pieces of different shapes as students and/or tasks and the learning outcome for the lesson or unit of work as the picture to be fitted together, we begin to see what a Jigsaw classroom might look like.

The task – perhaps to create a gymnastics routine or design a new net and wall game – is split into a number of 'pieces', aspects, or tasks and the students are assigned to one of these. We could divide the task into as many pieces as we want – after all, jigsaws come in many different denominations – but the prospect of a gymnastics routine being made up of 30 different movements or a new game having 30 different facets (all of which are independently designed) is not appealing. Similarly, the prospect of one student teaching the 29 others in their class their particular 'task' is not really changing the classroom structure of one expert and 30 novices (in other words, one teacher and 30 students). Furthermore, if you are going to maintain this structure then surely it is you (as an experienced and qualified adult) who should be the expert and it would make better sense for you to do the teaching in such a classroom structure. The fact is that this is what you/we are trying to move away from when using Cooperative Learning, so we need an alternative.

Experience and research tell us that six groups of five or five groups of six students are better ways of dividing a class and maximizing learning. If we consider FIFA's (2015) research into and justification for small-sided games (as opposed to full-sided 11-a-side games), we learn a number of important things.

- Players touch the ball five times more in 4-a-side football and twice as much in 7-sided games.
- Players are involved in three times as many one-on-one situations in 4-a-side football and twice as many in 7-sided games.
- On average, in 4-a-side football, goals are scored every two minutes, and every four minutes in 7-sided games.
- Goalkeepers make two to four times as many saves in 7-a-side football than they do in 11-a-side.
- The ball is out of play for eight per cent of the playing time in 4-a-side football, 14 per cent of the playing time in 7-sided games and 34 per cent in 11-a-side football.

Expanding these notions beyond football (soccer, for some of you) and into Physical Education and community sports, we quickly see the benefits of having children and young people working in smaller groups for sustained periods of time. Indeed, you could argue that if these ideas are applied to Physical Education and community settings then it is a little ridiculous that we would seek to encourage youngsters to work in larger groups. Happily, Cooperative Learning is not focused on large groups but on small and individual learning and Jigsaw certainly looks to take advantage of these and lots of other social learning theories.

Jigsaw

Jigsaw is not about dividing students randomly (Cooperative Learning never is) but about doing it heterogeneously and for longer periods of time. Cooperative Learning uses enduring groups that can last in the short- (1–2 lessons), medium- (3–15 lessons) and long-term (15+) but even the short groupings are longer than most small-sided teams stick together in traditional teaching and coaching. The difference with Jigsaw, over other Cooperative Learning Structures, however, is that the group/class is divided not once but twice.

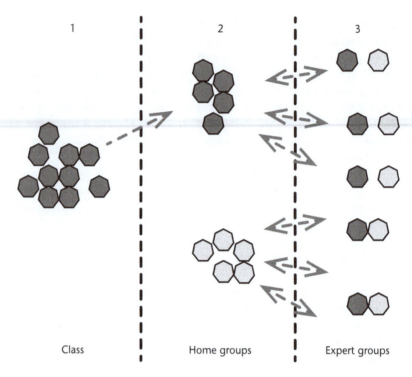

DIAGRAM 9.1 Dividing a class into a Jigsaw classroom

The first division (see Diagram 9.1) is into *home* or *base groups*. These teams are the heterogeneous ones and they need to be carefully selected. The rule of thumb that we always use is that every team should feel an equal mix of confidence and uncertainty. Confidence that, with a good performance in which every individual pulls together, they could beat any other team on their day. Equally they should feel that there is the very real potential to lose every game if they don't work together. It is a crude measure but it is surprising how often it is right.

Home groups are where the children will spend most of their time and these are the teams to which they should 'swear their allegiance', so to speak. Regardless of how the 'jigsaw' is divided up the children in each of these groups make up the full picture. The second division occurs when the 'jigsaw' is broken up and the children go to their *expert groups* (see Diagram 9.1). As you can see from the diagram, a class of ten becomes two *home groups* and five *expert groups*. These are ideal figures and more often than not they don't work exactly. You might end up with expert groups of six or indeed two or three groups of six and will have to double up. The important thing is that each *home group* needs to have a 'piece' in the *expert groups*. Without a representative they will have a piece missing from their jigsaw and they won't be able to complete their 'picture'.

Once the *expert groups* are divided up it is then time to give the children their pieces of the jigsaw. You don't give them the full picture but allocate each of them a unique piece of knowledge or an aspect of the routine that they will be solely responsible for (this is Individual Accountability). If you have two members of the same *home group* in an *expert group* then you will need to manage the situation so that every child has an individual role to play. When Ash teaches Jigsaw he starts with a little word game to show how the classroom works.

A Star Wars example

Dividing the groups as above, Ash will give each *expert group* a set of five cards. On the front of these is their number (and also the position of the word in the phrase or saying he is asking them to remember) and on the back is a word (or two) from the phrase he wants them to piece together in their *home groups*. Asking the children to remain silent at all times, he asks them to distribute the cards and then return with them to their *home groups*. Silence is very important because it is very tempting to shout out, and while this wouldn't spoil the bigger task, it would certainly spoil this one.

Once they are in their *home groups* they should have started to put the phrase together. Imagine that expert group one had the word 'IN', group two had 'A GALAXY', three 'FAR', four 'FAR', and five 'AWAY'. Putting these together in the correct order gives us the expression 'In a galaxy far, far away'. This is a simple, and quick, demonstration of Jigsaw, but what it shows us is how Jigsaw works. Each student is individually accountable for his or her piece of the jigsaw and without his or her word the whole expression is incomplete. The group is positive interdependent and they have to use interpersonal interactions and small group skills to put the jigsaw together – and this is just in a simple word challenge. When the task is made much bigger then the stakes are higher but the process remains fairly much the same.

Gymnastics (or dance) example

Often we ask children to develop their own dance or gymnastic routines and then perform them in front of their peers. For those who can dance this is a great opportunity, but for others, who might lack confidence or feel inexperienced, this can be a daunting task. Making a routine is hard enough when you're proficient and experienced but to do it alone is daunting. We often ask children to learn a dance routine that we have created (or found on the Internet) and then their responsibility is simpler – learn and perform the routine. This, however, robs them of the creative opportunities that come from choreographing a routine of their own and reduces the possibility that they will be asked to perform appropriate movements (i.e. movements that stretch them but which they still feel able to do, albeit with practice). When we (as teachers and coaches) develop routines we tend to try and find the middle ground and second guess what the children can and can't do. So some are doing moves that are too easy and others moves that are too hard.

Imagine instead that we made the class a Jigsaw class. Dividing the students up into six *home groups* (each of which would perform as a group in the final performance), we could then divide the class again into five *expert groups*. Each expert group would then be responsible for creating an element of the routine in their experts groups. As these sub-routines (say, five moments or eight beats' worth of a dance) are developed the individual *experts* are developing a piece of bespoke knowledge that no one else in their *home group* is privy to. Talk about Individual Accountability.

To achieve this division of knowledge we might set up our practical space as in Diagram 9.2. By dividing the space up as shown we create expert subsets within each class and go a long way to ensuring that individuals are positively interdependent and promotive in their interactions. They would need to engage in Promotive Face-to-Face Interactions, have good Small Group Skills and engage in regular reflections through Group Processing.

Once the five *expert group* routines (in this example, gymnastics) have been created and learned, the *experts* go back to their *home groups* and undertake to teach their teammates their section of the routine. To do this we need to reconfigure the practical space (see Diagrams 9.3 and 9.4) to allow every group to practice.

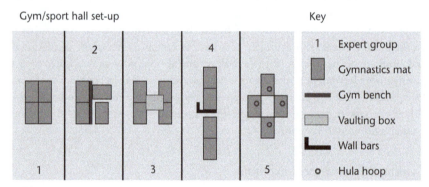

DIAGRAM 9.2   Set-up for *expert group* routine development and practice

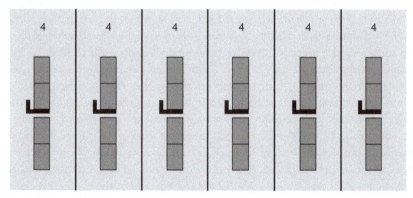

DIAGRAM 9.3   Set-up for *home group* practice (week four)

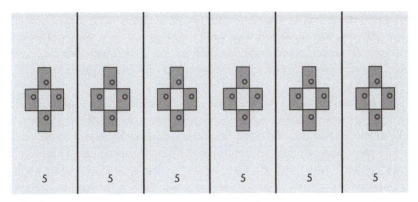

DIAGRAM 9.4   Set-up for *home group* practice (week five)

Using the space in such a way allows each *expert* to take a role in the learning of their peers. They hold a unique piece of knowledge and if they can't let their group mates in on the 'secret' then they can't succeed as a group. To put it bluntly, they sink or swim together. But what is your role? As the teacher or coach we are not suggesting that you take on the role of passive observer (this is certainly not a chance to catch up on your correspondence) but that you be the facilitator. You broker discussions and help solve disputes. You listen and ask relevant questions and you cut any potentially disruptive or non-cooperative behavior off at the pass. You don't need to know all the routines (although having the children write them down is useful) because there are many other *experts* in the room who can help teach other groups.

Once the five sub-routines are learned, then the *home groups* need to put them together and practice for their group performance. The practical space will need to be set up again as per Diagram 9.2 and the groups will need to be helped to manage the space (as there are five spaces and six groups), but experience tells us that by this stage of this cooperative process the groups are willing to work together.

Come the final performance there are *experts* around you who can help you mark the performances. They know what each section should look like and, in theory at least, every routine should be identical. The *experts* can provide feedback on accuracy, etc., leaving you to assess the key criteria you laid out at the start of the unit of work.

Games-making example

One of the things Ash likes to use *Jigsaw* for is making games, and he often does this with his students (be they elementary, high school or university students) as a simple way of introducing Jigsaw (once he's played the Star Wars word game with them). Using a similar set-up (see Diagram 9.5), he divides his classes first into *home groups* (these will be the teams they play their games in) and then into *expert groups*. He then tells them that they will be playing tag or 'it' games but that the games are yet to be invented because they are going to invent them. The *expert groups* are then given the task to invent a portion of the rules (in the example, 25 per cent).

As a teacher or coach your role is to ensure that the rules are appropriate and safe and pick appropriate boundaries for the games to be played in, etc. The children should feel that the game helps them develop because they are focused on fair play, participation, self-improvement, and cooperation. That said, the games shouldn't be perfect. At least not in the first or second (maybe even the sixth or seventh) instance. Rules made in isolation are not designed to fit together seamlessly, and one of the purposes of Jigsaw games making is to find the rough edges and the sticking points where the different rules simply don't align. Then, when they return to their *expert groups*, the children can keep negotiating the rules until they find something that works. This certainly helps with Promotive Face-to-Face Interaction and Small Group Skills.

But how does it work in reality?

The expert groups start with some basic rules (and experience tells us they tend to be quite basic, although they can also be overly complicated). For example, we have seen pitches as squares with hoops as safe zones, and children running to be tagged with a single touch anywhere on the body. The 'tagged' then stand still until they are untagged by a teammate (again with a single touch). Alternatively we have seen doughnut-shaped pitches with safe zones in the center. The children are on all fours like a crab, tagging with one appendage and doing a plank when waiting

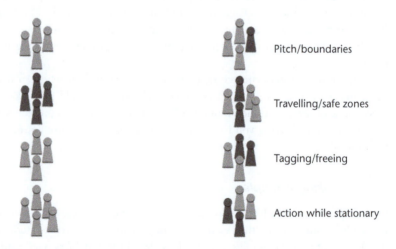

Pitch/boundaries

Travelling/safe zones

Tagging/freeing

Action while stationary

DIAGRAM 9.5 Roles for tag/tig/it games

to be freed. Neither works particularly well (as the children quickly work out) but that is why Jigsaw works so well. It is easy to go back to the *expert groups* with the *home group's* ideas and re-conceptualize the games.

The five elements in a Jigsaw classroom

In the previous sections we have shown how the Jigsaw classroom works and have alluded to the ways in which the five elements might be implemented/used to help enhance the student experience. In the next section it is our aim to make this explicit, one element at a time.

Individual Accountability – Being a piece in the jigsaw puzzle that is your *home group's* final task means that, as a student, you have a responsibility to the whole group. In other words, you are accountable. There is no safety net. When the teacher provides all the instruction in a class then you can always ask someone else nearby for some help. If you daydream or 'switch off' then someone can help you. In a Jigsaw classroom this is not so easy. To ask for help you have to do it a little more overtly and this means acknowledging that you don't know. Put simply, if you don't know and can't help your group then your group will sink rather than swim through their task.

Positive Interdependence – Dividing up knowledge into bespoke and yet isolated pieces means that not only do you hold your students Individually Accountable, you also make them Positively Interdependent. Jigsaw moves the classroom away from a dependence on one expert (i.e. the teacher or coach) and creates multiple experts instead. Each group has their own expert; four or five of them in fact. This means that to swim they need to rely on one another. This means facilitating interactions and working together to achieve a group goal.

Promotive Face-to-Face Interaction – Promotive follows on and complements positive. In their interactions in their *expert* and *home groups* students need to negotiate ideas and understanding. They are in close proximity to one another – toe-to-toe and face-to-face in fact – and it would be easy to resort to telling each other what to do and being 'bossy'. Instead they need to help each other to understand their new *expertise* and then they need to help their peers. When they are learning they need to be able to ask questions and challenge one another, but in a way that enhances their understanding. When they are teaching they need to be patient and help their group mates to understand. Above everything they need to promote each other's successes, support, encourage, and praise each other.

Small Group and Interpersonal Skills – It would be easy to assume that 'Small Group and Interpersonal Skills' is just another way of saying Promotive Face-to-Face Interaction. But it isn't. Working 'cooperatively is inherently more complex than competitive or individualistic learning' (Johnson et al., 1994, p. 10) because students must also understand how to provide leadership and manage conflict. They need to make decisions, build trust, and communicate their ideas.

Group Processing – In trying to achieve all of the other elements the students need time to reflect on their achievements and discuss how they can move forward together. In our previous book we argued that Group Processing provided the foundation that underpinned the model in Physical Education (Casey & Dyson, 2012). Indeed, in the same book, Lafont (2012) found that those who engaged in frequent social interactions between sequences of play turned out to be more effective than those who just performed. Giving children a chance to talk through their learning is often seen as being contrary to the movement-rich Physical Education we desire. Yet it has been shown that Group Processing helps them to continuously improve their learning and helps them to work together.

It is important to remember that using Cooperative Learning requires deliberate action on your behalf. These five elements don't just help the students to work cooperatively, they help you deliberately create Cooperative Learning between and amongst your students.

Self-processing / A time to reflect

Self-processing questions

1. Jigsaw is about dividing up the learning you want the students to do into equal and well-considered parts. We have used examples from gymnastics and games making but anything should work. Different shots in badminton or defensive formations in basketball would work equally well. How would you do this?
2. When placing the students into Jigsaw groups and asking them to develop a new expertise it is important that you don't undermine them. If you need to talk to them then do so in a way that helps them to maintain their expertise. How can you ensure that they take ownership and develop their expertise?

Our reflections

Ben

I have found that when you mention Cooperative Learning to folks they often think of cooperative games or group work. But when you say, 'Have you heard of Jigsaw?' they often say, 'Yeah we've done that before.' When you ask the details their answers vary a great deal. Now that might make you think 'Great! You know different kinds of jigsaw.' But unfortunately most of the time people have a poor understanding of Jigsaw and they certainly don't have the ability to adapt and modify it as Ash has in this chapter. Jigsaw is a great example of a Cooperative Learning Structure and perhaps the most recognizable, so enjoy playing with it.

Ash

I love using Jigsaw and from the very first time I used it it has remained a personal favorite. I think it's a great springboard into using Cooperative Learning and into more extravagant and risky uses of the model. It really helps you to get your head around the five elements (at least it did with me) and the different groups and roles help the students to understand what it means to learn Cooperatively.

References

Casey, A. & Dyson, B. (2012). Putting cooperative learning and physical activity into practice with primary students. In B. Dyson & A. Casey (Eds.). *Cooperative learning in physical education: A research-based approach* (pp. 59–74). London: Routledge.

FIFA. (2015). Small sided matches. Retrieved from http://www.fifa.com/aboutfifa/footballdevelopment/technicalsupport/grassroots/smallsidedmatches.html

Johnson, D. W., Johnson, R. T., & Holubec, E. (1994). *Cooperative learning in the classroom.* Alexndria, VA: ASCD.

Lafont, L. (2012). Cooperative learning and tutoring in sports and physical activities. In B. Dyson & A. Casey (Eds.). *Cooperative learning in physical education: A research-based approach* (pp. 136–149). London: Routledge.

10

LEARNING TEAMS, TEAM GAME TOURNAMENTS AND OTHER CLASSROOM STRUCTURES: PROMOTING COOPERATION

Chapter overview

Games – especially team games – have long formed the heart of Physical Education. However, research also suggests that students are often positioned as players in games and not as learners of games (Casey & Quennerstedt, 2015). This chapter shows how true competition can be achieved within a Cooperative Learning classroom. Structures such as Team Game Tournaments will be used to show how students' understanding of physical activity and games can be enhanced through the use of Cooperative Learning. Lesson plans and examples from multiple contexts will be used to show how team games can be used to teach cooperation, leadership, and teamwork.

We believe that

1. At the heart of competition is cooperation.
2. Children and young people need to be taught that competition is not just about winning and losing.
3. At its heart, Cooperative Learning aims to teach leadership and teamwork.
4. Kids learn that they are winners (i.e. good) or losers (i.e. bad) and improvements only count if it means you can become a winner. Getting better and still losing doesn't seem to incentivize many children, but perhaps it should.
5. Physical Education is part of a lifelong aspiration to be physically active. If we put kids in categories then how can we hope to encourage them, as losers, to continue to be active?
6. We need to rethink our relationships with one another, and the whole notion of survival of the fittest in Physical Education seems very outdated.

Imagine the scene

The children prepare for a sprint race but instead of knowing who will win they are excited by the ambiguity of the outcome. The last time they ran Sophie won, but since then they have been working in their teams on sprint starts and they don't know who will win now. Besides, this is just one of five races for the team trophy and every one of the students might have improved enough to win the race. What's more they are not just being judged on their time or finishing position but also on how much they have improved.

'On your marks!'

The runners move forwards and get into the sprint start position. None of them even tried this in the first race, so that could make a difference. They have also worked on different aspects of their running, so it could be anything that tips the balance, and this is why they're excited.

'Get set!'

Silence descends but the rumble of butterflies in every tummy is almost audible. No one can predict the result and everyone is excited for his or her group mates.

'Go!' The race – in its true sense – is underway.

Cooperation as an integral facet of competition

When arguing for a more cooperative approach to teaching and learning in Physical Education and youth sport we're frequently asked why we need a specific pedagogical model or models-based approach to achieve something that competitive games – team games in particular – already do on their own. When we reply and ask the same people to define the concept(s) at the heart of competition they frequently answer 'winning and losing'. When then asked to explain why, they reply 'it just IS.' As, if not more, frequently we are told that children need to learn how to win and lose because life is a competition and they need to get used to that. There seems to be a commonly held, perhaps near universal, belief that life is harsh and if you're not winning then someone else is – survival of the fittest and all that other stuff.

One of the core problems that we (as academics and former teachers, alongside (we believe) many of our colleagues researching and writing about Physical Education and sport, and many of our students both past and present) see is in the equation that dominates Physical Education, sport, and physical activity:

$$\text{Competition} = \text{Winning and Losing}$$

This equation is missing all of the 'bits' that teams games are expected to do – the bits, in our opinion, that Cooperative Learning does so well. In other words, the 'character building' and 'team building' traits outcomes that are reported to emerge from games – that is, the good stuff. As practitioners we are often blinded to the gap that exists between the idea of competitive team games and the practiced reality, and we speak from our own personal experiences as teachers and coaches.

The reality is, 'we' often see competition as winning and losing in which displays of power, dominance, and control prevail (Harvey & O'Donovan, 2013). We may argue that we see it as cooperation among teams and between teams, between individuals who are united in pursuit of personal achievement and who use different tactics and strategies to achieve their aims, but this isn't always born out in our practices. Furthermore, if you ask those around us – administrators, colleagues, and parents – they would, in all probability, use a cliché like 'winning and losing is part of life and therefore must be part of school and growing up'. You only have to scour the Internet or walk around the touchline of any mini or junior practice or match to see examples of this idea being played out. The motivational quotes we see on office walls or Physical Education flyers are enough to show us the ways, as a society, we have bought into the ideas surround winning and losing.

If we're honest about the games we play and the activities we pursue they are all pretty silly in and of themselves. Why would you look to run two laps of a 400-meter track to get to a finish point when the shortest route is across the middle? And, having agreed on those rules, why would you cheat? Why would you spend five days playing a game of cricket only to decide on a draw? Who in their right mind would consciously walk five hundred meters, carrying a bag of clubs and trying to put a tiny white ball in a hole nearly as tiny in the middle of a well-manicured field and then repeat it 18 times?

None of these examples are the easiest way of achieving these objectives. We could, for example, just walk to the hole and deposit our ball – a 'hole in one' every time. Although, in many respects why would we want to do that? It's almost as silly, if not sillier than, the club-wielding, ball-hitting version we call golf.

Don't get us wrong. We like golf, but when we agree to play 'a round' we also agree to play by the rules. We agree that we will play from tee to hole. We agree that we will cooperate with each other; take our turn; congratulate each other on a good shot and commiserate each other on a bad one. We agree to look for lost balls and keep an accurate score card and count every shot – even those that connect with nothing but air. And yet, in the equation above, we lose much, if not all of this in our pursuit of winning and not losing.

Equally we lose these facets of game play in Physical Education and youth sport when we assume the character building qualities of sport and physical activity are being developed even when focusing exclusively on winning and not losing. When our programs revert to winning and losing as 'THE' outcome at the expense of the game or activity and its broader facets, and when skill is valued over cooperation, we fail to make the wider qualities of sport and physical activity explicit.

We see this in the way that particular forms of sport (e.g. invasion games) and particular sports (e.g. volleyball, basketball, rugby, handball, American football, baseball, soccer, and track and field) are privileged over other forms of sport and/ or physical activity (e.g. dance, swimming, martial arts, and recreational/lifetime activities). We see this when there is what Harvey and O'Donovan (2013) referred to as 'a "hardening" of a hierarchy of activities well established with Physical Education which continue to feature sport and competitive games at the apex'

(p. 768). We see this in the million-dollar varsity football and basketball programs in the USA and the school scholarship programs in English, Australian, and New Zealand public/private (i.e. fee paying) schools. We see this in national curricula and school curricula when they repeat and reuse the same list of activities and the same timetables year on year.

This chapter looks at ways in which Cooperative Learning can supplement, enhance, and even replace the competition equation that prevails. That is not to say that we see competition as a bad thing – it's just that we see it as an immature and underdeveloped thing in its current (and dominant) guise. Consequently, this chapter explores ways in which we can allow competition to survive in a fuller form and how we can make the cooperative aspects of competition more meaningful to our students' learning and development. We do this specifically by looking at two Cooperative Learning Structures, Learning Teams and Team Games Tournament (TGT), and using them to rethink our traditional teaching of Physical Education.

Learning Teams

Learning Teams (Dyson, Linehan, & Hastie, 2001) is the most popular Cooperative Learning Structure (at least according to a recent review of literature on Cooperative Learning research (Casey & Goodyear, 2015)). It is based on Student Teams-Achievement Divisions (Slavin, 1980) and Learning Together (Johnson et al., 1994). We explored STAD in Chapter 8 but it is safe to say that the key concepts of 'learning together' underpin much of what is discussed in this book. With particular reference to Learning Teams, Johnson et al.'s (1984, p. 35) idea that learning together helps students in a number of ways seems key:

> Contributing ideas, asking questions, expressing feelings, actively listening, expressing support and acceptance (toward ideas), expressing warmth and liking (toward group members and group), encouraging all members to participate, summarizing, checking for understanding, relieving tension by joking, and giving direction to the group work.

Dyson and Grineski (2001) envisioned that learning teams would give students the opportunity to lead and share leadership with their group mates, take on roles with unique responsibilities, and use collaborative skills to achieve group goals. As part of the Learning Teams approach students take on two types of roles. First they are positioned as performers (as they would be in any traditional Physical Education lesson) and secondly they adopt roles such as recorder, encourager, coach, and equipment manager. For example, the recorder might be responsible for recording everyone's attendance, the number of attempts he or she makes, and/ or their final scores. The encourager would be high fiving his or her group mates, congratulating them on successful attempts, consoling them when things didn't go well, and generally being a positive influence for the group. The coach would lead the session planned by the teacher or the group and would use his or her under-standing of the intended learning outcomes to steer and guide the group in their actions. The equipment manager would collect and return the group's folder and take responsibility for its use in the lesson.

In the past we have used Learning Teams in different ways. They have been successful in tennis, volleyball, handball, and athletics where worksheets and equipment buckets were used, for example, to help the groups. They have also been used successfully with older students where, as the facilitator, we have called over the coaches from each group (while the rest of the group have been involved in a warm-up) and demonstrated the practice we would like them to do with their groups. Both of these approaches ensure that our interactions, as teachers, fit the Cooperative Learning rather than the traditional expectations that Johnson et al., (1984, p. 10) had for learning together (see Table 10.1).

The big question is, 'How do Learning Teams work?' In the example below we follow (and update) Dyson and Grineski's (2001) original explanation of Learning Teams in an effort to provide you with a framework around which to build your first lesson or unit.

How To:

1. Heterogeneous teams of three to five are selected and roles (other than that of performer) are given to or selected by the students. NB (note well): The roles 'other than that of performer' are fantastic because they ensure (as Ash often says) that there are no non-participants in a lesson, only non-performers. So any child who can't physically take part in Physical Education is actively involved from the start.

TABLE 10.1   What's the difference between Cooperative Learning and Traditional Learning groups? (Adapted from Johnson, Johnson, & Holubec 1994)

Cooperative Learning groups	Traditional Learning groups
Positive Interdependence	No interdependence
Individual Accountability	No Individual Accountability
Heterogeneous	Homogeneous
Shared leadership	One appointed leader
Shared responsibility for each other	Responsibility only for self
Task and maintenance emphasized	Only task emphasized
Social skills directly taught	Social skills assumed and ignored
Teacher observes and intervenes	Teacher ignores group functioning
Groups process their effectiveness	No Group Processing

2. As the teacher you provide an explanation, and/or a demonstration of a skill, practice or task, and then check for student understanding. This can be done through a teacher demonstration or a worksheet. Just remember that you are aiming for shared responsibility, student leadership, and a classroom where you observe and intervene, so don't take on too much of this task directly – at least not in front of the whole group. Remember, we're not looking for the 'sage on the stage' but the 'guide on the side'.

3. You describe the outcomes you aspire to (both academic and social) and help the students to understand the physical, cognitive, social, and/or affective skills you would hope to see when the group achieves their goal. These can be listed on a task sheet for the recorder to note or the encourager to shout out about.

4. Watch carefully for students doing their roles. For example, because you want the coach to provide specific feedback to the group members to improve their performance, you would listen out for this. If they get it right then encourage and congratulate them. If they don't, however, remember to talk to them individually. It's important that you don't undermine them. Other examples of roles that Dyson and Grineski (2001) suggested were that the student in the role of checker is asked to check that every student completes the task; the recorder records each student's performance on a task sheet; the demonstrator demonstrates the task; and the encourager encourages everyone to be involved.

5. Students carry out their assigned role during the task but these are not permanent and roles can/should be changed for the next task, so as to allow all students to attempt each role. In early lessons we feel that it is best to rotate the roles as this gives everyone a chance to try everything and stops certain children from commandeering what they see as the key (or at least the most recognizable) role of coach. In later units, as their confidence grows, you might allow students to select the roles to which they feel they are best suited. Just watch out for any child who might look to dominate or those too shy to ask.

6. Group members should assess each other on a skill or tactical practice using a task sheet. You shouldn't assess them yourself. You might (and probably will) keep your own records but don't make them public (at least not during the lesson). You need to give the students the chance to be leaders and you need to afford value to their new roles. If you override their decisions or correct them publically then you will undermine them (both in the short and long term) and other students will keep coming to you for help and advice because they don't trust their group mates. Why should they? You don't.

7. Remember to allocate time towards the end of the session for Group Processing. This time will allow the students to talk about their skill or tactical practice, their successes and failures, and set goals for the next lesson.

Example activity: the relay baton changeover in a 4x100-meter relay (track and field – what would be called athletics in the UK). In their groups/teams students are assigned roles and then asked to think of possible ways of exchanging in the relay. The objective is a safe exchange that doesn't slow the speed of the baton and which occurs in the 20-meter exchange zone. NB: the exchange zone is preceded by a 10-meter acceleration zone (for the receiver) and this should be accounted for in the student's thinking. Possible feedback/learning questions/prompts are:

1. Which hand will you pass/receive the baton with/in? Should these be the same or different?
2. How long does it take for you to match the speed of the incoming runner? And why is it important that you do?
3. You can use the acceleration zone to get up to speed but the exchange must take place in the 20-meter zone.

(These questions/prompts are listed on a task sheet).

Each student individually thinks through the scenario and comes up with their own solution. Group mates then share ideas. As a group they now try out each group member's idea. Students then choose the best tactic for their group. This might be a mixture of different students' ideas. Each group of students then races against another team to use their tactic in a modified relay situation. At the end of class students discuss their tactics in a Group Processing session facilitated by their teacher.

If at any stage the groups look like they are struggling then call the coaches in and give them some ideas. Given recent leaps in mobile technology you might show them a video (https://www.youtube.com/watch?v=VVeM508Ds10) or provide a link to a website (try this: http://www.wikihow.com/Run-a-4X100-Relay). Of course, you might demonstrate different types of exchange yourself but we wouldn't necessarily do this as our default options; but you know your students best and you should always do what works best for them.

Of all the hundreds of structures available to teachers, the Learning Teams structure has proven very popular in the Physical Education research. Its flexibility and ease of use have seen it used in multiple activities. We have used it in team games, athletics, aquatics, and aesthetics but are confident that it could be used in almost anything. That said, it's not the only structure, not by any means, and in the next section we will explore another structure that could be used in Physical Education.

Team Game Tournaments

A Team Game Tournament (TGT) is organized in a similar way to many other Cooperative Learning Structures, but most particularly STAD (Student Teams-Achievement Divisions), which we explored in Chapter 8. The idea of STAD, if you recall, is that once students are divided into their heterogeneous teams they engage in a group practice and then complete an assessment. The same happens in TGT. Unlike STAD, however, the scores in TGT are ranked and then compared to the corresponding ranks from every other team. Not only does this set up a personal and peer-group benchmark, it also allows every member of the team to potentially score points for their team and thus contribute to the team's success. In other words, it isn't one winner that emerges but a team that needs to work together to succeed.

Once the initial assessment is undertaken then the teams work as individual teams to improve their combined and individual assessment scores. Because each team is working in isolation from the others, and because the students can't see the improvement that others are making, they are encouraged to work as hard as they can to improve their scores. The students know the difference at the first assessment point between the teams and the different ranks and should be made aware that small gains in individual performances can be significant in the final assessment.

Once the team-led practice time has finished there is a second assessment point and points are awarded in the same way. Bonus points could be awarded for big gains in performance and/or for positive attributes such as team cohesion, cooperation, support, etc. Because there are multiple mini competitions contributing to the overall team competition, it ensures that everyone contributes to the team's score, and how many times have we seen a league won by a single point!

In the example that follows we show how this might be done in track and field: in this case in sprinting.

The TGT 'Olympics'

Track and field forms a core component of many Physical Education programs around the world. Unfortunately, anecdotal evidence (gathered when we talk to our students, visit schools, and think back on our own experiences as teachers and students) tells us that the most prominent feature of track and field is measuring or timing and the most commonly used bits of equipment are the measuring tape and the stopwatch. Furthermore, as suggested above, success in track and field is defined through competition where winners and losers are crowned. There is little in the way of cooperation or even, sadly, personal development. The limited time in lessons, the large number of students and (in the UK and NZ at least) the need to produce teams for the annual district championships and school sports day (not unlike an intra-mural school Olympics) means that finding the winner outweighs the need to educate and teach everyone and afford them a chance to improve. It also means that learning in track and field is limited to one run (be it sprinting or a middle distance) and/or three throws or jumps in a single lesson. Consequently, there is little or no incentive to do well (at least not for those students outside of the medal places) and improvement often comes as a consequence of maturation and not increased competence.

Even if track and field wasn't so prevalent in schools, sprinting has long been taught. It is one of the key elements in most games and the expression 'there's no substitute for pace' has certainly formed part of our sporting background. The problem is, in terms of a single race, there is only one winner and it is not designed to be cooperative – with the exception of the relay. The question is, therefore, how do you make it cooperative?

First you need heterogeneity in terms of team selection. Odds on you know your students' speed but if not (or if you want confirmation) then videoing a 20-meter sprint by the whole class at the end of the previous lesson will give you the evidence you need to pick teams. Once you've picked them, undertake task 1 in the worksheet (see Figure 10.1). Each group is responsible for recording each member's sprint time over 20 meters and entering it into their team table. A commonly asked question at this point is, 'Won't some children run slower in the first trial so they can make the biggest improvement?' The answer is almost certainly 'yes'. Some will, but big differences in time will be easy to notice and this can help you to discourage such practices in the future. At some point we have to trust our students and they need to learn that they enter into any competition agreeing to 'play by the rules'.

Once task 1 is completed then task 2, 'Same Rank Races', occurs. The idea here is to record the initial times and positions of each runner. This will form the basis of the initial competition but will also give each group a starting point for improvement. It is important that these scores do count for something, otherwise children might opt for slower times and therefore bigger improvements. Therefore, for example, in this case they could count as initial forms of assessment. At every point the students must feel that they are individually accountable for their performance and positively interdependent on one another so that the team can succeed.

Once the 'Same Rank Races' have been run and the initial team competition has been calculated (and the results are known) then the teams work individually to improve their times. Given the short distance of the race, three phases of sprinting will be significant: (a) the start, (b) the pick up (i.e. the first few strides of the race), and (c) the acceleration. Worksheets or demonstrations (as with Learning Teams above) can be provided for each of these phases and teams might work on different aspects simultaneously. It will be important that individual students – with support from their peers – can work on the aspect(s) of the race that will afford them the biggest improvement potential.

Once the practice time has finished then the students rerun the 'Same Rank Races' and the competition is recalculated. With points awarded for improvements (as in a STAD) and for overall positioning both in ranks and between teams, there are multiple ways that students can contribute to the lesson. In this way we rip up the competition equation and see that cooperation is integral to the process and that winning and losing are not the only result. Yes, children still win and lose, but they do it together and their contribution and improvement is measurable alongside their performance.

In both of the examples used in this chapter learning across the four domains is seen as important and physical learning becomes one facet of Cooperative

Task 1: Record each team member's sprint time over 20 m and then rank your team 1–6; 1 = fastest, 6 = slowest time. (Comparisons will be made with later times and dramatic improvements will be noted. So do your best at all times.)

Team member	Time	Rank

Task 2: All team members will now compete against their same rank from other teams, e.g. all 1s will race against the 1s from all four teams.
Rotate responsibilities for the events within your team dependent on your rank number.

	Runner	Starter	Timekeeper	Place judge	Recorder	Team supporter
Race 1	1	2	3	4	5	6
Race 2	2	3	4	5	6	1
Race 3	3	4	5	6	1	2
Race 4	4	5	6	1	2	3
Race 5	5	6	7	1	2	3
Race 6	6	1	2	3	4	5

Record where your team member is placed and the amount of points they receive (this is the job of the recorder) 1st = 8 points, 2nd 6 points, 3rd 4 points, 4th 2 points

	Time	Place	Points
Rank 1			
Rank 2			
Rank 3			
Rank 4			
Rank 5			
Rank 6			
			Total team points:

Task 3: Your aim is to try to beat your team's points and to have a high team improvement score. The winning team is the team that improves the most.

Task 4: Repeat task 2 (same point system)

	Time	Place	Points
Rank 1			
Rank 2			
Rank 3			
Rank 4			
Rank 5			
Rank 6			
			Total team points:

Team improvement score: ....

FIGURE 10.1 Team Game Tournament

TABLE 10.2 Team Game Tournament record sheet

Team	Lane 1 (5m) team representative		Lane 2 (6m) team representative		Lane 3 (7m) team representative		Lane 4 (8m) team representative		Lane 5 (9m) team representative		Team's total points
	Time	Points	Time	Points	Time	Points	Time	Points	Time	Points	

5 points 1st place; 4 points 2nd place; 3 points 3rd place; 2 points 4th place; 1 point 5th place Rota: Race 1- T1 = run T2 = start T3 = time T4 = record (move up the order began, e.g. T1 moves to start, T4 moves to run)

Learning lessons. Students are not forced to compare their performances with those of others and repeatedly see a gulf between winning and losing but instead see competition as a holistic and social process to which everyone contributes.

Self-processing / A time to reflect

Self-processing questions

1. Think about which equation you might apply to competition. Is it Competition = Winning and Losing?
2. Do you feel that Physical Education teaches things like leadership and teamwork? We have found that it does, but only when you make these outcomes explicit, set goals, and do not simply expect them to happen.
3. Changing up the way children and adults view competition is not an easy process but teams that work together and contribute ideas, who support and accept others and their ideas – indeed, do all the things that Johnson et al. (1984) suggested – do better. Do you agree with the experts Johnson et al.?

Our reflections

Ben

Competition is a part of our lives whether we like it or not. But that doesn't mean we need to get sucked into the Vince Lombardi mentality, 'Winning isn't everything, it's the only thing.' Competition isn't bad, it's how we use it in our teaching and coaching. For students in sport, physical activities, and/or Outdoor Education it's about setting appropriate goals for themselves. However, in Cooperative Learning we add another dimension and that is the social interaction between ourselves and others. We are part of the group, we provide a contribution that no one else has, and when we do that it feels good. In Cooperative Learning we can still be winners but we are assisting the goal shooter or passing to the inside player to shoot, or somehow supporting the completion of the task. And when we are *truly positively interdependent* then that sure does feel good and this can be part of healthy competition.

Ash

For a long time I saw winning as the sole outcome of competition. Changing my own mind wasn't easy, but over a number of years and through research-informed teaching I have come to see that there is so much more to it than being the winner. I was lucky at school I guess because I often finished somewhere near the top of the class in Physical Education, but many of my friends, inevitably, didn't. I wonder what I would have learned had my Physical Education not favored and advantaged me over my peers?

References

Casey, A. & Goodyear, V. (2015). Can cooperative learning achieve the four learning outcomes of physical education? A review of literature. *Quest, 67*(1), 56–72. http://doi.org/10.1080/00336297.2014.984733

Casey, A. & Quennerstedt, M. (2015). 'I just remember rugby': Remembering physical education as more than a sport. *Research Quarterly for Exercise and Sport, 86*(1), 40–50. http://doi.org/10.1080/02701367.2014.977430

Dyson, B. & Grineski, S. (2001). Using cooperative learning structures in physical education. *Journal of Physical Education, Recreation & Dance, 72*(2), 28–31. http://doi.org/10.1080/07303084.2001.10605831

Dyson, B., Linehan, N. R., & Hastie, P. A. (2010). The ecology of cooperative learning in elementary physical education classes. *Journal of Teaching in Physical Education, 29*, 113–130.

Harvey, S. & O'Donovan, T. (2013). Pre-service physical education teachers' beliefs about competition in physical education. *Sport, Education and Society, 18*(6), 767–787. http://doi.org/10.1080/13573322.2011.610784

Johnson, D. W., Johnson, R. T., Johnson-Holubec, E., & Roy, P. (1984). *Circles of learning: Cooperation in the classroom.* Alexandria, VA: Association for Supervision and Curriculum Development.

Johnson, D. W., Johnson, R. T., & Holubec, E. (1994). *Cooperative learning in the classroom.* Alexndria, VA: ASCD.

Slavin, R. E. (1980). Cooperative learning. *Review of Educational Research, 50*(2), 315–342. http://doi.org/10.3102/00346543050002315

11

HOW COOPERATIVE LEARNING IS RELATED TO THE DIFFERENT CONTEXTS FOR LEARNING: WORKING WITH PERSONS WITH DISABILITIES AT THE MIDDLE AND SECONDARY LEVEL

Chapter overview

This chapter explores the potential utility of Cooperative Learning as a pedagogical model for persons with disabilities at the middle and secondary levels. In Chapter 7 we argued that Cooperative Learning can be used as a teaching tool to foster social interaction between *all* students to create a truly inclusive learning environment. Using specific examples from research currently being conducted in the UK, Australian, and US contexts we highlight how preparing for and implementing Cooperative Learning in a secondary school inclusive Physical Education class can either promote or discourage interactions (Dowler, 2012; Grenier & Yeaton, 2012). Specifically the chapter discusses the use of Cooperative Learning in the creation of an inclusive Physical Education class.

We believe that

1. Disability does not equate to a lack of ability.
2. Ability is a dynamic rather than a static concept.
3. Neither teachers nor students should allow (or be allowed) to exclude anyone just so they can play the games they want to play.
4. Students should never be segregated or excluded from Physical Education and youth sport because they 'fall outside' of our perceptions of 'normal'.
5. There must be a commitment to removing all barriers to the full participation of everyone as equally valued and unique individuals.
6. A disabled person and/or the learner with 'special educational needs' labels should not have to merely 'fit in' to pre-existing structures, attitudes, and an unaltered environment.
7. Disabled people should not be forced to lead a separate life from their peers in education or society.

Imagine the scene

Jack MacDonald has been at the Ashville High School for four years and, truth be told, he spent the majority of his PE lesson in the library. His teacher didn't really know how to include him in the lessons and it was easier to keep the majority of the students active than modify or adapt what was planned and risk losing the rest of the class. So Jack went to the library. Jack knows his parents had hoped things would get better but year on year the same activities were taught – activities that weren't suitable to a student in a wheelchair – and so Jack came to know Mrs. Tarter and the Dewey decimal system rather than Mr. Roper and cardiovascular endurance.

That was last year, though. When Mr. Roper retired Mr. Fell arrived, and his approach to PE was very different. First he insisted that there be no non-participants in his lessons. Second, rather than send Jack to the library he brought him to the center of the classroom. His peers were asked to get to know Jack and devise ways of including him. Volunteers were sought (and found) who would work with Jack. There weren't many at first because the students had never worked with Jack (or anyone like Jack) before. Eventually everyone was involved. The students and Mr. Fell quickly got to know what Jack could already do and what he couldn't and began to understand what his real (and imagined) limitations might be. Basketball hoops and modified equipment that the children built themselves were frequently used in PE and the tasks they did were about everyone succeeding (including Jack). The students had quickly found that Jack was a great observer and had a keen analytical mind and he could build stuff that helped them all to understand. He saw mistakes before anyone else and was great at explaining things.

Truth be told, Jack doesn't have to adapt to PE (or the library) anymore because it adapts to him. He has made new friends and is even joining a wheelchair basketball team. He gets to practice with his friends because that's what they play now in lessons and he is one of the most able in the class. He still sees Mrs. Tarter but mainly when she comes to see him play rather than when he arrives at the library for his 'PE' lesson. He doesn't miss Mr. Roper at all but he would miss PE if he weren't included.

Rethinking ability and talent

One of the big problems in Physical Education and youth sport is the way we view ability and talent and, contrariwise, how we view disability and talentlessness. Talent and ability seem to equal performance and there seems to be a certain inevitability of 'talent' and 'talentlessness' (Evans, 2004; Fitzgerald, 2005). When ability and talent are measured in terms of young people's aptitude in playing traditional sports then ability and talent become fixed and only those who match the specific criteria of specific activities will ever be deemed as talented or possessing ability (Evans, 2004).

When using Cooperative Learning, and when including learning in the physical, cognitive, social, and affective domains (Casey & Goodyear, 2015), we are seeking to look beyond these well-establish notions of talent and are trying instead to develop the hidden potential of students. Instead of reinforcing the idea of ability we need to find new ways of understanding what our students are capable of achieving. Unfortunately the construction of 'ability' and its use as the benchmark of achievement are so ingrained that they operate at a core and unchallenged level in sport and Physical Education. To bypass and move beyond this we need to make a conscious and deliberate effort to change the way in which we teach.

One of the key obstacles lies in the ways we use 'dis' and 'less' to describe those who lack ability and talent or who present particular 'challenges' (Evans, 2004; Fitzgerald, 2005). Such students can become defined by their (dis)ability or talent(less)ness and their identity in all things becomes one of 'dis' or 'less'. Consequently they become labeled as deficient and this label subordinates them in respect to their peers (Grenier & Yeaton, 2012).

Only by making ourselves (as pedagogues) aware of our practices, our precon-ceptions, and our assumptions can we begin to challenge them and then operate beyond them. These are not challenges that relate only to disabled students but to any students whose experiences have been decided because of the 'ability' they possess and the ways in which, as educators, we determine what they are capable of achieving (Evans, 2004; Fitzgerald, 2005). This is particularly important given the widely expressed, yet unsubstantiated, opinion that we live in a time of inclusion and equity (Fitzgerald, 2005).

It could be argued that we live in a time when society increasingly talks of inclusion. However, this has only improved things at a superficial level (Fitzgerald, 2005). Until we can move beyond deep-seated ideas of what it is to be normal and what ability and talent are and how they are defined, then those who are disabled will have a difficult time. They are unlikely to be 'able to work towards, or achieve, a level of competence recognized as reflecting a "good" performance' (Fitzgerald, 2005, p.50) and therefore they are destined to fail and suffer exclusion and derision as a consequence of something that is beyond their ability to control. In short, they fail before they even enter the gymnasium or sports field and before they've ever had a chance to succeed.

This almost predetermined acceptance that people with a disability will fail is only reinforced by our behavior. Fitzgerald (2005) argued that any student, and not just those who were disabled, could publically be humiliated with exasperated moans of 'Aw Sir, do we have to?' or 'No way are we having him' before the indignity of being allocated to a random team like 'a spare piece of luggage that no one can be bothered to carry' (p. 43). Yes, kids can sometimes be mean, but somewhere in every lesson is a teacher allowing this to happen.

There are other ways, however, of excluding disabled students in an apparently integrated classroom. When peers refuse to interact with disabled students (by not passing to them, for example) then they purposefully exclude them and don't allow them to interfere with the game. This peer-driven exclusion, alongside the lack of cooperation and affiliation, are clear when you see a lesson where participation isn't equal and where the most able clearly dominate all aspects of the game.

As a consequence of such peer-driven exclusion, and a lack of cooperation and affiliation, quality Physical Education that makes a difference to children's 'ability' is lost and 'ability' is not seen as a problematic concept (Evans, 2004). Ability seems to be fixed and teachers compensate for individuals (or it could be argued that they teach to the middle level of ability and don't compensate) rather than seeing 'ability' as a 'dynamic process'. At present 'ability' is seen as a form of 'physical intelligence' – a 'God-given, homogenous, immutable construct – that separates the able from the less able. It allows PE to show when children have reached or surpassed their potential but not when PE has surpassed its role in education' (Evans, 2004, p. 71). What we argue in this book and in this chapter is that we need to rewrite these definitions and find ways for every child to be included and thrive.

Inclusion – not integration, segregation, or exclusion

Inclusion is an aspiration for all teachers and coaches and yet we're often caught between conflicting agendas. We've talked in previous chapters about the different 'responsibilities' that fall on the Physical Education teacher and the sports coach. Pedagogues, in whatever guise they take, have multiple roles to play, be it match and trophy winning coach, provider of the next world champion, solver of the obesity epidemic, or community developer. And yet, amidst all these other agendas, *the individual child* is being lost both as a person and as a decision maker.

At the heart of educational discussions is the 'dilemma of coupling the concept of equality with the need for efficiency' (Grenier & Yeaton, 2012, p. 120). How do we balance all of the agendas above and still provide equality? One of the problems is that society has seen differences as deficits and used teaching strategies that isolate individuals with disabilities. There are, and have long been, accepted courses of action for students with disabilities (Grenier & Yeaton, 2012). Indeed, we work in systems that see any disability as a 'failed human condition', and that 'people with disabilities are viewed as deviations from the norm especially when physical or psychological dispositions fall outside established codes of behaviour' (Grenier & Yeaton, 2012, p. 120).

In the euphoria that surrounded and followed the London 2012 Olympics and Paralympics much was made of the respective successes of each event. Never before had a Paralympics been so popular and there were repeated calls for a meaningful and sustained participation 'legacy' (especially in the UK) to follow on from both events. Yet less than a year, later Baroness Tanni Grey-Thompson (an eleven-time gold medal-winning Paralympian) was accursing the British Government of failing disabled children because many mainstream schools did not know how to teach sports to disabled children.

> Still an awful lot of disabled children are sent to the library because teachers don't feel equipped or able, in many cases, to integrate them properly into lessons.
>
> *(Grey-Thompson, in Silverman, 2013)*

Consequently, students are segregated or excluded from 'normal' Physical Education and youth sport experiences because they 'fall outside' of our perceptions of 'normal' and because, as educators or as an education system, we are challenged or, perhaps, suffer from a 'failure of imagination' (MacIntyne, 1999, p. 75) when it comes to inclusion.

One of the best visual representations we have seen to explain the key concepts in this debate can be seen in Figure 11.1. We would like to be able to credit this diagram to the author(s)/artist(s) but have been unable to do so. It appeared on Ash's Twitter feed and we haven't been able to authenticate a source. However, it serves as a stark illustration of what we should aspire to and yet often fail to achieve and for that we are grateful to the unknown creator(s).

Fundamentally everyone deserves access to the same experiences, and yet education has been slow in realizing this aspiration. In trying to explain the differences that we see between these four ideas we have drawn heavily on the work of The Alliance for Inclusive Education (The Alliance for Inclusive Education, 2015) around inclusion and the Joseph Rowntree Foundation's (Osler et al., 2002) work with girls and exclusion. Table 11.1 shows their aspirations and hopes for inclusion and defines the realities they perceive with the other terms.

Considering what we have already explored in this chapter, and in applying these definitions and aspirations for Physical Education and youth sport, then we might (and probably should) argue that many of the things we 'do' at best integrate and at worse segregate or exclude some young people from Physical Education. The Centre for Studies on Inclusive Education (Centre for Studies on Inclusive

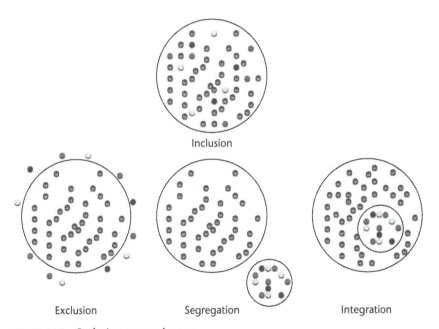

Inclusion

Exclusion   Segregation   Integration

FIGURE 11.1   Inclusion versus the rest

TABLE 11.1 Definitions and aspirations for inclusion

Term	Definition/aspiration
Inclusion	Disabled people of all ages and/or those learners with 'Special Educational Needs' labels being educated in mainstream education settings alongside their nondisabled peers, where there is a commitment to removing all barriers to the full participation of everyone as equally valued and unique individuals. For example: Education for ALL (The Alliance for Inclusive Education, 2015)
Integration	Disabled people of all ages and/or those learners with 'Special Educational Needs' labels being placed in mainstream education settings with some adaptations and resources, but on condition that the disabled person and/or the learner with 'Special Educational Needs' labels can fit in with pre-existing structures, attitudes, and an unaltered environment. For example: The child is required to 'fit in' to what already exists in the school. (The Alliance for Inclusive Education, 2015)
Segregation	Disabled people of all ages and/or those learners with 'Special Educational Needs' labels being placed in any form of segregated education setting. This tends to force disabled people to lead a separate life. For example: Separate special school, college or separate unit within school/college or on separate segregated courses within mainstream education settings. (The Alliance for Inclusive Education, 2015)
Exclusion	The definition of 'exclusion from school' … goes beyond the 'physical' and 'formal' definitions that tend to focus on school procedures and classroom management issues. [Students] may become excluded from school either officially or unofficially. Those who have disengaged from learning are effectively excluded, whether or not they have drawn attention to their needs through behavioural problems. (Joseph Rowntree Foundation, 2002)

Education, 2015) suggests that there are a number of ways of foregrounding inclusion in education. We don't have space here to explore them all but have selected a few for the purpose of this book and our focus on Physical Education. This is not a hierarchical list (and in some ways it might be considered as a list of convenience) but it hints at what is involved when we wish to foreground inclusion in education:

- putting inclusive values into action;
- supporting everyone to feel that they belong;
- reducing exclusion, discrimination, and barriers to learning and participation;
- restructuring cultures, policies, and practices to respond to diversity in ways that value everyone equally;
- learning from the reduction of barriers for some children to benefit children more widely.

Currently, and with our focus not only on ability and disability but also on physical prowess, we are failing to put our inclusive values into action. In the very act of foregrounding success in terms of physically doing something well we immediately make disability a huge negative. For example, imagine if you gave every child in a class a ball of paper. Now imagine you asked them to make a ball and throw it into the waste paper bin at the front of the class. OK, but now you say that they had to do so from the desk at which they were sitting. Now imagine you told them they would be judged from now on based on their ability to succeed in this one task. It didn't matter how much they improved, or how much they contributed; all that mattered was their ability to throw a paper ball into a bin that is located different distances away from each student. Cries of 'that's not fair' wouldn't follow far behind such a statement.

Albert Einstein famously argued, 'If you judge a fish by its ability to climb a tree, it will live its whole life believing that it is stupid.' If we judge children by their ability to perform set tasks in a set way then we condemn them to a life not unlike the fish's. The key, to us, therefore, seems to be in expanding our thinking around inclusion and findings ways of supporting everyone to belong. We don't need to adapt the child to the task but adapt (or scrap) the task for the child. In other words, we need to start out planning with the different children in our classes firmly in our minds. The expression 'they didn't learn it wrong, we taught it wrong' seems to sum this up.

Why is Cooperative Learning suitable?

> The Cooperative Learning Model has been considered internationally as a promising approach for the inclusion of students with disabilities into mainstream physical education classes (Grenier 2006, Grenier & Yeaton, 2012; Nyit & Hsieh 1993).
>
> (cited in Dowler, 2014, p. 19)

Inclusion is a big issue in all forms of education – both formal (i.e. schools) and informal (i.e. youth sport and community programs). That doesn't mean finding a single approach that works, but tailoring what you do to suit the different individuals in your care. In terms of using Cooperative Learning in Physical Education (and as mentioned in Chapter 7), Wendy Dowler (Australia) and Michelle Grenier and Pat Yeaton (USA) have been at the vanguard when it comes to developing our understanding of how Cooperative Learning might be used to support students with intellectual disabilities (Dowler, 2014) and physical disabilities (Grenier & Yeaton, 2012). It is with recognition to them and their work that we move forward in this chapter to describe some ways that Cooperative Learning might be used to shift the structural and attitudinal barriers that exist for students with disabilities in physical education.

Self-made materials as an example of an inclusive form of Cooperative Learning

Alongside Michelle, Wendy, and Pat we've had the opportunity to work with a number of other colleagues from around the world; colleagues who have pioneered the use of Cooperative Learning in Physical Education in many different settings. While we can't draw specifically on everyone's writing for this book we want to use the work of Javier Fernandez-Rio and Antonio Mendez-Gimenez around 'self-made materials' to show how different aspects of Cooperative Learning and Physical Education can be combined to create a more inclusive experience for young people.

The origins of self-made materials come from a very real need to meet the learning needs of students on extremely small, perhaps even non-existent budgets. Poorly financed Physical Education departments and/or youth sport and/or community programs don't lend themselves to expansive or innovative experiences for young people. When this is coupled with the diverse learning needs of students with different disabilities, and the expectation that specialized equipment might solve some of our concerns, then cost becomes a real issue. Indeed, it has been repeatedly argued elsewhere that budgets (or the lack of them) are one of the biggest limiting aspects of change in Physical Education.

Beyond the basic need to have (and therefore build) equipment, self-made materials provide an important educational experience for young people (Fernandez-Rio & Mendez-Gimenez, 2014). Indeed, a second and significant reason for using self-made materials, given the context of this chapter, is 'the search for resources that could fit the needs of all students to create developmentally appropriate equipment (i.e., size, shape and weight)' (p. 29). Thirdly, by designing and building developmentally appropriate equipment (i.e. equipment that the builder and his or her group mates can use in the context of Physical Education) the emphasis is taken away from ability as a physical outcome and focused in many different areas.

Fernandez-Rio and Mendez-Gimenez (2011) report that the outcomes of designing and building self-made materials include the following: they increase students' participation time; they are adaptable enough to fit each student's needs; they are low cost; they promote students' creativity; motivate students; engage students and their families in the students' learning process; and they allow for multidisciplinary projects. But how do they work?

Imagine that instead of simply playing a game the students had to design their own equipment. The very act of building equipment takes the emphasis away from the immediate (and traditional) focus on the game and starts to get students thinking about the different elements of the game that make it playable and fun. If we take, as our example, popular striking and fielding games such as baseball or softball, or alternatives like rounders, cricket, or Danish long ball, then we might start by thinking about the bat we might use. Baseball and softball use a long bat, which is held in two hands and swung horizontally. Rounders uses a smaller bat that is also swung horizontally but held with one hand. Danish long ball uses a round paddle bat, which is swung one-handed. Finally, cricket uses a two-handed bat, which has one flat 'blade' and a separate handle. All of these require participants to think differently about their 'build'.

Let's imagine that we now wish to use this in a lesson (or more probably a unit of work) that includes learners with diverse needs, that is, a physical and/or mental disability, then we might prompt different learners to think about the best-shaped bat they might design for hitting the ball. Weight, length, and width might all be elements that help different learners to eventually succeed in the game. In the sub-sections that follow we will explore some possible self-build projects (see Figures 11.2 and 11.3).

Keeping the students individually accountable and positively interdependent

Fernandez-Rio and Mendez-Gimenez (2014) suggest that it is important to monitor the build process and decide how 'good' the built materials are, i.e. are they too big, small, weak, difficult to use, etc. This is a key element in using self-build materials in your lessons as it ensures that everything is 'fit for purpose'. It also keeps the students 'honest' in their endeavors and focuses on other aspects of physical activity other than who has talent and who's talentless which, in turn, breaks up the normal course of things in Physical Education and youth sport.

In designing their own equipment students are also required to think about what best serves their needs. In helping each other in the build they are also made aware of different people's feelings, their understanding, their aspirations, and their limitations. When young people are presented with a challenge to overcome they are required to think more deeply and to consider others. In a recent piece Casey, Hastie, and Jump (2014) argued that traditional Physical Education teaches children to play the game well. Not playing the game well, they argued, was a bad thing, while playing it well meant that individuals conformed to a tight set of expectations around what it means to be a player. By inventing their own games, the young people involved played the game for appreciation rather than simply for the sake of playing it well (Casey et al., 2014). When these ideas are transferred to inclusion and/or self-made material then the learning outcome for a given session, unit, or season can change.

Think inclusion

It's been noted previously that sticking young people into groups does not make those groups cooperative. Likewise, simply creating heterogeneous groups that place students with learning or physical disabilities alongside students without recognized disabilities does not mean everyone is included. Inclusion doesn't happen by chance but by design. It is a conscious decision. Cooperative Learning is not a pedagogy of performance but is one that, through the combination of social

What do you think the most important elements of designing a bat are? Put the following in order of priority where 1 is very important and 5 is not very important.

	1	2	3	4	5
1. Big hitting surface:					
2. I can swing it with two hands:					
3. I can swing it with one hand:					
4. I can swing it fast:					
5. It is very easy to hit the ball:					

What do you think the consequences are of having a big hitting surface?
What sort of shape allows you to swing the bat faster?
Do you want to hit the ball more often or further?
What factors will help you to succeed?
Now we need to make our bat.

Baseball/Softball bat

Materials: 2/3/4 sheets of newspaper, masking tape
Instructions: Lay the newspaper out with the longest side facing you and start to roll it very tightly. The tighter and more uniform the roll the more solid the eventual bat will be. Once the whole sheet is rolled then use the masking tape to maintain the shape and protect the final bat. Roll a second piece of newspaper, this time with the shorter side facing you around one end of the first role. The idea is to keep one end slightly thinner so it can serve as a handgrip. When the second roll is made use the masking tape to cover the bat again. Once again the tighter the roll the stronger and more robust the ball will be. Repeat the process until you have a bat that is thick enough and heavy enough for your purposes.
Hint: The more cooperative you and your teammates are the more compact the bat will be.

Rounders bat

The process is the same as above, just start with the short side facing you on the first roll and on the second roll fold or cut the piece of newspaper in half.

Danish long ball

Materials: cardboard, newspaper, scissors/cutter, glue, and colored masking tape.
Instructions
For the bat: Draw two identical circles in the cardboard and carefully cut them out. If you want a thicker bat then increase the number of circles you cut. Glue the pieces of cardboard together and then put the colored masking tape around them.
For the handle: Lay the newspaper out with either the longest or the shortest side facing you and start to roll it very tightly. If you want a longer handle then use the longer side and vice versa. The tighter and more uniform the roll the more solid the eventual bat handle will be. Once the whole sheet is rolled then use the masking tape to maintain the shape and protect the final bat.
Joining them together: Lay the circles face down and lay the handle across the back. Then use the masking tape to fix the two together. The more tape you use the more secure the handle will be but the heavier the bat will be.

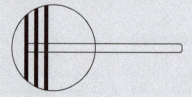

Cricket Bat

FIGURE 11.2 Making a striking and fielding game – bat design task

The process is the same as above, just cut rectangles instead of circles.

Handle paddles

Materials: cardboard, scissors, elastic tape, glue, a stapler, and colored masking tape
Instructions: Trace four circles bigger than your open hand and cut them out. Place your hand on one of the circles and make marks on either side of each finger and on either side of your wrist. Cut open the marks and feed the elastic tape through the slots. Staple the elastic on the other side to the one where your hand is. You should now have finger wrist straps. Glue a second circle on top of the staples and strap up the paddle with tape to keep the two pieces of cardboard together. Repeat for the other hand.

Ball

Materials: plastic shopping bags, masking tape
Instructions: Scrunch/crush/crumple one of the bags into a ball. Then either a) wrap the 'ball' in masking tape to make a small ball or b) wrap a second, third, or fourth bag around the outside. Once the ball is the required size then wrap in masking tape. For a game like softball you might want a bigger ball but for baseball, rounders, cricket, or Danish long ball a smaller one.
Hint: The tighter you scrunch the bag the harder the ball will be.

FIGURE 11.2 (cont'd)

Material: _____
Builder: _____
Evaluator: _____

Check and use the material with your peers. After a few minutes, evaluate it using this scale:

1	2	3	4	5
NO	FEW/LITTLE	SOME	MUCH	VERY MUCH

1. Safety: Is it dangerous?	1	2	3	4	5
2. Robustness: Does it break easily?	1	2	3	4	5
3. Utility: Does it work well?	1	2	3	4	5
4. Adequacy: Is it appropriate?	1	2	3	4	5
5. Aesthetics: Is it designed well?	1	2	3	4	5
6. Effort: Did it take time to build?	1	2	3	4	5

Total score:_____

Observations:

FIGURE 11.3 Self-made material assessment sheet

and academic learning, seeks to promote students' interpersonal skills and their ability to interact and achieve (Casey & Goodyear, 2015). The learning outcomes attributed to the model have been summarized as 'academic achievement (an ability to apply and understand content), interpersonal skill development and relations (communication skills and/or peer relations), enhanced participation (engagement with learning tasks), and an improvement in young people's psychological health (self-esteem and/or motivation)' (p. 57). None of these focuses on ability and all serve as a means through which we might focus on inclusion.

In the examples above we tried to show how by changing the desired outcomes – the whole focus in fact – of a lesson we change what can be achieved. The first decision comes when we create the relationships that exist between the students in our classes, and in Cooperative Learning that means creating opportunities to work together in meaningful ways. Initially there are some extra factors that you need to consider. It is important that as the teacher or coach you choose students who will be supportive of any student with a disability. You need to carefully consider the selection of the higher ability students who have the capacity to interact with the student with a disability and the rest of the group and you need to give all students time to interact and get to know one another. When working towards an inclusive classroom it is often good to think of Cooperative Learning as involving two phases – a preparation phase and an application phase.

In the *preparation phases* students would be given the opportunity to learn social skills necessary to work together, such as active listening, nonverbal communication, how to explain and give feedback, decision making, problem solving, learning group roles, and group bonding activities. After these have been used then the *application phase* can begin. The key is to not try and rush through things but, instead, to realize that inclusion takes time and it requires everyone to think a little differently about learning in Physical Education. It also requires us to think differently about Physical Education and move away from a focus on ability and/ or disability.

Fundamentally, learning outcomes in Physical Education shouldn't be about one type of performance or one conception of ability. It shouldn't be about who's the best or who's the worst but about who's engaged and who's improved. It should be about lifelong learning. Cooperative Learning is not a pedagogical model that endorses and inflates egos but one that embraces mastery – everyone's mastery.

Self-processing / A time to reflect

Self-processing questions

1 Being inclusive is more than fitting students into what we already do. How do we create experiences that suit everyone and their learning needs?
2 It is not as simple as creating a tweak here and there. How can we approach our teaching from a different angle altogether even if it's not so easy?
3 Is it worth it? Hell yes!!! Our work with teachers using Cooperative Learning

shows that, yes, it's different and it takes a little bit of time to 'get your head around it' but it's better than what they did before – better than what we (as the authors) did before.

Our reflections

Ben

We believe that inclusion of all students in Physical Education, coaching, Outdoor Education, or any community-based PA program should be considered normal. Unfortunately, as educators we get distracted by the perceived barriers to the inclusion of *all* when we should be focusing on working with the student and their Cooperative Group to adapt and modify the activity so that *all* students make a contribution to the completion of the task. Cooperative Learning sets this up as a prerequisite. Think about *Positive Interdependence* and *Individual Accountability* – it's not some of the group members that contribute but *all* group members that contribute to the completion of the task or scoring the goal or defending the space from an attack in a game. Let's work towards being inclusive – we can do this!

Ash

Writing this chapter has presented more challenges to me than any of the others because it was an area that was so new to me. Sometimes it is difficult to think outside the boxes in which we find ourselves and to find new ways of doing teaching. It can be a frustrating process, but as I often say to my students, there is no such thing as writer's block, there is only reader's block. You can't write because you don't know enough about what you want to talk about. Put down the pen, step away from the keyboard, and go and explore the world and find something to inspire you. I had to do that with this chapter and now I sit writing this reflection and think, 'That was tough but it was well worth it.' I hope using Cooperative Learning as an inclusive approach to teaching will give you the same satisfaction.

References

The Alliance for Inclusive Education. (2015). Integration is not inclusion. Retrieved May 8, 2015, from http://www.allfie.org.uk/pages/useful info/integration.html

Casey, A. & Goodyear, V. (2015). Can Cooperative Learning achieve the four learning outcomes of physical education? A review of literature. *Quest*, *67*(1), 56–72. http://doi.org/10.1080/00336297.2014.984733

Casey, A., Hastie, P., & Jump, S. (2014). Examining student-designed games through Suits' theory of games. *Sport, Education and Society*, 1–19. http://doi.org/10.1080/13573322.2014.994174

Centre for Studies on Inclusive Education. (2015). What is inclusion? Retrieved May 8, 2015, from http://www.csie.org.uk/inclusion/what.shtm

Dowler, W. (2012). Cooperative learning and interactions in inclusive secondary school physical education classes in Australia. In B. Dyson & A. Casey (Eds.). *Cooperative learning in physical education: A research-based approach*. (pp. 159–165). London: Routledge.

Dowler, W. (2014). Cooperative learning as a promising approach for the inclusion of students with disabilities. *ACHPER Active and Healthy Magazine, 21*(2), 19–24.

Evans, J. (2004). Making a difference? Education and 'ability' in physical education. *European Physical Education Review, 10*(1), 95–108. http://doi.org/10.1177/1356336X04042158

Fernandez-Rio, J. & Mendez-Gimenez, A. (2011). Self-made materials as a resource to enhance the cooperative learning model. Limerick: AIESEP International Conference.

Fernandez-Rio, J. & Mendez-Gimenez, A. (2014). Self-made materials, cooperative learning and games invention: Great combination for physical education. *Active & Healthly Magazine, 21*(2/3), 29–32.

Fitzgerald, H. (2005). Still feeling like a spare piece of luggage? Embodied experiences of (dis)ability in physical education and school sport. *Physical Education and Sport Pedagogy, 10*(1), 41–59. http://doi.org/10.1080/1740898042000334908

Grenier, M. (2006). A social constructionist perspective of teaching and learning in inclusive physical education. *Adapted Physical Activity Quarterly, 23*, 245–260.

Grenier, M. & Yeaton, P. (2012). Cooperative learning as an inclusive pedagogical practice in physical education. In B. Dyson & A. Casey (Eds.). *Cooperative learning in physical education: A research-based approach* (pp. 119–135). London: Routledge.

MacIntyne, A. (1999). *Dependent rational animals: Why human beings need virtue.* Chicago: Open Court.

Nyit, C. K. & Hsieh, Y. T. (1993). *The effects of co-operative learning on teacher-student interactions and peer relationships: A case study of a student with mild intellectual challenges.* Unpublished manuscript. Taiwan Normal University, Taiwan.

Osler, A., Street, C., Lall, M., & Vincent, K. (2002). Girls and exclusion from school. Retrieved from http://www.jrf.org.uk/publications/girls-and-exclusion-school

Silverman, R. (2013). Disabled children 'sent to library' during PE. *Daily Telegraph*, 21 May. Retrieved from http://www.telegraph.co.uk/education/10071489/Disabled-children-sent-to-library-during-PE.html

12

HOW TO ASSESS IN PHYSICAL EDUCATION AND PHYSICAL ACTIVITY SETTINGS

Chapter overview

One of the perennial concerns in education is how to assess students' learning. This is important in an environment where cooperative and team interaction forms the heart of learning. How does the teacher or coach know what a student knows when he or she is always working in a collective or as a team? This chapter explores different ways of assessing students' individual learning and contributions to lessons. Furthermore, it shows how to avoid 'social loafing' and 'ghosting' (ways in which students pretend to be involved but instead rely on the work of others to gain a good grade) and shows how groups can become enthused about assessment and come to see it as a means of showing both the individual's and the group's collective development.

We believe that

1. Assessment in Physical Education is typically weak and erratic, and focused on physical attainment rather than cognitive, social, and affective development.
2. Assessment often occurs in teacher informal feedback and isn't systematic or based on students' attainment across multiple domains.
3. Quality authentic assessment takes time, planning, effort, and persistence.
4. Trial and error with a number of different assessments is a healthy and appropriate approach to teaching.
5. Teachers should work with their students to create different assessments.
6. Cooperative Learning is a pedagogical practice that promotes students to become *individually accountable*.
7. Peer assessments are an integral part of Cooperative Learning as a student-centered pedagogy.

8. We should measure what we treasure rather than treasuring what we measure, i.e. we should only measure what we see as important rather than making it important because we know how to measure it.

Imagine the scene

As you walk into the gymnasium you wonder what's going on. There appears to be little formal structure to the lesson, the students work on what looks like different tasks, and conversations seem to focus on so many diverse areas. At least that's what it looks like at first sight.

As you stand and watch you begin to notice that there is a pattern to the apparent chaos. You are used to watching Cooperative Learning lessons and you are not troubled by the lack of traditional structure (i.e. standing in lines and an emphasis of skills over learning) and are able to look 'beyond' these limited expectations. As you explore the room (both physically and with your eyes) you notice that all of the groups are working on a similar task – a team project – but all seem to have very different outcomes.

The lessons to date have focused on Ultimate Frisbee and as the unit of work draws to a close the students are developing a resource to give to younger students. Each group has been asked to make an electronic workbook that next year's class can use to learn about Ultimate Frisbee. As you watch you can see students debating ideas, drawing diagrams, and taking photographs (of equipment and different skills). You see the teacher circulating from group to group and helping them move their ideas forwards. She is not answering the questions but is scaffolding the students' understanding and encouraging them to think a little deeper.

Introduction

At some point we are asked to assess student learning. In doing this we are asked to create 'windows into students' minds' (Johnson, Johnson, & Holubec, 1994, p. 89) and try to understand what they are thinking and what they understand. In Cooperative Learning, with its emphasis on academic and social skills, we need to find ways of assessing students' academic and teamwork efforts. We need to understand not only skill execution (as an example of an academic outcome in the physical domain) but also leadership and responsibility (as examples of teamwork outcomes). To do this we need to assess not only what students do physically but also what they understand, how they interact, and how they value the learning of the group on a par with their own. This is not an easy task but in the sections that follow we hope to be able to give you some ideas and get you thinking. Before we do though we thought it would be useful to talk a little bit about assessment and how it can be used to create the 'windows' we might ultimately seek. The purpose of this chapter is to present an overview of different assessment pedagogical practices and the types of rubrics that can be used to assess some kind of learning. That learning could be in any of the domains of learning.

Standards-based assessment

In the US there has been a move towards much more standards-based assessment. In keeping with a body of thought that seeks to move the curricula we teach away from a focus on activities, and the associated assessment away from skill development (Lund & Tannehil, 2015), standards-based assessment recognizes the different skills, knowledge, and dispositions that students develop in order to be successful. Put simply, such a move is seen by some as an attempt to explain what schools and teachers should be trying to achieve when they assess in Physical Education if they are to show learning and development and not just skill acquisition (Lund & Tannehil, 2015; Ward, 2013). This represents a move away from testing and towards an emphasis on standards, assessment, and accountability. Such a shift in emphasis finds its origin in the publication of *A Nation at Risk* (Gardner, 1983), a document that indicated that students in the US did not seem to compete academically with students from around the world. The fallout from this, as Ward (2013) argued, is that we now have a strong focus in education on meaningful assessment and not just measurement.

Dyson et al. (2011b) reported that this type of accountability has led to a number of states 'requiring schools to report student progress toward meeting the standards on a state-based report card as a means of informing parents about student performance and for holding schools accountable for student learning' (p. 101). Unfortunately, many other countries have now taken this approach to education, which to varying degrees mirrors the NCLB movement in the US. For example, New Zealand has brought in National Standards for Numeracy and Literacy at the Primary Level. This move takes valuable time and resources away from specialist areas such as the Arts, Music, Health, and Physical Education (Dyson et al., 2011b).

While there has recently been a big shift in assessment policy in the UK, there has been a much less noticeable shift in assessment practice. Prior to the start of the academic year 2014/2015 every child was 'leveled' against a set of national standards and schools were expected to closely monitor each child's 'levels of progress'. Significantly, the government, and its national inspectors (the Office for Standards in Education, or OfSTED), then measured the school against its ability to increase each child's level by the requisite amount. However, in September 2014 that was supposed to change. Leveling was removed and replaced with a number of attainment targets (standards in the US context) against which teachers can plan their curriculum activities. This signified a move away from physical performance as the dominant measure and towards a curriculum that valued what children did, thought, and felt. However, saying that we should be assessing more than just performance has proven much more difficult for teachers to put into their practice. Teachers have been used to leveling for such a long time, indeed many have known no other way of assessing, that schools and consequently Physical Education departments have struggled to make changes. Even though the government has changed its expectations, teachers and schools have struggled to follow suit. Assessment has been about seeing progress (physical) for so long that sometimes we forget that it is also about what we think (cognitive) and what we feel (social and affective).

Assessments should (a) be closely connected to Physical Education pedagogy and must have clearly articulated learning intentions; and (b) be planned in detail; and, once taught, the assessment process should be critically reflected upon to create appropriate learning intentions and improve future assessments. Above all assessment should be seen as a pedagogical tool to enhance students' learning and not just as a tool to measure what and/or if students have learned. It should be both future-/forward-facing (i.e. it should look at where the student is going and how he or she might get there) and past-/backward-facing (i.e. looking at how, what, where, and when students have met and surpassed recognized standards).

One example of an approach to assessment in physical education that seeks to blend many of the aspects we have already talked about is the *PE Metrics* developed by the National Association of Sport and Physical Education's (NASPE) National Assessment Task Force (Dyson et al., 2011a; NASPE, 2010). While it is beyond the scope of this book to discuss *PE Metrics* there are a lot of great resources which the Cooperative Learning teacher or coach can connect with and use.

One aspect of *PE Metrics* we would like to discuss, however, is the Pedagogical Cycle of Assessment (see Figure 12.1), which was designed to assist teachers in their assessment process. In *PE Metrics* the Pedagogical Cycle of Assessment was promoted as a cyclical process of assessment (Dyson & Williams, 2012) that was proposed as a way for teachers to understand the complex process of assessment. Teachers were encouraged to think of assessment as a recurring process of inquiry while acknowledging that quality assessment takes a great deal of time for the trial and error of assessment and reflection on their students' progress to occur. The teacher is encouraged to create learning intentions, followed by planning the content, followed by teaching the content, followed by assessment of content, followed by reflecting, and then consequently creating new learning intentions for their students.

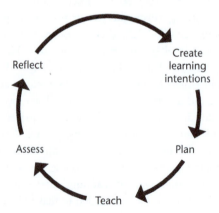

FIGURE 12.1 The Pedagogical Cycle of Assessment

Different types of assessment and assessing for what is important

There are also more things to assess than physical performance. Throughout this book we have talked about different domains of learning, i.e. physical, cognitive, social, and affective. Furthermore, and as we argued previously, 'our vision of Cooperative Learning in physical education moves group work from the random and short term associations commonly formed in the gymnasium … towards a state of "social interdependence" that is developed in a structured and purposeful manner' (Dyson & Casey, 2012, p. 172). Physical Education should not be just about working toward individual performance targets but also about how individuals interact and support other people. Yet for this to be meaningful and viewed as being important then we need to assess for it. For too long the significance of learning has been decided based on the mantra, 'Is it on the test?' If we don't assess for it then why would the teacher or students devote time for it? If we assess for 'dressing out' (i.e. getting changed into the correct clothing for Physical Education) but don't assess for learning or group work then what are we saying is important? If we value the five elements in Cooperative Learning then we need to find ways of assessing them.

Johnson et al. (1994) suggested that when assessing for different elements of Cooperative Learning we might adopt a 'Yes' or 'No, start over' approach. In suggesting a yes/no, start-over approach to assessment Johnson et al. (1994) positioned each of the elements as important and therefore encouraged the teacher to not only look for them in both their teaching and their students' learning but to be prepared to start over again if they weren't present. For them it wasn't a case of trying for the elements but (and much like in the pedagogical cycle of assessment above) reflecting on what is achieved in every lesson. They also suggested that assessment should be planned for and should take into account the process of the assessment, the outcomes of the assessment, and the setting of the assessment (Johnson et al., 1994).

In considering the process Johnson et al. (1994, p. 91) believed that 'it's important to focus on assessing the process of learning well to focus on outcomes'. In doing so you continuously improve the process of learning and therefore the quality and quantity of student learning will also continuously improve. The outcomes of learning have (as previously discussed) traditionally been measured in terms of performance-based assessment, but if we are considering other learning outcomes such as cognitive, social, and affective learning then we also need to consider how other types of assessment (maybe the compositions, exhibitions, demonstrations, video projects, surveys, and actual students' performances) might also be used to assess the outcomes of learning. The setting in which the assessment is to take place should be as authentic. It is not enough to simply assess, and consideration should be given to creating lifelike settings for solving real-life problems. Johnson et al. (1994) argue that to conduct an authentic assessment we might set students to work on real-life problems, for example working in research teams to find a cure for cancer. In a Physical Education setting, therefore, you might set teams the challenge of preparing for a 3-mile run or the district or regional championships.

Types of assessment

In considering the process, outcomes, and settings of assessment it is also important to consider the different types of assessment you might use. In what follows we therefore begin by providing some brief definitions around which we can position the examples that follow later in the chapter. There are many different types of assessment (e.g. formative assessment, summative assessment, and authentic assessment; for more details see Lund & Tannehil, 2015), but here we will only address three forms of assessment: formative assessment, summative assessment, and authentic assessment. The intention of formative assessment is to monitor student learning and provide ongoing feedback that can be used by teachers to improve their instruction and by students to improve their learning. Fundamentally, formative assessments are designed to help students identify their individual strengths and weaknesses and figure out areas that need work. Examples of formative assessments might include asking students to (a) create a defensive task to represent their understanding of soccer; (b) identify three learning cues for the forearm pass in volleyball; and/or (c) perform a bench press with safe technique and good form.

The intention of summative assessment is to evaluate student learning at the end of an instructional unit by comparing it against a standard or benchmark. Examples of summative assessments include (a) end-of-unit written or practical exam; (b) completion of a final project like a portfolio, and/or (c) scores on a fitness test. It is important to note that any evidence or information gained from summative assessments can be used to inform future tasks for students or teachers, and their intention should be to guide their future instruction.

Developing the ideas of Johnson et al. (1994) around assessment, Gillies (2007) argues that the more the assessment (be it formative or summative) takes place in 'real life', the more authentic it is. *Authentic* assessment is a form of criterion-referenced assessment intended to assess student learning in a real-life context against specific performance criteria or rubrics (Gillies, 2007). Authentic assessment involves the student, with the guidance of others, selecting pieces of their combined work over a period of time to demonstrate that they have made progress toward their learning intentions. In core subjects, such as Math and Literacy, students will often develop a portfolio or folder of artifacts that are explained as evidence of learning. Authentic assessment in Physical Education is an assessment done in the *real game situation* compared to the traditional isolated skill testing that has occurred in many Physical Education settings. The pedagogical approach for *authentic* assessment is grounded in the content or the context in which the activity occurs as opposed to the traditional idea of testing the skill in isolation. The notion in Cooperative Learning is that students are assessed in a more authentic manner.

That is, as opposed to just regurgitating answers on a test form or preforming a mindless fitness assessment students are often assessing each other using a peer assessment. Often students are part of creating the assessments under the facilitation of their teacher.

To ensure that assessment in Physical Education is authentic it is important that the assessment relates to our aspirations for students both inside and outside the classroom. Authentic assessments might be considered as *non-traditional* (i.e. drawing the cardio workout or weight training task for each workout, creating a poster for stretching, videotaping the correct form for a bench press, and so on). On many occasions this way of assessing allows students to create a performance or product that typically in the US the teacher will have to grade commonly using a rubric. A rubric is a rating scale and list of criteria by which student knowledge, skills, and/or performance can be assessed (Lund, 1992; Lund & Tannehil, 2015). The rating scale could be created to show levels of competence, that is, 1, 2, 3, or 4; or it could have more generally three levels of proficiency: emerging, developing, or proficient.

The form of assessment that we use in this book is an example of ongoing authentic assessment (Lund & Tannehil, 2015; Lund, 1992). These assessments are often qualitative rubrics. In doing so we do not position assessment as a one-off evaluation but rather as a way of gathering information or evidence to best inform better pedagogical practice. These *non-traditional* assessments tend to be more authentic, that is, related to the task or game being played (e.g. a rubric for the correct form for a bench press, a rubric for a poster on stretching, a rubric for a 2–3 minute iPad video on a physical skill, and so on). They also consider the process, outcomes, and setting of the assessment rather than just the need to see a technique or action.

Many of the assessments we describe can be used as peer assessments, either with partners in groups of two or in small groups of students. In peer assessments 'students are asked to consider the level, value or quality of the product produced' (Gillies, 2007, p. 160). 'Peer assessments are most helpful when they provide rich and detailed qualitative feedback' (Gillies, 2007, p. 163). In Physical Education we have known for years that peers learn from being able to assess their own ability and the ability of others' work (Dyson et al., 2010; Dyson, 2001).

Assessment examples

In this section we present some examples of assessments that could be used in Physical Education classes. We start with qualitative rubric rating scales to help you visualize this.

On a rating from level 1 to 4, grade 5 students are assessed for the overhand throw (see Figure 12.2). The competence level in this rubric is set at 3. In other words, if the student can throw with these essential elements then they are considered competent:

Level		Setting – Performs the same skills in a "real-life situation" (√/x)	Assessment
4	Displays all the selected essential elements with fluid motion and differentiated trunk rotation		
3	Throws with selected essential elements: a) Throwing elbow shoulder high, hand back, and side orientation in preparation for the throw b) Trunk rotation with elbow lagging behind hip c) Weight transfer to non-throwing forward foot		
2	Throws with 2 of 3 essential elements		
1	Throws with 1 or no essential elements		
0	Does not complete the assessment task		

FIGURE 12.2   Grade 5 overhand throw

- throwing elbow shoulder high, hand back, and side orientation in preparation for the throw;
- trunk rotation with elbow lagging behind hip;
- weight transfer to non-throwing forward foot.

Importantly, the student has also been asked to demonstrate that he or she can also throw in a 'real-life' context, e.g. to beat a batter to the nearest base (in baseball, softball, rounders, Danish long ball, etc.) (Figure 2.2).

Please note that further specifics for a rubric can be added or modified. This is often based on the content and the developmental level of the students participating. The next assessment refers to students creating a dance using different directional movements, different levels of movement, different non-locomotor movements, and different locomotor movements (Worksheet 12.1).

After the dance is completed the members of the group can assess their own unit performance or that of their group members during the dance (Figure 12.3, p. 170).

Ultimate Frisbee poster

Using the *Team Project* Cooperative Learning Structure (Kagan & Kagan, 2009, p. 135) during a unit on Ultimate Frisbee, Jackson from TK High School asked his grade 10 students to create a group poster. The Team Project is ideal for this undertaking as it was designed to help teams to work together to make a project. Once Jackson had explained the project and assigned roles the students worked

WORKSHEET 12.1   Create your own dance

Individual accountability	Positive interdependence	Interpersonal and small group skills	Face-to-face interaction	Group processing
Learning objective	Create your own dance using different directional movements, different levels of movement, different non-locomotor movements, and different locomotor movements.			
Students' role within the task	Create your own dance in your Cooperative Learning group using Jigsaw as a Cooperative Learning Structure (see Chapter 3 and Chapter 9 for more details). There are four parts to this dance: different directional movements, different levels of movement, different non-locomotor movements, and different locomotor movements.			
Equipment/ pre-lesson tasks	None required. Music optional.			
Task	Task: Create a group dance that uses at least: 1 Two different directional movements 2 Three different levels of movement 3 Two non-locomotor movements 4 Three locomotor movements 5 The creative dance must have a title and music to match the movements.			
Assessment	After the students create and present a creative group dance, the students hand in a written or visual representation of the dance using some dance terms learned in class.			
Rubric	Dance title: Music to match:			

Name:	Direction	Levels	Locomotor	Non-locomotor
Rachel				
Ioane				
Joshia				
Suz				

Students create a dance sequence that is rated a) Awesome or b) Needs some work:

That clearly demonstrates:

1 Two different directional movements
2 Three different levels of movement
3 Two locomotor movements
4 Three non-locomotor movements

together to make the poster. The key aim of project work in Cooperative Learning was that it be representative of the real world. Jackson asked his students how many jobs there are in the world where people simply receive information, memorize

	Awesome	Good	Needs work
Willingly supported other group members			
Made a contribution to the dance			
Could explain the creative dance			
Was able to perform the dance sequence			

Group Member #1: Thomas _____

	Awesome	Good	Needs work
Willingly supported other group members			
Made a contribution to the dance			
Could explain the creative dance			
Was able to perform the dance sequence			

Group Member #2: Maddy _____

	Awesome	Good	Needs work
Willingly supported other group members			
Made a contribution to the dance			
Could explain the creative dance			
Was able to perform the dance sequence			

Group Member #3: Brennan _____

	Awesome	Good	Needs work
Willingly supported other group members			
Made a contribution to the dance			
Could explain the creative dance			
Was able to perform the dance sequence			

Group Member #4: Lily _____

	Awesome	Good	Needs work
Willingly supported other group members			
Made a contribution to the dance			
Could explain the creative dance			
Was able to perform the dance sequence			

FIGURE 12.3 Group Processing dance

information, and then take a test on what they can remember. Instead they engage in teamwork and as such, structures such as Team Project are conceptualized as a way of replicating real life skills.

Task:

Students were asked to describe what they think of Ultimate Frisbee and how to play the game. The students were required to list some Ultimate Frisbee terms and provide comments or pictures of how to play the game. Parts of the poster had to include ways of passing, creating space on attack, using space in defense, teamwork, and learning cues to perform Ultimate Frisbee skills with good form.

For example, the highest scoring rubric level looked like this: The poster uses a number of Ultimate Frisbee terms. Terms are listed or written in short phrases or pictures are labeled. The students demonstrate understanding of Ultimate Frisbee by listing terms and comments or pictures of how to play the game: ways of passing, using space on attack, using space in defense, teamwork, and learning cues to perform Ultimate Frisbee skills with good form. (The Ultimate Frisbee poster rubric is presented in Box 12.1.)

BOX 12.1: ULTIMATE FRISBEE POSTER RUBRIC

Poster element	1 = Proficient 2 = Developing 3 = Emerging 4 = Excellent
Appropriate and accurate details support for each student's: different ways of passing	
Appropriate and accurate details support for each student's: using space on attack or defense	
Appropriate and accurate details support for each student's: teamwork	
Appropriate and accurate details support for each student's: learning cues	
Appropriate and accurate details support for each student's: using space in defense, and learning cues	
All illustrations, photographs, and drawings add to the purpose and interest of the poster.	
The lanague used is easy to understand while using technical langauge.	
Complex ideas are explained using appropriate media (e.g. digrams, pictures, links to Internet resources, etc.)	
Total (Out of 32)	

The Ultimate Frisbee poster is assessed by students, listing terms and comments or pictures of how to play the game, including ways of passing, using space on attack or using space in defense, teamwork, and learning cues to perform Ultimate Frisbee skills with good form (Box 12.1)

Video peer assessment

Students can learn to use an iPad to film their classmates as described in Chapter 7 with Pat Yeaton at North Hampton Elementary using the structure *Rally Coach* (see Chapter 3 for more details). If the teacher or coach wants to use iPads they need to be extremely well organized to avoid large amounts of waiting time. The instructions need to establish routines so that the students do not waste time using the iPad for fun or in an inappropriate manner.

Instructions for videotaping punting a rugby ball could be:

1. Video your group members on an iPad.
2. The video of each student should be no longer than 3 minutes.
3. Your video should be of the student punting a rugby ball.
4. Each member of the group should be assessed on the learning cue rubric.
5. Sign on your task sheet that all members of the group worked to produce the videos and assess each other's form on the rubric.

Group grading in Cooperative Learning

In Cooperative Learning students work with their group mates to complete the task. Group grading in Cooperative Learning should be explained explicitly to students. For example, the group score is a single product. That is, the group

---

BOX 12.2: ASSESSING THE RUGBY PUNT

Punting a rugby ball	Awesome	Good	Needs work
Hold ball at waist level with two hands.			
Drop the ball onto your foot. Do not toss it.			
Contact ball with your shoelaces.			
Step toward target with non-kicking foot.			
Kicking leg follows through to the air.			

Group members sign in:

1.   2.   3.   4.

works to produce a single dance, physical routine, presentation, or task sheet. The product is evaluated and all members receive the score awarded. When this method is used with a task sheet, a presentation, or sets of problems, the group members are required to reach consensus on each part of the task or question and be able to explain it to others. The Cooperative Learning Structure *Numbered Heads Together* is a strategy that can facilitate this process. The discussion within the group enhances the social interaction and problem resolution.

Johnson, Johnson, and Holubec (1994) found that the more frequently students experienced long-term Cooperative Learning experiences (several units of work), and the more Cooperative Learning was used in their classes, then the more likely the students agreed with a group score. Students reported that they believed that everyone who tries has an equal chance to succeed in class, that students get the grades they deserve, and that the grading system is fair. Johnson and Johnson (1999) found that group grades might be perceived to be unfair by students before the students have participated in a Cooperative Learning activity. In our experience, once cooperation has been experienced for some time, however, a single group grade is often perceived as the fairest method of evaluation. Box 12.3 represents a rubric for Group Processing whether the group worked well together.

There are many concepts in Cooperative Learning that teachers find difficult to assess. Here are some suggestions for basic authentic assessment rubrics. These can be a simple rubric to focus on one positive social behavior at a time or a more complicated rubric that can focus on three positive social behaviors, as presented in Box 12.4.

BOX 12.3: DID THE GROUP WORK WELL TOGETHER?

Works with the group all the time	Works with the group some of the time	Works with the group rarely/not often	Is disruptive to the group
Shows patience	Shows impatience at one time	Shows impatience more than one time	Shows impatience frequently
Contributes ideas for modification	Contributes some ideas for modification	Contributes few ideas for modification	Contributes no ideas for modification
Listens to others	Listens to others most of the time	Listens to others some of the time	Does not listen to others
Encourages other group mates	Encourages other group mates most of the time	Encourages other group mates some of the time	Does not encourage group mates

BOX 12.4: POSITIVE SOCIAL BEHAVIORS

Positive social behavior	Always	Sometimes	Rarely/ Not often	Not observed
Work together with their team: Students receive supportive comments from each other, cooperate positively with each other, act in encouraging manner.				
Supportive encouraging of peers: Helping others, positive comments about a play or move, positive pats on the back.				
Starts to act as a leader in groups: Student helps others with skills and tactics. Goes beyond encouraging. Leads others to be better players in skills suggesting offensive and defensive strategies.				
Student comments:				

Social loafing, ghosting, and the competent bystander

Social loafing, ghosting, and being a competent bystander are all terms that describe one type of behavior, that is, non-engagement. *Social loafing* was a term coined to highlight the way in which some people do very little in terms of group work and yet benefit from the hard work of others. This is a trait that is often seen in unstructured group work where groups of people are collectively assessed on a group project. The harder working and collaborative students end up doing the work of the less conscientious students simply to ensure they don't lose marks themselves. *Ghosting* and the Physical Education term *competent bystander*, developed by the qualitative research of Marielle Tousignant (Tousignant &

Siedentop, 1984), are terms that represent the act of looking like you're involved but not actually taking part. The child who stands in the queue with her or his peers but never makes it to the front to take their turn, or the child who takes part in a game but never puts her or himself in a position to make a pass or a tackle, might represent these ideas.

Teachers we've worked with have found that there are strategies to avoid social loafing and ghosting. In fact, we would argue, Cooperative Learning has built in elements to limit or remove the chances that people have to opt out. Some of the most effective strategies are to:

- Put students in small groups, with groups of four (numbers and absenteeism allowing) proving to be the best.
- Keep students in close proximity to each other so they can engage easily in Promotive Face-to-Face Interactions.
- Create a task that requires all students to participate and keep them individually accountable.
- Hold each student accountable for the task through Positive Interdependence and Individual Accountability.

The T-Chart

Peer assessments for the social and emotional domain can be part of the Group Processing session. Students could assess each other to determine if they are: encouraging, helpful, giving appropriate feedback, accepting feedback appropriately, and listening to each other. The questions below could be part of a way of 'checking in' with each other or assessing how the groups are functioning. One question for each lesson would be a good way to start. After the tasks as part of the Group Processing students ask each other:

- Did we provide encouraging comments or actions to each other?
- Did we help each other?
- Did we give feedback to each other in a nice way?
- Did we accept feedback from others without a fuss?
- Did we listen to each other's ideas?

From one of the questions above we have created a T-Chart that we have used in our Cooperative Learning programs (see Figure 7.2 in Chapter 7). The best and most authentic T-Charts are made by the students for the students in their learning contexts. The T-Chart below was made by year 5 students at Papatoetoe South School to assess pro-social behaviors.

The key is to ensure that young people can only succeed if their whole group succeeds, i.e. 'we sink or swim together'. The aim of assessment in this environment, therefore, is to help the group succeed by keeping both the group and the individuals that make up the group accountable for their progress and their

---

BOX 12.5: PROVIDING ENCOURAGING COMMENTS

T-Chart for providing encouraging comments or actions to each other:

Looks like	Sounds like
High five	"You did it"
Pat on the back	"Great pass"
Hand shake	"Way to follow through"

---

contributions. Assessment – formal and informal, summative and formative, but *authentic* – is used to map this process, to guide the learning process and to inform future decisions.

On a cautionary note, however, we must remember that the purpose of assessment is to enhance learning, not test memory. Furthermore, we need to make sure that we use rewards judiciously. Using rewards can provide short-term gains for students. But we must be aware of the traps of too many extrinsic rewards as Kohn (1991) reminds us that intrinsic rewards are far stronger than extrinsic rewards. He argues that '[p]eople who think of themselves as working for reward feel controlled by it, and this lack of self-determination interferes with creativity' (p. 84).

Self-processing / A time to reflect

Self-processing questions

1 What assessment do you currently use in your Physical Education, coaching, or Outdoor Education?
2 What assessment presented in this chapter will you try to use?
3 Will you try authentic assessment even if it takes time, planning, effort, and persistence?
4 Do you have the patience to trial and error a number of different assessments?
5 Can you shift the responsibility to students to create different assessments?
6 Will you challenge yourself to try peer assessment?
7 Are you willing to take up the challenge of group assessments?

Our reflection

Ben

Whether we like it or not the world is moving towards more accountability. We are now seeing standards being assessed in schools, particularly in core subjects such as Math, Literacy, and Science. We have to figure out more authentic ways to assess our learning intentions and more appropriate assessments for our students. We believe Cooperative Learning is a pedagogical practice that helps promote more authentic forms of assessment. Remember one of the key elements of Cooperative Learning is *Individual Accountability*. I do not support standardized assessment in Physical Education but I do think we need to work towards better ways of collecting evidence about what students do in our classes and move towards more *authentic* assessment.

Ash

Assessment is a part of life. We are assessed on our ability to drive by driving. We are assessed on our ability to work as a team by the way in which our team works in real situations. These are authentic real world and real life situations. In Physical Education and community sport we are often assessed on abstract and/or out of context aspects of the game (my least favorite being how well we dribble around a cone). We are also almost exclusively assessed on our physical performance and not on our cognitive, social, and/or affective development. Cooperative Learning provides us with the opportunity to do things differently. When we place value on group work and Positive Interdependence, for example, then so will our students. When we put these things 'on the test' then the students will see the value we place in them. In this way we must assess what we value rather than simply valuing what we assess.

References

Dyson, B. (2001). Cooperative learning in an elementary physical education program. *Journal of Teaching in Physical Education, 20*(August 2015), 264–281. http://doi.org/10.1080/07303084.2003.10608363

Dyson, B. & Casey, A. (2012). *Cooperative learning in physical education: A research-based approach.* London: Routledge.

Dyson, B. & Williams, L. (2012). The Role of PE metrics in physical education teacher education. *Journal of Physical Education, Recreation & Dance, 83*(5), 29–32. http://doi.org/10.1080/07303084.2012.10598777

Dyson, B., Linehan, N. R., & Hastie, P. A. (2010). The ecology of cooperative learning in elementary physical education classes. *Journal of Teaching in Physical Education, 29,* 113–130.

Dyson, B., Gordon, B., & Cowan, J. (2011a). What is physical education in primary schools in Aotearoa / New Zealand? *Asia-Pacific Journal of Health, Sport & Physical Education, 2*(3/4), 5–16.

Dyson, B., Placek, J. H., Graber, K. C., Fisette, J. L., Rink, J., Zhu, W., … Park, Y. (2011b). Development of PE metrics elementary assessments for national physical education standard 1. *Measurement in Physical Education and Exercise Science.*

Gardner, D. P. (1983). *A nation at risk.* Washington, DC: The National Commission on Excellence in Education, US Department of Education.

Gillies, R. M. (2007). *Cooperative learning: Integrating theory and practice.* Thousand Oaks, CA: SAGE.

Johnson, D. W. & Johnson, R. T. (1999). Making cooperative learning work. *Theory Into Practice, 38*(2), 67–73. http://doi.org/10.1080/00405849909543834

Johnson, D. W., Johnson, R. T., & Holubec, E. (1994). *Cooperative learning in the classroom.* Alexandria, VA: ASCD.

Kagan, S. & Kagan, M. (2009). *Kagan cooperative learning.* San Clemente, CA: Kagan.

Kohn, A. (1991). Group grade grubbing versus cooperative learning. *Educational Leadership,* 83–87. Retrieved from http://www.indiana.edu/~tchsotl/part3/KohnGrubbing.pdf

Lund, J. (1992). Assessment and accountability in secondary physical education. *Quest, 44,* 352–360.

Lund, J. & Tannehil, D. (2015). *Standards-based physical education curriulum development* (3rd ed.). Sudbury, MA: Barlett and Jones.

NASPE. (2010). *PE metrics: Assessing the national standards: Standard 1 elementary.* Reston, VA: NASPE.

Tousignant, M. & Siedentop, D. (1984). A qualitative analysis of task structures in required secondary physical education classes. *Journal of Teaching in Physical Education, 3*(1), 47–57.

Ward, P. (2013). The role of content knowledge in conceptions of teaching effectiveness in physical education. *Research Quarterly for Exercise and Sport, 84*(4), 431–440. http://doi.org/10.1080/02701367.2013.844045

13

BEYOND THE BOOK: A GUIDE TO DEVELOPING AND MAINTAINING A COOPERATIVE LEARNING PEDAGOGY IN PHYSICAL EDUCATION AND PHYSICAL ACTIVITY SETTINGS

Chapter overview

This chapter is written as a guide for teachers, coaches, and other educators related specifically to the implementation of Cooperative Learning in their schools or educational settings. Drawing on cutting-edge research (as yet unpublished), it will show how teachers and coaches can begin to adapt the model to their own context and the learning needs of individual learners. For example, drawing on the work of Goodyear (2015) it will show how teachers at a secondary school in the UK initially learned about and adopted the model as a departmental approach to teaching physical education. It shows how they became an award-winning department and role models for other users of the approach.

The chapter outlines a whole school approach to Cooperative Learning from the work of Dyson et al. (2014) from a New Zealand elementary school. This chapter draws on the authors' work in schools and on social media sites and shows how – step-by-step – teachers and coaches can become highly skilled in the use of Cooperative Learning both in their local setting and beyond. It offers some advanced examples of how the model might be used and challenges the reader to make lasting change in their classrooms, schools, outdoor education settings, sport teams, and their communities.

We believe that

1. Cooperative Learning can make a difference in the lives of the learners to develop physical, cognitive, emotional, and social skills.
2. Positive Interdependence can create a mind-set that 'we can sink or swim together'.
3. To implement Cooperative Learning or any innovative pedagogy successfully takes time, effort, persistence, and the help of others.

4. Continuing Professional Development is hard work for teachers, coaches, and facilitators but can have significant benefits.
5. *Teaching as Inquiry* can enable the collection of relevant and meaningful evidence to support and develop the implementation of any innovative pedagogical practice.
6. Critical reflection allows for ongoing growth and development as an educator.
7. Social media can play an important role in teaching and learning in many different settings.

Imagine the scene

You no longer see yourself as the teacher of your classes – at least not in the traditional sense – but instead view yourself as a co-participant or a co-learner in the journey that the young people in your care are undertaking. You feel that your role is not to know everything or to direct kids toward the right answers but is, instead, to be a learning guide on their unique and individual journeys. To do this you immerse yourself in their development and focus on what they want/feel they need to learn.

Entering the room, you see the children disperse to their home groups and begin to engage in their tasks for the day. This is part of a semester-long project and they have been engaging in it across multiple platforms. They are linked with students in different countries and different schools and they use social media outlets and communication technologies (such as YouTube and Skype) to share the work they are doing. You have been gathering resources and making connections for this lesson but know that your place is not to force your ideas on your students but to help them find their own direction. There was a time when you would have told them they were right or wrong and then told them what they needed to do to improve. Those days are behind you now and you feel that there is more to be learned from making a mistake that they can acknowledge themselves than there is from being told what to do.

You are far from idle and you travel the room constantly (both physically and with your senses) yet you don't interject unless you are either invited to or required to for safety reasons. The students know they can ask for help at any time and that you are always there to help if needed. They often seek your advice and they value your contributions but they certainly don't depend on them solely. They see you as a co-learner/co-participant – albeit one with more knowledge and understanding – but a co-learner nonetheless. They know they have taught you things and they also know that they are benefiting from the learning you have undertaken with other classes over the years. Your knowledge has been refined and enhanced across many years of doing this and they appreciate the role that hundreds of your students have played in enhancing their learning.

You see one group engaged in a collaborative meeting via Skype with some students from Spain and you move across to see what is happening. Both of the groups involved in the conversation have been involved in designing their own equipment for a new game they have co-created and they are discussing the various merits of different materials. The language barrier is a bit of an issue but different forms of communication (and Google translate) are helping them to get their ideas across. Your language skills are no better than theirs but you have passed the students a 'vocabulary sheet' that you co-created with Javier on Google Docs before the lesson. He has passed on the same sheet (but from a Spanish language perspective) to his students and the conversation picks up. Moving on, you continue to play a vital, if somewhat peripheral, part in the lesson.

Introduction

For educators to become experts in the use of Cooperative Learning at school, in their districts, in the community setting, and beyond takes a great deal of time, effort, and persistence, as we have found over the years (Casey & Dyson, 2012). We started using Cooperative Learning more than a decade (in Ash's case) or two (in Ben's case) ago and yet we are constantly refining and expanding our practices. We learn from our own use of Cooperative Learning in our daily teaching and in seeing and reading about how others are using it. We don't consider ourselves to be experts and know we have much still to learn. What we do have is a desire to get better at this and a willingness and desire to become co-learners with you in this process. Like the teacher above we have developed international and local collaborations and have a thirst for learning. In working through this book we hope you have developed a similar thirst for learning and an understanding that this is a long-term undertaking.

That is not to say that you can't make rapid progress in your use of Cooperative Learning. This book should act as a resource for you, a support for you to achieve some of your educational goals. Our advice is to start small and set reasonable goals while aspiring big and planning for your use of the model over weeks, months, and years. We encourage you to celebrate your successes, however small, and please share them with us so we can continue to learn. As educators we are often not very patient and we want instant results. We have seen student teachers and established professionals try something new and give up almost immediately because they 'can't do it'. Change is not measured in minutes or hours but in weeks, months, and years. We need to learn to be more patient but at the same time be prepared to put in that big effort and be persistent. Receiving appreciation and support is important for our students, but it is also important for us as educators to receive appreciation and support as well.

As we have said throughout this book, start small and play to your strengths (work with content that you are comfortable with and of which you have high content knowledge). It is also useful to find a friend or collaborator as two minds and two lots of determination can make a real difference. Just like starting up a new fitness program or taking up a new hobby it helps when there is someone to push you along or someone who needs prompting. Often it is easier to let ourselves down than it is to let someone else down. Ben found it useful to think *playfully* and allocate the time for trial and error (Dyson et al., 2004). This shouldn't be too hard or too boring in the first instance. Make it fun for yourself, and the children will see and feel that fun and enjoy themselves all the more as a result. Enjoy yourself and the reworking of your curriculum won't feel like a chore. Remember that sinking feeling when you bite off more than you can chew (you know, the one you get when you set out to tidy the garage or the loft but realize that it was a massive job); you don't want that in your curriculum. Think of change in terms of multiple units and not a single afternoon or lesson and you are at about the right level. Small steps. One piece of the jigsaw at a time. Remember, Rome wasn't built in a day. To keep it manageable we suggest starting small with peer tutoring or Reciprocal Teaching as described in Chapter 6. Or try out some of the same lessons that we have exampled throughout the book. One or two elements at a time and then reflect. Start with a partner activity or one task that is not complex. In Chapter 6 we describe Think-Pair-Share and Reciprocal Teaching; these provide some useful examples, but the book is full of them. So remember:

1. **Play to your strengths**, that is, work with content that you are comfortable with and have high content knowledge of. This is content you have experience with and something you like to teach or coach. Areas of expertise for us would be stretching, middle distance running, volleyball, rugby, cricket, tennis, swimming, kayaking, and hiking.
2. **Find a friend or collaborator to work with**. This may well be a teacher in a different subject area or level. It may be a friend who is an outdoor educator or a colleague who is working in the community. You need a 'buddy'. We have been buddies for several years – colleagues and friends – but we have other buddies who can help us out if needed. You will benefit from having someone who you can work with, someone you trust to share things with, and someone who will provide you critique but not be too hard on you. But that feedback needs to be constructive. We always tell our students to provide the learner with positive feedback first, so take the advice for yourselves too.
3. **Think playfully and think enjoyment**. When we were younger we used to think more playfully. In fact, Kretchmar (2012) would argue that our generation is growing up 'play disabled', that is, we have learned to grow up with a diminishing amount of play. We work very hard and do mostly structured activities but how often do we spend time in 'free play', like we did when we were kids? So we encourage you to approach your teaching and coaching *playfully*. Physical Education, physical activity, coaching, Outdoor Education, and community activities should be fun – they should be pleasurable movement experiences for students (Pringle, 2010). We want students to be motivated so that they will want to play in the future. As adults we don't play enough – we're too busy.
4. **Take your time**. In our work with teachers we have found that it takes a great deal of time and persistence to move Cooperative Learning from a trial and error beginning phase to the phase of using Cooperative Learning with seamless transitions from one task to the next. In a seamless transition the educator can use Cooperative Learning to teach most content in Physical Education, Outdoor Education, and PA.

Learning to teach in a new way

At the heart of rethinking your teaching is the idea that you are learning to teach in a new way.

For us there are two key elements that we keep coming back to: Positive Interdependence and Individual Accountability. There are four schools of thought with regards to Cooperative Learning and, while all the main proponents might disagree on the make-up of the key elements, they agree that Positive Interdependence and Individual Accountability are key. For educators to develop Positive Interdependence (and perhaps, for example, Promotive Face-to-Face Interaction) we suggest that using the role of 'encourager' helps a great deal. In what follows we use a real-life example of how one teacher did this. Ben worked with one teacher in New Hampshire, USA and it took him two years of persuasion before she would agree that having the role of *encourager* as part of the Cooperative Learning group was a good idea. Up until that time she commented frequently that she didn't want to have a separate role for encourager because she 'want[ed] all my students to encourage each other'. Ben agreed that all her students should encourage each other but after two years he succeeded in providing enough evidence to her about her students that she agreed she needed to use the role of 'encourager' so that all students would learn how to encourage each other. One strategy to help her students encourage each other was to develop a T-Chart for encouraging positive reinforcement (the T-Chart is presented in Chapter 12). As a direct result of this change in focus – from a holistic to a specific notion of encouragement – the teacher saw a significant change in the positive interactions of her students. In many ways the students understood that encouragement and positivity were important in their lessons but they didn't understand what it took to be encouraging. When they were faced with the reality of being the primary encourager then they were also 'forced' to think differently and more proactively about this role. By making encouragement and positive interactions explicit, the students had to face up to their responsibilities.

When thinking about teaching in a new way we also need to think about the type of learners we want to support and encourage. As we indicated in Chapter 5, learning interpersonal skills, relating to others, and cooperative physical activities (among other things) are becoming key aspects of the global story of learning in Physical Education (EfD, 2014; MOE, 2007; NASPE, 2013). The impact of using Cooperative Learning or what Cohen (1994) called 'small group learning' has huge potential for the future of teaching and learning. In a recent Futures Report on innovative learning environments the Organisation for Economic Co-operation and Development (OECD, 2013) has emphasized re-thinking of the core elements fundamental to schools in order to create innovative learning environments that emphasize student-centered pedagogies. To create innovative learning environments, the report proposed several principles (OECD, 2013). To be most effective, learning environments should:

- Ensure that learning is social and often collaborative.
- Be highly attuned to learner motivations and emotions.
- Be acutely sensitive to individual differences.
- Be demanding for each learner but without excessive overload.
- Use assessments consistent with learning aims, with strong emphasis on formative feedback.

We would argue that throughout this book we have presented each one of the OECD (2013) principles. In addition, OECD's (2013) Futures Report suggested that Cooperative Learning is one of the six innovative pedagogical approaches that should be used to create effective student-centered learning environments in the twenty-first century.

In Ben's research at Papatoetoe South School in South Auckland, New Zealand, a more advanced approach to Cooperative Learning as a pedagogy practice has been used to create a whole-school focus on the inclusion of Pasifika and Maori (indigenous peoples in New Zealand) students in the school's curriculum. For the last three years Ben has developed a collaborative relationship with the school and with its teachers and students in order to include (rather than simply integrate – see Chapter 11) the indigenous peoples of New Zealand into everything that they do. The school also developed a Professional Learning Group in Cooperative Learning. To make this truly collaborative and cooperative a number of steps needed to occur.

First, the school leaders (administration) have bought into this process. They have allocated time for teachers to be involved in Continuing Professional Development (CPD) and have specifically allocated a significant portion of time to Professional Development meetings over a three-year period. While this CPD has been facilitated/activated by Ben it has been led by teachers who have adopted a focus on an *inquiry* approach to teaching. For those not acquainted with the New Zealand Curriculum (MOE, 2007) it is enough at this time to say that it is framed by notions of effective pedagogy that are grounded in inquiry. The basic premise of *Teaching as Inquiry* encourages teachers to collect evidence about themselves and their students in a critically reflective process. This evidence must be authentic, that is, relevant and meaningful to the teacher and their students. *Teaching as Inquiry* should enable ongoing critical reflection that continues to work to improve the teacher's pedagogical practice and student learning (MOE, 2007; Timperley et al., 2014).

Secondly, the senior leadership team (made up of the principal and three deputy principals) has invested not just time but money in the collaboration. It paid for 20 out of 30 teachers from the school to attend a Kagan Cooperative Learning workshop for three days over the last two years. Following the workshops, Ben has run additional professional development workshops with the entire staff of the school to consolidate and develop their understanding of Cooperative Learning.

Thirdly, following these two CPD events (both through the workshop and through Ben) a Professional Learning Group in Cooperative Learning (PLG in

CL) emerged organically from the teachers. The PLG in CL is made up of seven teachers, two senior leadership team members, and a graduate student. Ben and this group have met nine times across the three years in an effort to support and guide both the PLG in CL and the use of Cooperative Learning in the school more generally. Topics for discussion and inquiry have included:

- Cooperative Learning Structures;
- praise phrase and team building;
- Group Processing;
- behavior management strategies;
- social skills development; and
- translating the Kagan workshop to a broader Cooperative Learning approach unique to this school's context.

This work has highlighted the support and scaffolding of learning required both to develop and sustain the use of Cooperative Learning in a school. More importantly it has shown the efforts that are required to ensure the inclusion of Pasifika and Maori students in the school's curriculum, which was an overarching aim of the project. Of course, all of this takes a great deal of time, effort, and dedication. We don't have all the answers but we are working hard to improve students' educational experiences and researching the impact of Cooperative Learning in a meaningful and purposeful way.

In a separate study, Vicky Goodyear (initially with the support of Ash but now working independently) has supported a school in the south of England to develop a longitudinal approach to the use of Cooperative Learning. While it is beyond the scope of this book to discuss this longitudinal study in detail (and Vicky's prerogative to talk about this innovative and groundbreaking work) we present a few, already published, details below as a second example of the positive impact that Cooperative Learning can have on a school community (for more details see Goodyear & Casey, 2013).

In the academic year 2011/2012 the Buckingham School Physical Education department used the Cooperative Learning model to enhance students' learning. As a result of the huge success of this initial year-long adaption of the model across the department (success that led the department to be described as outstanding by the senior leaders in the school) Cooperative Learning was prioritized as the focus for whole-school improvement. The Cooperative Learning model was used across the school including in Science, Technology, English, and Math subjects.

The school instigated a Professional Development program that included:

1. The use of Cooperative Learning buddies (i.e. a person in each subject area who would become a subject-specific Cooperative Learning leader).
2. INSET (or in service training) workshops led by members of the Physical Education department to (a) develop teachers' understanding of Cooperative

Learning, (b) develop the teachers' current use of the model, and (c) afford teachers time to plan.

3. The use of applied tasks (e.g. teachers are challenged to use one or two elements and then reflect on their implementation of the model and plan forward).

4. Scheduled time of discussions within the working week to allow teachers to (a) share good practice, (b) share ideas, (c) share resources, and (d) receive support from their buddies (and or Vicky).

The impact of these approaches was noticeable across the school. Teachers consistently received higher evaluations of their teaching, students' learning was enhanced, and teachers were engaged. It was also noticed by the then Secretary of State for Education, Michael Gove, who described the school as a 'centre for innovative excellence', and OfSTED, who said that 'the department is recognised as a centre of excellence in the UK and abroad … lessons using Cooperative Learning were textbook outstanding.'

Both of these examples, one from New Zealand and one from the UK, go a little way toward showing the positive impact that Cooperative Learning can have when a school and/or Physical Education group or Physical Education community invest in changing and bettering the ways in which they teach. In addition, throughout this book we have shared other examples of Cooperative Learning from the USA, France, Spain, and Germany.

Creating a positive Cooperative Learning environment

We suggest that creating a positive Cooperative Learning environment requires an equity pedagogy. To us an equity pedagogy means inclusion (see Chapters 7 and 11). Inclusive programs are caring and empathetic to the needs of *all* students. Inclusion requires re-thinking of current practices and re-organizing current classroom and school systems. We have discussed inclusion in Chapter 7 and Chapter 11 but believe it is important to come back to this in our final chapter.

We believe one thing that Cooperative Learning can do is help people work together. Often when we are isolated and disconnected from each other we feel less confident and unsure. There are many educators and coaches who work in isolation. Working together we can harness strength, enthusiasm, and energy from one another. In isolation teachers, coaches, and educators can achieve a great deal but often they need the support of others at crucial times to be able to sustain their good work. This brings us back to one of the underlying messages of this book. We want to emphasize that 'we sink or swim together' and that 'two heads are better than one' in this education process; that is, for us, the imperious construct of Positive Interdependence. Therefore, we encourage you to work in a positive interdependent way with others. Johnson and Johnson (2009) think so highly of this construct that recently, based on their research of 20 years, they have published a seminal article on 'social interdependence theory' (please see Johnson & Johnson, 2009). Clearly, one of the basic tenets of Cooperative Learning is Positive Interdependence.

Working in isolation is the reality for some teachers but it doesn't need to be. Much of Ash's recent work has been around the use of social networking sites (SNSs, such as Twitter and Facebook) in teacher professional development. It is an increasingly small world that is connected, in an instant, to a wider professional community. Using social media can be a great way of finding people – finding those Cooperative Learning buddies or training partners you might seek to help you make changes. Hashtags such as #physed, #pechat, #pegeeks, and #peblogs can bring you into contact with many innovative and likeminded teachers. Ash has made many friends and confidants on Twitter and he can certainly help you meet people (find him as @DrAshCasey – or Drash to his closest Twitter colleagues). The Twittersphere is just one example of a PLN (professional learning network) that exists on SNSs. Dive in and give it a go!

Hauora or Bildung

The more, we would argue most, effective educators establish a learning environment that provides opportunities for students to work in situations that are positive and supportive in order to develop their physical, social, emotional, and academic needs. In fact, if we refer to the New Zealand Curriculum (MOE, 2007) it emphasizes the development of the health and well-being of each child, referred to in NZ as *Hauora*. This is an important Maori educational concept and germane to Physical Education in NZ. Hauora is a concept that entwines the physical, social, emotional, spiritual, and mental needs of the student.

In the Germanic/Scandinavian cultures there is a notion/idea called *Bildung* that was explained to us by Ingrid Bähr and Jonas Wibowo (2012) in our edited book. Ingrid and Jonas explained that there are two different words in the German language that refer to educational philosophy: *Bildung* and *Erziehung*. They suggest that 'Bildung can be done only by the student him- or herself, where as education (Erziehung) is the job of the teacher' (p. 28).

In considering both of these ideas we suggest that Cooperative Learning puts the child or the learner at the center and can incorporate all domains of learning. By considering and acknowledging that there are some things that only the student can do for him or herself then we need to create an environment that invites students to self-activity. We cannot force them to work as a team but we can create environments in which they choose to do all or some of these things.

If we position Cooperative Learning as a student-centered pedagogy (and we do) then as educators we should also strive to view the learners as distinctive and having different propensities to learn. If the educator concentrates on the student, has knowledge of how the student learns, and has respect for the student's own perspective or opinion then they are being truly student-centered. Sapon-Shevin (2010) suggested that children are motivated to learn more favorably when the teacher establishes a *positive* learning environment, *adapts* instruction to individual differences, and *facilitates* students' learning and thinking skills.

We all come from different backgrounds and we all have different experiences as educators so it is not surprising that Bähr and Wibowo (2012) believe that teachers have different perspectives about what student-centered learning means. That is, we need to make sure that when we are working with a group of teachers, coaches, outdoor educators, or community workers, we discuss our specific understandings of student-centered learning. When establishing student-centered learning, Gillies (2007) suggested that teachers do not always appreciate the important role that discussion plays in developing a relationship, learning social skills, and the scaffolding of new learning. Furthermore, teachers do not always recognize that it is not imperative that they motivate students through the process of grading. As we discussed in Chapter 12, assessment should be used as part of the teaching and learning process and not as a summative evaluation of students. When the students are engaged in different facets of their own and each other's learning then they are motivated in different ways. Grading is a way of showing what they have achieved collectively and not just how they did against a grading sheet.

Future-focused teaching

Given that the classroom of the future is more likely to involve more students working on tasks in small groups around different social media or multiple types of different media, we suggest that Cooperative Learning could be a pedagogy that activates and enhances the ways in which teachers interact with their students. If we take note of the principles recommended by the OECD (2013) it is highly likely that the structure of future learning environments will be more open-plan and have more flexible grouping arrangements that will enable students to move among small groups to work on different types of tasks. That is, students will be expected to assume more responsibility for their own learning and educators will act in the role of facilitator of learning. Furthermore, such learning could easily be occurring in multiple contexts (both nationally and internationally) and with a mobile device serving as the conduit for such interaction.

Cooperative Learning has the potential to provide differentiated instruction through interesting and varied tasks. We propose that students will become more like partners in the learning process, as Ash found in his research (Casey, 2013). We come from a constructive position so we will suggest that the students can become the creative learner, the active learner, and the social learner (Dyson, 2002). The interpersonal or social skills that students develop in Cooperative Learning are immensely important for their future success in their learning. Gillies (2007) stated: 'to be able to interact effectively with others, students need to have the social skills that will facilitate such interactions… When students' social skills are well developed they learn to listen to what others have to say, share materials and ideas, deal with differences through discussion, and resolve conflicts amicably' (p. 239). There is plenty of research and evidence to suggest that students work better and perform more favorably when they have developed a high level of Interpersonal and Small Group Skills. Students in future classrooms will need these social skills because they will be more involved with their peers in small learning groups, and this will be possible if they are encouraged to set up their own team-based tasks using Cooperative Learning Structures. Given what we suggested at the beginning of the chapter they could be using technology to break down language barriers and geographical limitations that would have previously made any such work impossible.

We believe that Information Communication Technology (ICT) will play a significant role in the creation of student-centered learning environments in the future. Technology will be integrated into our teaching and learning programs to enable students to access information from multiple sources, engage in active problem solving, and work together to create innovative conceptualization and knowledge that do not exist at present. To make such a thing possible we will need to consider what our e-pedagogies might look like and how students will be prepared to work through and with ICT.

Currently there is little definitive evidence to suggest that e-learning is more effective than more conventional methods (Mehanna, 2004). Garrison and Anderson (2003) attributed this lack of impact to education's dogged adherence to a transmission model (i.e. the face-to-face delivery of knowledge) that has hampered the capabilities of e-learning to create a 'new learning ecology' (p. 61). In contrast, e-pedagogy should challenge us to 'develop a new understanding of effective pedagogies that are specific to these learning contexts' (Mehanna, 2004, p. 280). Cooperative Learning is certainly an approach that places the student at the heart of their own and others' learning and potentially creates new classroom and community positive learning environments.

Self-processing / A time to reflect

Self-processing questions

Many concepts in this book should appeal to educators in the twenty-first century. There is growing research support for the skills and tactics taught by Cooperative Learning. These skills not only support the academic but the physical, emotional, and social development of the student that they need for success in life. Cooperative Learning can improve students' attitudes to school and toward a more productive life.

1. What questions do you have to answer in order to implement Cooperative Learning?
2. How will you start to use Cooperative Learning in your teaching, coaching, and community work?
3. Do you have a friend or colleague that you can work with? Could you 'sink or swim together'?
4. In the twenty-first century can you afford not to collect relevant evidence on your own teaching or coaching and that of your students or your players? If

you agree with this statement then you have already started the 'Teaching as Inquiry' process.

Our reflections

Ben

We believe Cooperative Learning has huge potential, but like any innovative pedagogy it requires a concentrated amount of time, effort, and perspiration to become an effective pedagogy. Teachers we have worked with would argue that it takes two to three years to have Cooperative Learning up and running in their school. Just like any pedagogical practice it requires continual critical reflection. I like the notion of *Teaching as Inquiry*. The basic premise of *Teaching as Inquiry* encourages teachers to collect evidence about themselves and their students. This evidence must be authentic, that is, relevant and meaningful to the teacher and their students. *Teaching as Inquiry* should enable ongoing critical reflection that continues to work to improve the teacher's pedagogical practice and student learning – good luck to y'all!

Ash

I use Cooperative Learning in my daily teaching and I can't give a higher accolade than that. It works for me in multiple ways and with many different groups. It is adaptable and it keeps surprising me. It can be used with diverse learners and across many different platforms. It lends itself to collaboration – both with your students and your colleagues. I hope you enjoy using it as much as I have. Happy teaching.

References

Bähr, I. & Wibowo, J. (2012). Teacher action in the cooperative learning model in the physical education classroom. In B. Dyson & A. Casey (Eds.). *Cooperative learning in physical education: A research-based approach* (pp. 27–41). London: Routledge.

Casey, A. (2013). 'Seeing the trees not just the wood': Steps and not just journeys in teacher action research. *Educational Action Research, 21*(2), 147–163. http://doi.org/10.1080/09 650792.2013.789704

Casey, A. & Dyson, B. (2012). Putting cooperative learning and physical activity into practice with primary students. In B. Dyson & A. Casey (Eds.). *Cooperative learning in physical education: A research-based approach* (pp. 59–74). London: Routledge.

Cohen, E. G. (1994). Restructuring the classroom: Conditions for productive small groups. *Review of Educational Research, 64*(1), 1–35. http://doi.org/10.3102/00346543064001001

Dyson, B. (2002). The implementation of cooperative learning in an elementary physical education program. *Journal of Teaching in Physical Education, 22*(1), 69–85.

Dyson, B., Griffin, L. L., & Hastie, P. (2004). Sport education, tactical games, and cooperative learning: Theoretical and pedagogical considerations. *Quest, 56*(2), 226–240.

Dyson, B., Barratt, M. Berry, S., Colby, R. & Dryden, C. (2014). Cooperative learning as models based practice: Pedagogy of the possible. Paper presented at Physical Education New Zealand Conference, Christchurch, New Zealand.

EfD. (2014). National curriculum in England for physical education. Retrieved May

8, 2015, from https://www.gov.uk/government/publications/national-curriculum-in-england-physical-education-programmes-of-study/national-curriculum-in-england-physical-education-programmes-of-study

Garrison, G. R. & Anderson, B. (2003). *E-learning in the 21st century: A framework for research and practice.* Netherlands: OpenUniversititNederland.

Gillies, R. M. (2007). *Cooperative learning: Integrating theory and practice.* Thousand Oaks, CA: SAGE.

Goodyear, V. (2015). Developing students' promotive interactions over time: Teachers' adaptions to and interactions within the cooperative learning model. AIESEP International conference. July, 2015, Madrid, Spain.

Goodyear, V. & Casey, A. (2013). Innovation with change: Developing a community of practice to help teachers move beyond the 'honeymoon' of pedagogical renovation. *Physical Education & Sport Pedagogy,* September, 1–18. http://doi.org/10.1080/174089 89.2013.817012

Johnson, D. W. & Johnson, R. T. (2009). An educational psychology success story: Social interdependence theory and cooperative learning. *Educational Researcher, 38*(5), 365–379. http://doi.org/10.3102/0013189X09339057

Kretchmar, R. S. (2012). Play disabilities: A reason for physical educators to rethink the boundaries of special education. *Quest, 64*(2), 79–86. http://doi.org/10.1080/003362 97.2012.669316

Mehanna, W. N. (2004). e-Pedagogy: The pedagogies of e-learning. *ALT-J, Research in Learning Technology, 12*(3).

MOE. (2007). *The New Zealand Curriculum.* Wellington, New Zealand: Learning Media.

NASPE. (2013). *National standards & grade-level outcomes for K–12 physical education.* Champaign, IL: Human Kinetics.

OECD. (2013). Health at a glance 2013: OECD indicators. *OECD Publishing,* 210. http://doi.org/10.1787/health_glance-2013-en

Pringle, R. (2010). Finding pleasure in physical education: A critical examination of the educative value of positive movement affects. *Quest, 62,* 119–134.

Sapon-Shevin, M. (2010). *Because we can change the world: A practical guide to building cooperative, inclusive classroom communities* (2nd ed.). Thousand Oaks, CA: Corwin.

Timperley, H., Kaser, L., & Halbert, J. (2014). A framework for transforming learning in schools: Innovation and the spiral of inquiry. *Centre for Strategic Education, Seminar Series Paper Number 234.*

INDEX

Please note that references to non-textual material such as Figures or Tables will be in *italics*.

Taylor & Francis eBooks

Helping you to choose the right eBooks for your Library

Add Routledge titles to your library's digital collection today. Taylor and Francis ebooks contains over 50,000 titles in the Humanities, Social Sciences, Behavioural Sciences, Built Environment and Law.

Choose from a range of subject packages or create your own!

Benefits for you

» Free MARC records
» COUNTER-compliant usage statistics
» Flexible purchase and pricing options
» All titles DRM-free.

Benefits for your user

» Off-site, anytime access via Athens or referring URL
» Print or copy pages or chapters
» Full content search
» Bookmark, highlight and annotate text
» Access to thousands of pages of quality research at the click of a button.

REQUEST YOUR **FREE** INSTITUTIONAL TRIAL TODAY	**Free Trials Available** We offer free trials to qualifying academic, corporate and government customers.

eCollections – Choose from over 30 subject eCollections, including:

Archaeology	Language Learning
Architecture	Law
Asian Studies	Literature
Business & Management	Media & Communication
Classical Studies	Middle East Studies
Construction	Music
Creative & Media Arts	Philosophy
Criminology & Criminal Justice	Planning
Economics	Politics
Education	Psychology & Mental Health
Energy	Religion
Engineering	Security
English Language & Linguistics	Social Work
Environment & Sustainability	Sociology
Geography	Sport
Health Studies	Theatre & Performance
History	Tourism, Hospitality & Events

For more information, pricing enquiries or to order a free trial, please contact your local sales team: www.tandfebooks.com/page/sales

 Routledge Taylor & Francis Group | The home of Routledge books

www.tandfebooks.com